brilliant
Microsoft® office 2003
POCKET BOOK

Joe Habraken

WITHDRAWN FROM SWINDON LIBRARIES

PEARSON
Prentice Hall

Harlow, England • London • New York • Boston • San Francisco • Toronto
Sydney • Tokyo • Singapore • Hong Kong • Seoul • Taipei • New Delhi
Cape Town • Madrid • Mexico City • Amsterdam • Munich • Paris • Milan

Pearson Education Limited
Edinburgh Gate
Harlow
Essex CM20 2JE
England

and Associated Companies throughout the world

Visit us on the World Wide Web at:
www.pearsoned.co.uk

Original edition appeared in, Microsoft® Office 2003 All-in-One, 1st edition, 0789729369 by Joe Habraken, published by Que Publishing, Copyright © Que Publishing.

All rights reserved. No part of this publication may be reproduced or transmitted in any form or by any means, electronic, mechanical, including photocopying, recording or by any information storage retrieval system without permission from Pearson Education, Inc.

This UK edition published by PEARSON EDUCATION LTD, Copyright © 2006

The right of Joe Habraken to be identified as author of this work has been asserted by him in accordance with the Copyright, Designs and Patents Act 1988.

All trademarks used herein are the property of their respective owners. The use of any trademark in this text does not vest in the author or publisher any trademark ownership rights in such trademarks, nor does the use of such trademarks imply any affiliation with or endorsement of this book by such owners.

ISBN-13: 978-0-13-175726-4
ISBN-10: 0-13-175726-1

British Library Cataloguing-in-Publication Data
A catalogue record for this book is available from the British Library

10 9 8 7 6 5 4 3 2 1
10 09 08 07 06

Typeset in 9.5pt Helvetica by 30
Printed and bound in Great Britain by Ashford Colour Press Ltd, Gosport, Hampshire

The Publisher's policy is to use paper manufactured from sustainable forests.

Swindon Borough Council Library Services	
Askews	
005.5	£7.99

Brilliant Pocket Books

What you need to know – when you need it!

When you're working on your PC and come up against a problem that you're unsure how to solve, or want to accomplish something in an application that you aren't sure how to do, where do you look? If you are fed up with wading through pages of background information in unwieldy manuals and training guides trying to find the piece of information or advice that you need RIGHT NOW, and if you find that helplines really aren't that helpful, then Brilliant Pocket Books are the answer!

Brilliant Pocket Books have been developed to allow you to find the info that you need easily and without fuss and to guide you through each task using a highly visual step-by-step approach – providing exactly what you need to know, when you need it!

Brilliant Pocket Books are concise, easy-to-access guides to all of the most common important and useful tasks in all of the applications in the Office 2003 suite. Short, concise lessons make it really easy to learn any particular feature, or master any task or problem that you will come across in day-to-day use of the applications.

When you are faced with any task on your PC, whether major or minor, that you are unsure about, your Brilliant Pocket Book will provide you with the answer – almost before you know what the question is!

Contents

Introduction   xiii

Office Introduction and Shared Features   1

1 What's New in Office 2003?   3
- → Introducing Microsoft Office 2003   3
- → Office 2003 and the Document Workspace   4
- → Getting Help in Office 2003   6
- → Using the New Research Feature   7
- → Faxing over the Internet   7
- → Office 2003 and XML Data   8
- → Office Instant Messaging   9

2 Using Common Office Features   11
- → Starting Office Applications   11
  - Starting an Application by Choosing a Document Template   11
  - Creating Desktop Icons   12
- → Using the Menu System   13
- → Using Shortcut Menus   14
- → Working with Toolbars   15
- → Understanding Dialog Boxes   17

3 Using Office Task Panes   19
- → Understanding the Task Pane   19
- → The Research Task Pane   21
- → The Basic File Search Task Pane   23
- → Other Standard Task Panes   24
  - The Clip Art Task Pane   24
  - Using the Office Clipboard   25

4 Getting Help in Microsoft Office   27
- → Help: What's Available?   27
- → Using the Ask a Question Box   27

→ Using the Office Assistant	28
– Turning the Office Assistant On and Off	28
– Asking the Office Assistant a Question	29
→ Using the Help Task Pane	30
→ Searching for Help Online	31

5 Customizing Your Office Applications — 33

- → Navigating Options Settings — 33
- → Setting Options in Word — 35
- → Setting Options in Excel — 37
- → Setting Options in PowerPoint — 38
- → Setting Special Options in Access — 39
- → Customizing Toolbars — 40

6 Faxing and E-Mailing in Office 2003 — 43

- → Understanding E-Mails and Faxes in Office — 43
- → Using the Word Fax Wizard — 44
- → Sending Faxes from Other Office Applications — 47
- → Sending E-mails from Office Applications — 48

Outlook — 51

1 Getting Started in Outlook — 53

- → Starting Outlook — 53
- → Understanding the Outlook Window — 54
- → Working Offline — 56
- → Exiting Outlook — 56

2 Using Outlook's Tools — 57

- → Using the Navigation Pane — 57
- → Using the Folder List — 59
- → Using Outlook Today — 60

3 Creating Mail — 63

- → Composing a Message — 63
- → Formatting Text — 66

→ Checking Spelling	69
→ Adding a Signature	71
– Creating a Signature	71
– Inserting the Signature	72
→ Sending Mail	72
→ Recalling a Message	73

4 Working with Received Mail   75

→ Reading Mail	75
→ Saving an Attachment	78
→ Answering Mail	80
→ Printing Mail	81

5 Managing Mail   83

→ Deleting Mail	83
– Undeleting Items	83
– Emptying the Deleted Items Folder	85
→ Forwarding Mail	86
→ Creating Folders	88
→ Moving and Copying Items to Another Folder	90

6 Attaching Files and Items to a Message   93

→ Attaching a File	93
→ Attaching Outlook Items	97

7 Using the Outlook Address Books   99

→ Understanding the Outlook Address Books	99
→ Using the Address Book	100
– Finding Records in an Address Book	101
– Adding Records to an Address Book	102

8 Using the Calendar   105

→ Navigating the Calendar	105
→ Creating an Appointment	107

Word   109

1 Working in Word   111

- → Starting Word   111
- → Understanding the Word Environment   112
- → Using Menus and Toolbars   114
  - The Word Menu Bar   115
  - Shortcut Menus   117
  - Word Toolbars   118
- → Exiting Word   120

2 Working with Documents   121

- → Starting a New Document   121
  - Using Document Templates   123
  - Using Word Wizards   125
  - Creating a New Document From an Existing Document   127
- → Entering Text   128
- → Saving a Document   129
- → Closing a Document   131
- → Opening a Document   131

3 Editing Documents   133

- → Adding or Replacing Text and Moving in the Document   133
  - Adding New Text   133
  - Replacing Text with Typeover   134
  - Moving Around the Document   135
- → Selecting Text   136
  - Selecting Text with the Mouse   137
  - Selecting Text with the Keyboard   138
- → Deleting, Copying and Moving Text   139
  - Deleting Text   139
  - Copying, Cutting and Pasting Text   139
  - Using the Office Clipboard to Copy and Move Multiple Items   141
  - Using Drag and Drop   143
- → Copying and Moving Text Between Documents   143

4 Using Proofreading and Research Tools — 145

- → Proofing As You Type — 145
  - Correcting Individual Spelling Errors — 148
  - Correcting Individual Grammatical Errors — 149
- → Using the Spelling and Grammar Checker — 150
- → Finding Synonyms Using the Thesaurus — 152
- → Adding Research Services — 155
- → Working with AutoCorrect — 156

5 Changing How Text Looks — 159

- → Understanding Fonts — 159
- → Changing Font Attributes — 160
- → Working in the Font Dialog Box — 161
- → Aligning Text — 163
- → Aligning Text with Click and Type — 165
- → Automatically Deleting Formatting Inconsistencies — 166
- → Reveal Formatting — 167

6 Printing Documents — 169

- → Sending Your Document to the Printer — 169
- → Changing Print Settings — 170
- → Selecting Paper Trays, Draft Quality, and Other Options — 173

Excel — 175

1 Creating a New Workbook — 177

- → Starting Excel — 177
- → Understanding the Excel Window — 177
- → Starting a New Workbook — 180
- → Saving and Naming a Workbook — 182
- → Saving a Workbook Under a New Name or Location — 184
- → Opening an Existing Workbook — 184
- → Closing Workbooks — 185
- → Exiting Excel — 186

2 Entering Data into the Worksheet — 187

- → Understanding Excel Data Types — 187
- → Entering Text — 188
  - Tips on Entering Column and Row Labels — 189
  - Adding Comments to Cells — 190
- → Entering Numbers — 192
- → Entering Dates and Times — 193
- → Copying Data to Other Cells — 194
  - Entering a Series of Numbers, Dates and Other Data — 195
  - Entering a Custom Series — 196
- → Taking Advantage of AutoComplete — 197

3 Performing Simple Calculations — 199

- → Understanding Excel Formulas — 199
  - Formula Operators — 200
  - Order of Operations — 201
- → Entering Formulas — 201
- → Using the Status Bar AutoCalculate Feature — 203
- → Displaying Formulas — 204
- → Editing Formulas — 205

4 Editing Worksheets — 207

- → Correcting Data — 207
- → Undoing an Action — 208
- → Using the Replace Feature — 208
- → Checking Your Spelling — 211
- → Copying and Moving Data — 212
  - Using Drag and Drop — 213
  - Moving Data — 214
  - Using Drag and Drop to Move Data — 214
- → Using the Office Clipboard — 214
- → Deleting Data — 216

PowerPoint — 217

1 Working in PowerPoint — 219

- → Starting PowerPoint — 219

- → Getting Comfortable with the PowerPoint Window   220
- → Exiting PowerPoint   223

2 Creating a New Presentation   225

- → Starting a New Presentation   225
  - Creating a New Presentation with the AutoContent Wizard   226
  - Creating a New Presentation with a Design Template   228
  - Creating a New Presentation from an Existing Presentation   230
  - Creating a Blank Presentation   232
- → Saving a Presentation   232
- → Closing a Presentation   233
- → Opening a Presentation   233
- → Finding a Presentation File   234

3 Working with Slides in Different Views   237

- → Understanding PowerPoint's Different Views   237
- → Moving from Slide to Slide   238
- → Introduction to Inserting Slide Text   240
- → Editing Text in the Slide Pane   240
  - Editing Text in the Outline Pane   241
  - Moving Text in the Outline Pane   242
  - Rearranging Text in the Outline Pane   244

4 Changing A Presentation's Look   245

- → Giving Your Slides a Professional Look   245
- → Applying a Different Design Template   246
- → Using Colour Schemes   249
- → Changing the Background Fill   250

5 Inserting, Deleting, and Copying Slides   253

- → Inserting Slides into a Presentation   253
  - Inserting a New, Blank Slide   253
  - Inserting Slides from Another Presentation   254
- → Creating Slides from a Document Outline   255
- → Deleting Slides   256
- → Cutting, Copying and Pasting Slides   256

6 Adding and Modifying Slide Text — 259

→ Creating a Text Box — 259
 – Sizing and Moving Text Boxes — 260
 – Deleting a Text Box — 261
→ Changing Font Attributes — 261
 – Using the Font Dialog Box — 262
 – Formatting Text with the Formatting Toolbar — 263
→ Copying Text Formats — 265
→ Changing the Text Alignment and Line Spacing — 265
→ Adding a WordArt Object — 267

7 Adding Graphics to a Slide — 271

→ Using the Clip Art Task Pane — 271
→ Inserting an Image from the Task Pane — 272
→ Inserting an Image from an Image Box — 273
→ Inserting a Clip from a File — 275
→ Managing Images in the Clip Organizer — 277

Introduction

Welcome to the *Brilliant Microsoft® Office Pocket Book* – a handy visual quick reference that will give you a basic grounding in the common features and tasks that you will need to master to use Microsoft® Office 2003 in any day-to-day situation. Keep it on your desk, in your briefcase or bag – or even in your pocket! – and you will always have the answer to hand for any problem or task that you come across.

Find out what you need to know – when you need it!

You don't have to read this book in any particular order. It is designed so that you can jump in, get the information you need and jump out – just look up the task in the contents list, turn to the right page, read the introduction, follow the step-by-step instructions – and you're done!

How this book works

Each section in this book includes foolproof step-by-step instructions for performing specific tasks, using screenshots to illustrate each step. Additional information is included to help increase your understanding and develop your skills – these are identified by the following icons:

Jargon buster – New or unfamiliar terms are defined and explained in plain English to help you as you work through a section.

Timesaver tip – These tips give you ideas that cut corners and confusion. They also give you additional information related to the topic that you are currently learning. Use them to expand your knowledge of a particular feature or concept.

Important – This identifies areas where new users often run into trouble, and offers practical hints and solutions to these problems.

Brilliant Pocket Books are a handy, accessible resource that you will find yourself turning to time and time again when you are faced with a problem or an unfamiliar task and need an answer at your fingertips – or in your pocket!

Office Introduction and Shared Features

1 What's New in Office 2003?

In this lesson, you learn about the new features that the Office 2003 application suite provides.

→ Introducing Microsoft Office 2003

Microsoft Office 2003 is the latest version of the popular Office application suite. Microsoft Office 2003 comes in different editions that include a different set of Office applications. For example, the Microsoft Office Professional Edition, which we cover in this book, includes Word 2003, Excel 2003, PowerPoint 2003, Outlook 2003 with the Business Contact Manager, Publisher, and Access 2003. Table 1.1 provides a look at each of the Microsoft Office 2003 editions.

Table 1.1 The different editions of Microsoft Office 2003

Edition:	Microsoft Office Professional Edition 2003	Microsoft Office Small Business Edition 2003	Microsoft Office Standard Edition 2003	Microsoft Office Student and Teacher Edition 2003
Applications Included	Word 2003 Excel 2003 PowerPoint 2003 Outlook 2003 with Business Contact Manager Publisher 2003 Access 2003	Word 2003 Excel 2003 PowerPoint 2003 Outlook 2003 with Business Contact Manager Publisher 2003	Word 2003 Excel 2003 PowerPoint 2003 Outlook 2003	Word 2003 Excel 2003 PowerPoint 2003 Outlook 2003

No matter which edition of Office you use, you are provided with different software applications that you can use to tackle a large variety of business and personal tasks on the computer. For example, Word allows you to create reports, letters, and other documents, and Excel allows you to tackle spreadsheets, invoices, and do a wide variety of number-crunching tasks. Each application provides a specialized set of tools and environments for addressing your productivity needs.

Microsoft Office 2003 offers a number of new enhancements to the Office suite. This lesson serves as a quick overview of some of these new features.

→ Office 2003 and the Document Workspace

An exciting new feature, the Document Workspace, allows users who don't have the option of sharing documents on a corporate network to collaborate on the Web. The Document Workspace is actually an extension of Microsoft Windows SharePoint Services, which allows you to store documents for collaboration on a SharePoint server. Multiple users can access the document in the shared workspace, and tasks can be assigned associated with the collaborative effort.

The Document Workspace is a fairly advanced feature offered by Office 2003, so the full details related to the use of this powerful feature are beyond the scope of this introduction. However, creating a new workspace is surprisingly easy. It does, however, require that you are connected to the Internet and have access to a SharePoint server maintained by your company or you have subscribed to a SharePoint hosting service such as those offered by Microsoft. Let's take a look at creating a Document Workspace in Microsoft Word.

To create a Document Workspace, follow these steps (these steps assume Microsoft Word is already open):

1. Open the document that will be available in the shared workspace.
2. Select **Tools** and then **Shared Workspace**. The Shared Workspace task pane opens as shown in Figure 1.1.
3. Type the URL (Uniform Resource Locator or Web address) for the workspace that will serve as the holding area for the shared document in the Location for New Workspace box.
4. Click the **Create** button in the task pane.
5. A connection box will appear that requires you to enter your user name and password for the shared workspace. After entering the information, click OK.

6 The shared workspace will be created (on the Web site you designated) and a copy of the current document is placed in the workspace.

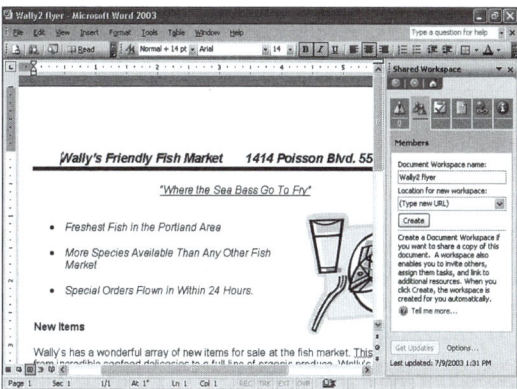

Figure 1.1 A shared workspace can be created for your Office documents.

As the creator of the site, you are designated as the site owner. This allows you to add new members to the site, add additional documents, and manage the workspace. You can also view who is currently online and working on the document. Figure 1.2 shows a document that is shared in a workspace. Note that the Shared Workspace task pane lists the current users of the workspace and whether or not they are currently online. Tools provided in the task pane allow you to quickly e-mail workspace users and to update the workspace status.

Timesaver tip

Tasks Can be Created Using the Shared Workspace Task Pane A useful feature related to the Shared Workspace feature is the ability to create tasks and assign them to users of the workspace. Click the **Tasks** icon at the top of the Shared Workspace task pane and then click the **Add New Task** link. To name the task, use the Task dialog box that appears, and set the other task parameters, such as who the task is assigned to and when the task is due.

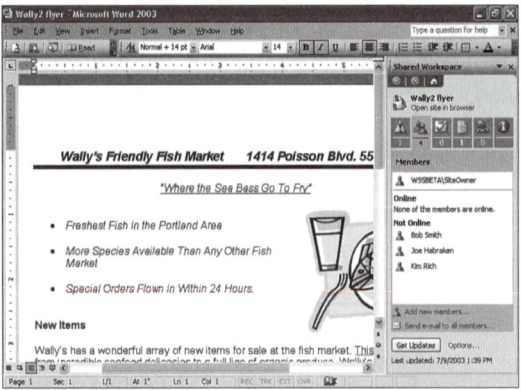

Figure 1.2 The Shared Workspace task pane allows you to manage the workspace and its users.

→ Getting Help in Office 2003

Microsoft Office 2003 uses a streamlined Help system that is primarily accessed using the new Help task pane. Options available in previous versions of Office such as the Office Assistant and the Ask a Question box are also available in Office 2003 for accessing help.

You can open the Help task pane by selecting the **Help** menu and then accessing the Help command for the current application. For example, to access the Help task pane in Word, select **Help** and then **Microsoft Word Help**. The Help task pane appears as shown in Figure 1.3.

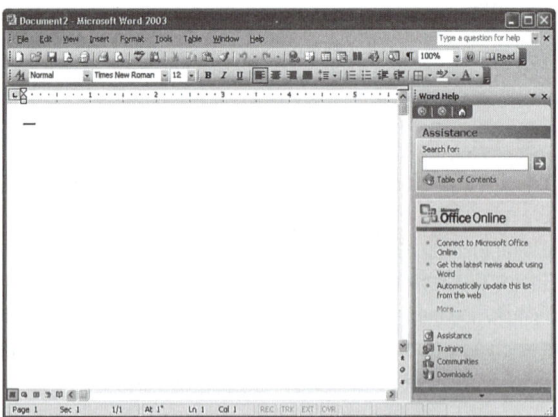

Figure 1.3 The Help task pane allows you to search for help and access online Office resources.

The Help task pane enables you to search using keywords. You also have access to up-to-date help via Office online.

→ Using the New Research Feature

Another new feature that Office 2003 provides is the Research task pane. The Research task pane allows you to access basic tools such as the Thesaurus, but it also provides you with the ability to access online resources that range from business Web sites, to stock information, to online encyclopedias such as Microsoft's Expedia.

For example, I might want to search for information on a key term as shown in Figure 1.4. The Research task pane is discussed in more detail in Lesson 3, "Using Office Task Panes."

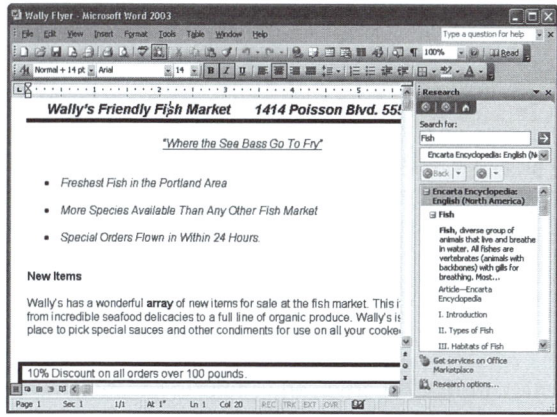

Figure 1.4 The Research task pane allows you to search for business data and other information from inside your Office application.

→ Faxing over the Internet

Another addition to Office 2003 is the ability to send faxes from your Office applications over the Internet. This feature requires that you sign up for an Internet fax service. These services provide you with the ability to send and receive faxes over the Internet. This means that you do not require a fax modem on your computer to work with faxes.

Sending the current document from any Office application as an Internet fax is quite easy: You click the **File** menu, point at **Send To**, and then select **Recipient Using Internet Fax Service**. The first time you use this command, you will have the option of being taken to a Web page that allows you to sign up for a fax service. Pricing for this service varies by provider as do the steps required to prepare a fax cover page and send your Office document. Faxing is discussed in more detail in Lesson 6, "Faxing and E-Mailing in Office 2003."

→ Office 2003 and XML Data

XML (Extensible Markup Language) is fast becoming the standard for data exchange on the World Wide Web. In Office 2003, instead of saving documents in their default formats, you can save Office documents as XML documents.

> **Jargon buster**
>
> **XML** or Extensible Markup Language is a markup language (HTML being an example of another markup language) that can be used to tag data so that it can be transferred between applications and also interpreted and validated. XML is rapidly becoming an important format for moving data between servers on the Web.

Saving in XML format is particularly useful in situations where you want to convert Excel or Access data to an XML format for use on the Web. Although using XML data on the Web is beyond the scope of this book, you will find that if required, you can quickly save data in an Office application such as Excel in the XML format.

Follow these steps:

1 Select **File**, then **Save As**. The Save As dialog box will open.

2 In the Save As dialog box, select the **Save as Type** drop-down box and select **XML Data** (see Figure 1.5). You can also change the filename if you want.

3 When you have made the necessary changes in the Save As dialog box, click **Save**.

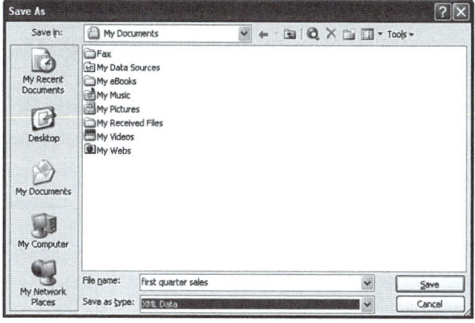

Figure 1.5 Office data can be saved in the XML format.

→ Office Instant Messaging

Microsoft Office XP introduced smart tags to the Office applications. A *smart tag* is a special shortcut menu that provides you with additional options related to a particular feature. There are paste smart tags, AutoCorrect smart tags, and smart tags for dates, times, and addresses that you place in your Office documents. Office 2003 has added a new Person Name smart tag that flags contact names that you have added to your Outlook Contacts list and provides the Windows Messenger address for the contact.

Timesaver tip

Make Sure the Person Name Smart Tag Is Active The Person Name smart tag must be applied to names in your documents if you want to send instant messages. Select **Tools**, then **AutoCorrect Options**. In the AutoCorrect dialog box, click the **Smart Tags** tab and make sure that the **Person Name (English)** smart tag has a check mark next to it.

For example, if you create a document that includes the person's name, the name will be flagged with the Person Name tag (the name will be underlined with a dashed red line). Point at the name and click the smart tag icon that appears (the icon looks like the Windows Messenger icon, see Figure 1.6). On the menu that appears, select **Send Instant Message**.

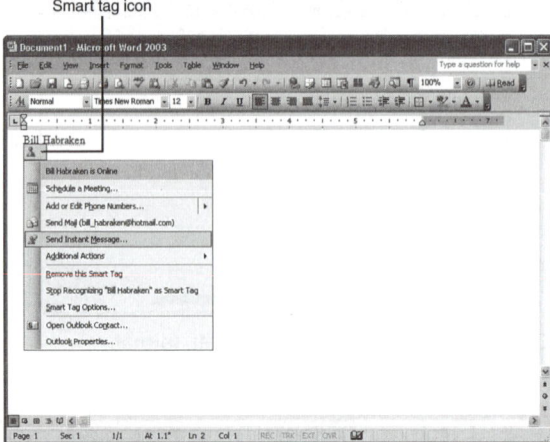

Figure 1.6 Send instant messages directly from your Office applications using the Person Name smart tag.

A Windows Messenger window will open. You can now send your instant message as needed.

Important

Your Message Recipient Must Be Online To send an instant message to a person using the new Person Name smart tag, that person must currently be online using Windows Messenger. If they are not online, the Send Instant Message menu choice is not available.

2 Using Common Office Features

In this lesson, you learn how to use common Office features such as menus, toolbars, and dialog boxes.

→ Starting Office Applications

The Microsoft Office applications can be quickly started from the Windows Start menu. Desktop icons can also be quickly created for an Office application to provide quick access to that application.

To start an Office application from the Start menu, follow these steps:

1 From the Windows XP desktop, click **Start**, point at **All Programs**, and then point at the **Microsoft Office** folder. The Office programs installed on your computer will appear as shown in Figure 2.1 (for Windows 2000, point at **Programs**, then **Microsoft Office**).

2 To open a particular Office application, click that application's icon on the menu. The program window for that application appears.

Starting an Application by Choosing a Document Template

You can also start a particular Office application by choosing the type of Office document that you are going to create. This is done using the Start menu.

1 From the Windows desktop, click **Start**, **All Programs**, then **New Office Document**. The New Office Document dialog box appears (see Figure 2.2).

2 All the Office application templates are available on the different tabs of the New Office Document dialog box. You can create blank documents or special documents from the templates that are provided (specific templates are discussed in more detail in the various parts of this book as they relate to a particular Office application). Select a particular template in the dialog box.

Figure 2.1 Use the Start menu to start your Office applications.

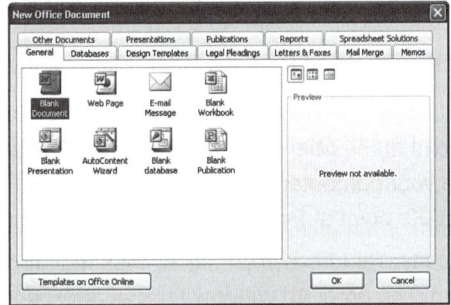

Figure 2.2 The New Office Document dialog box can be used to quickly start a new document in any Office application.

3 Click **OK**. The application that uses that particular template opens (such as Word if you select the Blank Document icon), and the new document appears in the application window.

Creating Desktop Icons

You can also create shortcut icons for your Office applications on the Windows desktop. To create desktop icons for Office applications, follow these steps:

1 From the Windows desktop, click **Start** and then point at **All Programs**, **Microsoft Office**.

2 Right-click the Office application icon that you want to use to create the desktop icon.

3 Select **Copy** from the shortcut menu that appears.

4 Click anywhere on the desktop to close the Start menu.

5 Right-click the Windows desktop and select **Paste Shortcut** from the shortcut menu that appears.

A desktop icon for the selected application appears on the Windows desktop. You can double-click the icon to start the specific application. You can also use the steps discussed in this section to create shortcut icons for your other programs (including non-Office applications), as needed.

Timesaver tip

More Shortcuts You can also pin an application to the Start menu in Windows XP. This provides quick access to the application. Right-click on a Start menu icon and select Pin to Start menu.

→ Using the Menu System

The menu bar that you find in the Office applications gives you access to all the commands and features a particular application provides. These specific menu systems are found below the title bar and are activated by selecting a particular menu choice. The menu then opens, providing you with a set of command choices.

The Office 2003 applications use a personalized menu system that was first introduced in Microsoft Office 2000. It enables you to quickly access the commands you use most often. When you first choose a particular menu, you find a short list of menu commands. As you use commands, the Office application adds them to the menu list.

To access a particular menu, follow these steps:

1 Select the menu by clicking its title. The most recently used commands appear; hover the mouse pointer for just a moment and all the commands on a particular menu appear; if you don't like to hover, click the Expand icon (the double down-pointing arrow on the bottom of the menu) to view all the menu choices.

2 Select the command on the menu that invokes a particular feature.

You will find that several of the commands found on the menu are followed by an ellipsis (…). These commands, when selected, open a dialog box or a task pane. Dialog boxes require you to provide the application with additional information before the particular feature or command can be used (more information on working with dialog boxes appears later in this lesson).

Some of the menus also contain a submenu or a cascading menu that you can use to make your choices. The menu commands that produce a submenu are indicated by an arrow to the right of the menu choice. If a submenu is present, you point at the command (marked with the arrow) on the main menu to open the submenu.

> **Timesaver tip**
>
> **Activating Menus with the Keyboard** You can also activate a particular menu by holding down the **Alt** key and then pressing the keyboard key that matches the underscored letter, also called a hotkey, in the menu's name. For example, to activate the File menu in Office applications, press **Alt+F**.

If you would rather have access to all the menu commands (rather than just those you've used recently), you can turn off the personalized menu system. To do this, follow these steps in any Office application:

1 Click the **Tools** menu, and then click **Customize**.

2 In the Customize dialog box, click the **Options** tab.

3 To show all the commands on the menus (without delay), click the **Always Show Full Menus** check box.

4 Click **OK** to close the dialog box.

→ Using Shortcut Menus

A fast way to access commands that are related to a particular item on an Office document, such as selected text or a picture, is to right-click that item. This opens a shortcut menu that contains commands related to the particular item with which you are working.

For example, if you select a chart on an Excel worksheet, right-clicking the chart (see Figure 2.3) opens a shortcut menu with commands such as Cut, Copy, and Paste.

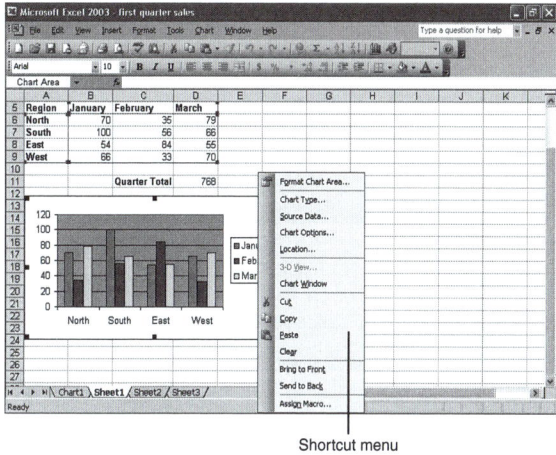

Figure 2.3 Shortcut menus provide quick access to application commands.

As you learned in Lesson 1, some items in your Office application documents are also marked with smart tags. Pointing at an item underscored with a dotted red line allows you to access the smart tag menu and access options related to that document item, such as a pasted item.

→ Working with Toolbars

Toolbars provide you with a very quick and straightforward way of accessing commands and features in the Office applications. When you first start one of the Office applications, you typically see the Standard and Formatting toolbars sharing one row, as shown in Figure 2.4.

To access a particular command using a toolbar button, click the button. Depending on the command, you see an immediate result in your document (such as the removal of selected text when you click the **Cut** button), or a dialog box might appear, requesting additional information from you.

> **Timesaver tip**
>
> **Finding a Toolbar Button's Purpose** You can place the mouse pointer on any toolbar button to view a ScreenTip that describes that tool's function.

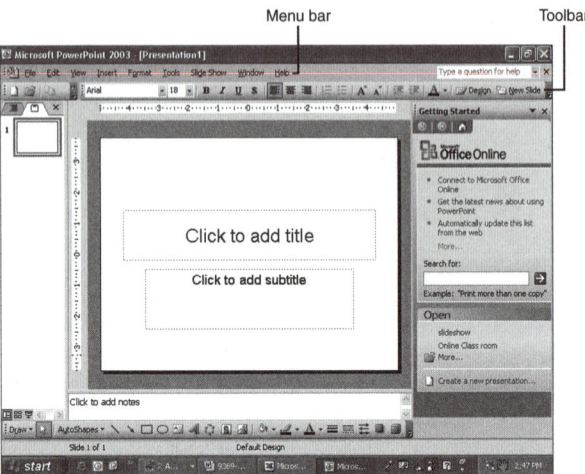

Figure 2.4 Toolbars, such as the Standard and Formatting toolbars in this PowerPoint window, provide quick access to an application's features and commands.

Other toolbars, such as the Drawing toolbar and toolbars that are specific to a particular Office application, open when you access a particular application. You can also open them manually by right-clicking any visible toolbar and then selecting the toolbar you want to use from the list that is provided. You can also use this method to close a toolbar you no longer need.

> **Important**
>
> **Missing Toolbar Buttons?** The Standard and Formatting toolbars have been configured to share one row by default, so you might not be able to see every button on the toolbars. To find a hidden button, click the **More Buttons** button on the end of either toolbar. Another alternative is to click the **Toolbar Options** button on the Standard or Formatting toolbar and select **Show Buttons on Two Rows**. This gives each toolbar its own row.

In Lesson 5, "Customizing Your Office Applications," you learn how to customize common Office features. We will work with toolbar settings and other options related to the various application settings.

→ Understanding Dialog Boxes

When you are working with the various commands and features found in Office applications, you will invariably come across dialog boxes. Dialog boxes are used when an Office application needs more information from you before it can complete a particular command or take advantage of a special feature. Dialog boxes always appear when you select a menu command that is followed by an ellipsis. Dialog boxes also appear when you invoke this same command using the appropriate toolbar button.

Figure 2.5 shows Word's Font dialog box. This dialog box enables you to make selections using check boxes and drop-down lists. Other dialog boxes use option buttons, spinner boxes, and other methods of enabling you to quickly make selections in a particular box.

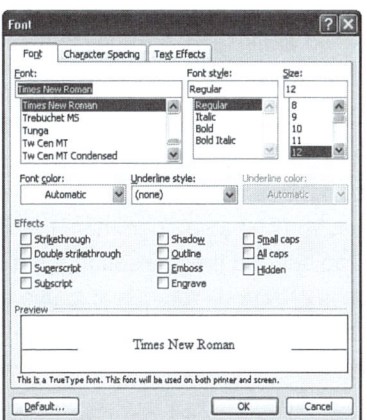

Figure 2.5 Dialog boxes enable you to make your choices related to a particular feature.

In most cases, when you complete your selections in a dialog box, you click the **OK** button to close the box and complete the command. You also have the option of clicking the **Cancel** button if you want to close the dialog box without saving any changes you made.

3 Using Office Task Panes

In this lesson, you learn how to use Office 2003's task panes.

→ Understanding the Task Pane

A major change to the previous version of Office, Office XP, was the introduction of task panes. Office 2003 also uses task panes, which have replaced many of the dialog boxes that were a common feature in Office 97 and Office 2000. Office 2003 has also added new task panes such as the Research task pane (which we discuss later in this lesson).

A task pane is a multipurpose window pane that appears on the right side of the window of an Office application. The list that follows describes the global task panes that you will find in all the Office applications:

- **New File Task Pane**—Enables you to start a new file in a particular application (for example, in Word it is called the New Document task pane; in Excel it is called the New Workbook task pane). It also provides access to various document templates and the capability to open recently used files.

- **Office Clipboard Task Pane**—Enables you to view items that you copy and cut to the Office Clipboard. You can manage up to 24 items on the Clipboard and paste them within an application or between applications.

- **Clip Art Task Pane**—Enables you to search the Office Clip Gallery and insert clip art into your Office application documents.

- **Search Task Pane**—Enables you to search for files from any of the Office applications.

- **Research Task Pane**—This new task pane allows you to take advantage of a number of research and reference services. A number of these references are accessed via online services such as Microsoft Encarta.

You look at the Research, Search, Clip Art, and Clipboard task panes in more detail later in the lesson.

Task panes also house features that handle specific purposes in each of the Office applications. For example, in PowerPoint, the Slide Layout task pane (shown in Figure 3.1) is used to select a design format for a new or existing PowerPoint presentation slide. You learn about the different task panes in the Office applications as you use them in the different parts of this book.

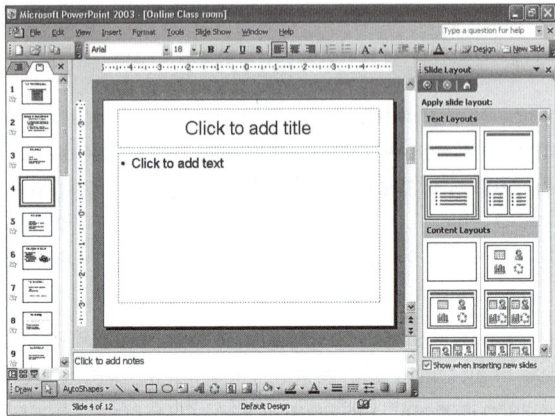

Figure 3.1 The task pane provides specific features in the different Office applications.

When you are working in an Office application, such as Word or Excel, you can open a task pane and switch between the different task pane features offered in that particular application. To open a task pane, follow these steps:

1. In the Office application window, select the **View** menu and select **Task Pane**. The New File task pane appears on the right side of the application window (the New File task pane is the default task pane for the Office applications).

2. To switch to a particular task pane that is available in the current Office application, click the task pane's drop-down arrow (see Figure 3.2).

3. Click the item on the task pane menu that you want to use.

You will find that the task pane also pops up when you select specific features in an application. For example, in Word, when you select

Format and then **Styles and Formatting**, the Styles and Formatting task pane appears in the Word window.

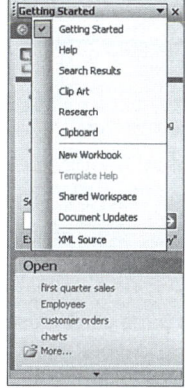

Figure 3.2 Use the task pane's menu to switch to a particular task pane in an application.

>
>
> **Timesaver tip**
>
> **Help Is Now a Task Pane**   Office Help is now accessed through a task pane. Getting help in Office is discussed in Lesson 4, "Getting Help in Microsoft Office."

→ The Research Task Pane

The newest Office task pane is the Research task pane. The Research task pane provides a tool that can be used to access all sorts of information related to a selection in a Word document, Excel worksheet, or PowerPoint Presentation. These tools can be standard tools such as the Thesaurus and can also consist of specialized data sources created to find specific kinds of information. For example, Figure 3.3 shows the results of a Research task pane search for the term "Microsoft." The results provide company information including employee numbers and yearly revenue.

To use the Research task pane, follow these steps:

1 From an Office application window, select the term or phrase that will be used in the Research task pane search.

Figure 3.3 The Research task pane can be used to find a variety of information from any Office application.

2 Select the **View** menu and then select **Task Pane** to open the task pane.

3 Select the task pane drop-down arrow and select Research. The Research task pane will open.

4 Your selected term or phrase will appear in the Search For box.

5 Click the **Services** drop-down list and select the research services you want to use for the search. You can select **All Research Sites**, **Factiva News Search**, **All Business and Financial Sites**, and a number of other resource services.

6 After selecting the service or services, the search will be performed. A list of found information will appear in the task pane.

7 To switch from the initial source to the next source (found in the search), click **Next**.

8 To expand any of the found information, click the plus symbol next to a source heading.

If you want to conduct another search, type the keyword or phrase in the Search For box and then click the **green Search arrow**. Results are returned in the task pane. When you have finished working with the Research task pane, click the **Close** button to close it.

→ The Basic File Search Task Pane

The Basic File Search task pane enables you to locate files stored on your computer or company network without leaving the Office application that is currently open. To use the Search task pane, follow these steps:

1 From an Office application window, select the **File** menu and then select **Search** to open the Search task pane (see Figure 3.4).

Figure 3.4 Use the Search task pane to locate files on your computer or network.

2 Type the keyword or keywords that you want to use for the search into the Search text box.

3 To specify the locations that should be searched, click the **Selected Locations** drop-down box. You can expand any of the locations listed, such as My Computer, by clicking the plus (+) symbol to the left of the location. This enables you to view folders and subfolders at that location. Use the check boxes to the left of each location to specify whether that location should be searched.

4 To specify the types of files that are located during the search, click the **Selected File Types** drop-down list. Select or deselect the check boxes for particular Office applications (such as Word or Excel) to specify the types of files that should be included in the search.

5 When you are ready to run the search, click the **Go** button.

The files that meet your search criteria appear in the Search task pane. To open one of the files (in the application that it was created in), click the filename.

> **Timesaver tip**
>
> **Run an Advanced Search** You can also click the Advanced Search link in the Search task pane to run an advanced search. The Advanced Search task pane enables you to create a search that uses conditional statements and allows you to search by file type, the date that the file was last modified, and a number of other parameters.

→ Other Standard Task Panes

Two other standard task panes that you will probably use a lot are the Clip Art and Office Clipboard task panes.

The Clip Art Task Pane

How you find and insert clip art in the Office applications has been made much easier by the introduction of the Clip Art task pane. This task pane enables you to quickly search for clip art using a keyword search. Clip art that matches your search parameters is then immediately shown in the Clip Art task pane as thumbnails.

To use the Clip Art task pane, follow these steps:

1 In an Office application such as Word or Excel, select **Insert**, point at **Picture**, and then select **Clip Art**. The Clip Art task pane appears (see Figure 3.5).

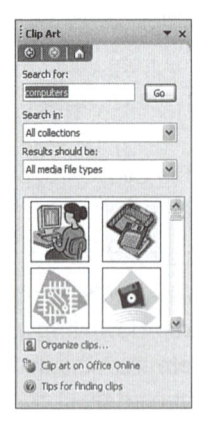

Figure 3.5 Search for clip art by keywords using the Clip Art task pane.

2 In the task pane's Search For box, type keywords that Office can use to find your clip art images.

3 Use the **Search In** drop-down box to specify the collections you want to include in the clip art search. Selected collections are marked with a check mark in their check box that you can toggle on and off with a simple click of the mouse.

4 Use the Results Should Be drop-down box to specify the type of files that should be included in the search. You can select or deselect file types such as Clip Art, Movies, and Sounds.

5 When you have finished setting your search parameters, click the **Search** button. When the search is complete, the clip art that meets your search criteria appears in the task pane.

6 In the Image list, locate the image that you want to place into your Office document. Then, click the image. The application inserts clip art document.

Using the Office Clipboard

Microsoft Office 2003 provides a new version of the Office Clipboard that enables you to accumulate a list of 24 copied or cut items. This makes it very easy to paste items within an Office document, between Office documents in an Office application, or to copy, cut, and paste items among your different Office applications.

To use the Office Clipboard, follow these steps:

1 In an Office application, select **Edit** and then select **Office Clipboard**. The Office Clipboard task pane opens.

2 As you cut or copy items from your various Office applications, the items are placed on the Office Clipboard, as shown in Figure 3.6.

3 To paste an item from the Clipboard, place the insertion point in your Office document at the place where you want to insert the item, and then click the item on the Office Clipboard task pane.

You can remove items from the Office Clipboard at any time by placing the mouse on the item. A drop-down arrow appears; click the drop-down arrow and select **Delete** from the shortcut menu that appears. You can clear the entire Clipboard by clicking the **Clear All** button at the top of the task pane.

Figure 3.6 Use the Office Clipboard to copy, cut, and paste multiple items in your Office applications.

4 Getting Help in Microsoft Office

In this lesson, you learn how to access and use the Help system in Microsoft Office.

→ Help: What's Available?

Microsoft Office supplies a Help system that makes it easy for you to look up information on application commands and features as you work in a particular Office application. Because people have different preferences, the Office Help system can be accessed in several ways. You can

- Ask a question in the Ask a Question box.
- Ask the Office Assistant for help.
- Use the Help task pane.
- Access the Office on Microsoft.com Web site to view Web pages containing help information (if you are connected to the Internet).

→ Using the Ask a Question Box

The Ask a Question box is the easiest way to quickly get help. An Ask a Question box resides at the top right of every Office application.

For example, if you are working in Excel and would like to get some help with Excel functions, type **functions** into the Ask a Question box. Then press the **Enter** key. A search will be performed on the Help system and the results of the search (based on your keywords) will appear in the Search Results task pane (see Figure 4.1).

To access one of the Help topics supplied, select the appropriate link in the Search Results task pane. The Help window will appear. In the Help window, you can use the links provided to navigate the Help system. Click on a particular link to read more about that topic. The

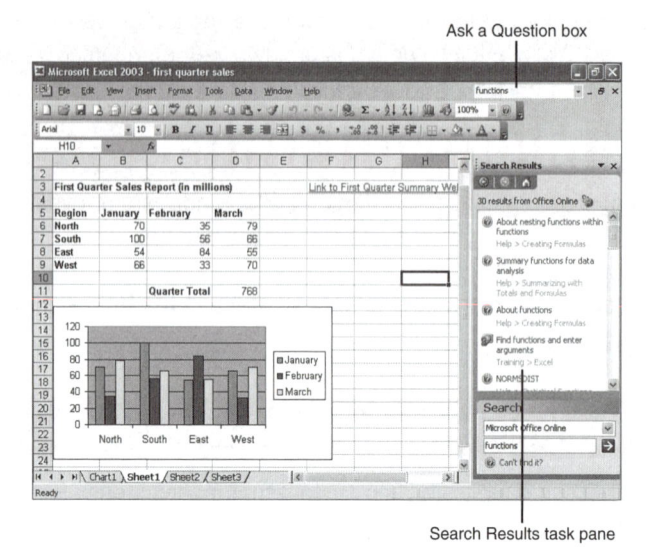

Figure 4.1 The Ask a Question box provides a list of Help topics in the Search Results task pane.

topic will be expanded in the Help window. When you have finished working with the Help window, click its Close button.

→ Using the Office Assistant

Another way to get help in an Office Application is to use the Office Assistant. The Office Assistant supplies the same type of access to the Help system as the Ask a Question box. You ask the Office Assistant a question, and it supplies you with a list of possible answers that provide links to various Help topics. The next two sections discuss how to use the Office Assistant.

Turning the Office Assistant On and Off

By default, the Office Assistant is off. To show the Office Assistant in your application window, select the **Help** menu and then select **Show the Office Assistant**.

You can also quickly hide the Office Assistant if you no longer want it in your application window. Right-click the Office Assistant and select **Hide**. If you want to get rid of the Office Assistant completely so that it isn't activated when you select the Help feature, right-click the Office

Assistant and select **Options**. Clear the **Use the Office Assistant** check box, and then click **OK**. You can always get the Office Assistant back by selecting **Help, Show Office Assistant**.

Asking the Office Assistant a Question

When you click the Office Assistant, a balloon appears above it, as shown in Figure 4.2. Type a question into the text box. Then click the **Search** button.

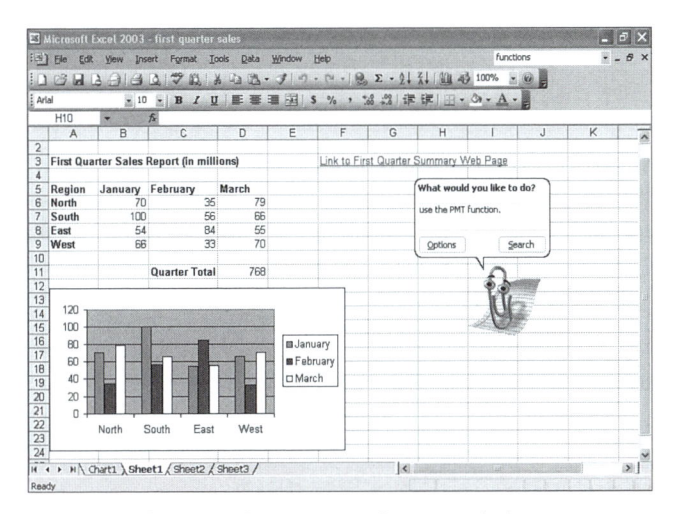

Figure 4.2 Ask the Office Assistant a question to get help.

When you click Search, the Search Results task pane appears, containing a list of results. Click a particular topic to open the Help window. Using the Office Assistant actually provides you with the same type of results you receive when you use the Ask a Question box.

Although not everyone likes the Office Assistant because having it enabled means that it is always sitting in your application window, it can be useful at times. For example, when you access particular features in an application, the Office Assistant can automatically provide you with context-sensitive help on that particular feature. If you are brand new to Microsoft Office, you might want to use the Office Assistant to help you learn the various features that the Office applications provide.

> **Timesaver tip**
>
> **Select Your Own Office Assistant** Several different Office Assistants are available in Microsoft Office. To select your favorite, click the Office Assistant and select the **Options** button. On the Office Assistant dialog box that appears, select the **Gallery** tab. Click the **Next** button repeatedly to see the different Office Assistants that are available. When you locate the assistant you want to use, click **OK**.

→ Using the Help Task Pane

You can also forgo either the Type a Question box or the Office Assistant and get your help from the Help task pane; select **Help** and then the help command for the application you are using, such as **Microsoft Word Help**. You can also press the **F1** key to make the Help task pane appear (see Figure 4.3).

Figure 4.3 Open the Help task pane to search for help by topic.

The Help task pane provides you with the ability to do a search using a keyword or keywords. You can also open the Help table of contents for the application that you are currently working in.

To do a search using the Help task pane, click in the Search box and type a keyword, phrase, or question. Then click the **Start Searching** arrow. The results of the search will appear in the Search Results task pane. Click a particular result and the Help window will open as shown in Figure 4.4.

To expand any of the help topics provided in the Help window, click a particular link. If you want to expand all the topics provided, click **Show All**.

> **Timesaver tip**
>
> **View the Help Window Tabs** If you don't see the different tabs in the Help window, click the **Show** button on the Help window toolbar.

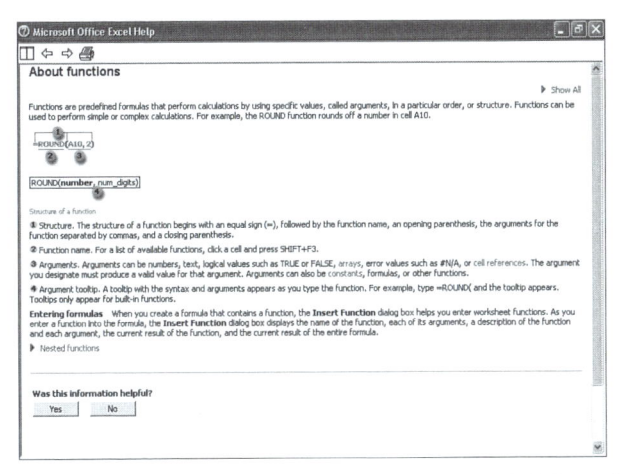

Figure 4.4 The Help window provides access to all the help information provided for a particular application.

→ Searching for Help Online

If you don't find the help you need using the different ways we discussed in this lesson to access the Help window, you can connect to the Microsoft Office Web site. The site provides a search engine and other information on the different Microsoft Office applications. To connect to the Office Web site, follow these steps:

1 Open the Help task pane (select **Help** and then your application's help command, or press **F1**).

2 In the Help task pane, click the **Connect to Office on Microsoft.com** link.

3 The Microsoft Office Web site will open in your Web browser window. Use the links to the various articles and the Search engine provided to find the help that you need.

> **Timesaver tip**
>
> **Take Advantage of ScreenTips** Another Help feature provided by the Office applications is the ScreenTip. All the buttons on the different toolbars provided by your Office applications have a ScreenTip. Other buttons or tools in an Office application window can also provide ScreenTips. Place the mouse on a particular button or icon, and the name of the item (which often helps you determine its function) appears in a ScreenTip.

5 Customizing Your Office Applications

In this lesson, you learn how to customize your Office applications.

→ Navigating Options Settings

Office applications provide you with a great deal of control over the desktop environment that you work in. You can control options such as how the application window looks for a particular Office application and where the application should store files, by default, when you save them.

Every one of the Office applications has an Options dialog box that provides access to different settings that you can customize. First, you take a look at how you open and navigate the Options dialog box in an Office application. Then, you look at several of the applications and some of the key options they offer that you might want to customize.

> **! Important**
>
> **Customizing Office Applications** You might want to work with the Office applications described in this book before you change a lot of options for the applications.

To open and navigate the Options dialog box in an Office application, follow these steps:

1. In an Office application (such as Word), select **Tools**, **Options**. The Options dialog box for that application appears (see Figure 5.1).
2. To switch between the different options, click the appropriate tab on the Options dialog box. Each tab controls a subset of the options available in that application.

Customizing Your Office Applications   33

3 To change settings on the various tabs, use the check boxes, drop-down lists, or spinner boxes to make your selections for various features.

4 When you have finished customizing the various options in the Options dialog box, click **OK**. You are returned to the application window.

Figure 5.1 The Options dialog box in an application enables you to customize various settings.

You will find that you can set a large number of options in the Options dialog box for each Office application. This doesn't mean that you have to change them all (if you're not sure what you're doing, in many cases you shouldn't change them). Next, take a look at some of the common settings that you might want to change in your Office applications.

→ Setting Options in Word

When you work in Word, you are probably going to create letters and envelopes for mailings. One of the options related to Word that you will want to set up is your user information. This way, the return address on any letters and envelopes you create with Word are inserted automatically into certain documents.

Another set of options that you might want to customize in Word are the options related to the Spelling and Grammar Checker. For example, you might want to customize the types of things that are automatically flagged by the Spelling and Grammar Checker when you run these features in Word.

To customize some of the Word options, follow these steps:

1 In Word, select **Tools** and then select **Options** to open the Options dialog box.

2 Click the **User Information** tab on the Options dialog box (see Figure 5.2).

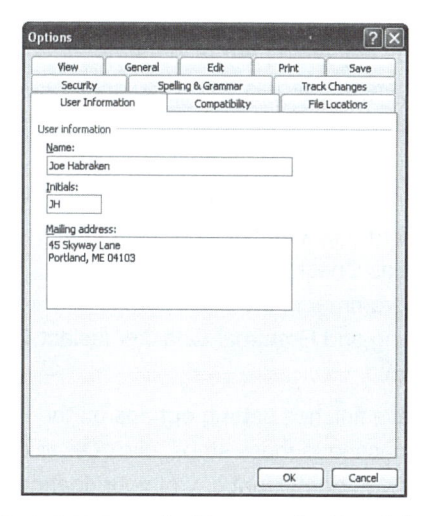

Figure 5.2 Provide your name and address on the User Information tab.

3 If necessary, type your name into the Name box on the User Information tab. Type your address into the Mailing Address box. That takes care of the User Information tab.

Customizing Your Office Applications

4 To set options related to the Spelling and Grammar features, click the **Spelling & Grammar** tab (see Figure 5.3).

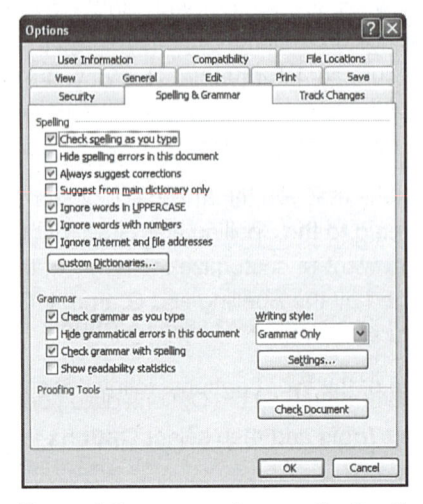

Figure 5.3 Set Spelling and Grammar options on the Spelling & Grammar tab.

5 Check boxes are provided that allow you to check spelling as you type or to hide any typing errors in the document (by default, typing errors are flagged as you type with a red underscore). You can also determine whether you want the Spelling feature to ignore uppercase words, words with numbers, and Internet and file addresses. Select or deselect check boxes as needed.

6 Use the Grammar box on the Spelling & Grammar tab to set options such as Check Grammar As You Type. You can also set whether the grammar in the document is checked whenever you run the Spelling and Grammar Checker (select **Check Grammar with Spelling**).

7 When you have finished setting options on the two Options dialog box tabs discussed in these steps, click **OK** to close the Options dialog box. If you don't want any of your changes to take effect, click **Cancel**.

→ Setting Options in Excel

When you work with Excel, you work with numbers and calculations. As you learn in the Excel section of this book, Excel is a number cruncher. It is built to do math and provide you with correct results when it does calculations.

Two of the options that you might want to adjust related to Excel specify when it recalculates all the formulas in an Excel workbook and the rules that it uses to check for errors in an Excel worksheet.

Follow these steps:

1 In Excel, select **Tools** and then select **Options**. The Options dialog box opens.

2 Click the **Calculation** tab on the Options dialog box (see Figure 5.4).

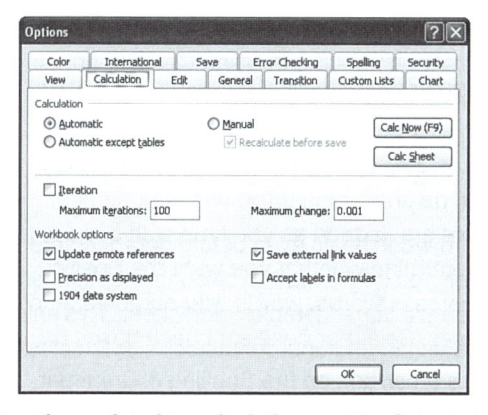

Figure 5.4 Set options related to calculations on the Calculation tab.

3 When you work with very large worksheets and worksheets that are linked to other Excel workbook files, your worksheet is recalculated every time you change or add data on the worksheet. If you have a computer with marginal processing power and memory, this process can take a while. You can turn off the automatic recalculation feature on the Calculations tab by clicking the **Manual** option button. If you do this, you must press **F9** to make Excel recalculate the sheet.

4 You might want to look at another set of options on the **Error Checking** tab (click it). This tab contains a list of errors that Excel can automatically check for as you work on your worksheet (see Figure 5.5).

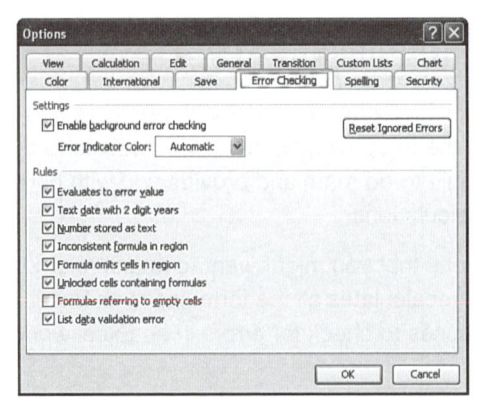

Figure 5.5 Error checking helps make sure that your worksheet data is entered correctly.

5 To set a default color for errors found in a worksheet, click the **Error Indicator Color** drop-down box and select a color from the color palette (because the Spelling Checker and smart tags use red, don't pick red).

6 You should probably leave the error rules listed all in force. However, notice in Figure 5.5 that the Formulas Referring to Empty Cells check box is not selected. This is because you typically enter formulas into worksheets even before data is entered. After creating a worksheet, you might want to select this option, especially if you are working on a large, complex worksheet. This ensures that you get all the data into the appropriate cells, or Excel will start sending error messages your way.

7 When you have finished setting these options, click **OK** to close the Options dialog box (or **Cancel** to discard changes).

→ Setting Options in PowerPoint

After you work in PowerPoint for a while, you might find that you want to specify a view to be the default view when you open presentations that you have created. Another option you might want to set is the default location where presentations that you save are placed.

Follow these steps to change these PowerPoint options:

1 In PowerPoint, select **Tools** and then select **Options** to open the Options dialog box.

2 Click the **View** tab on the Options dialog box (see Figure 5.6).

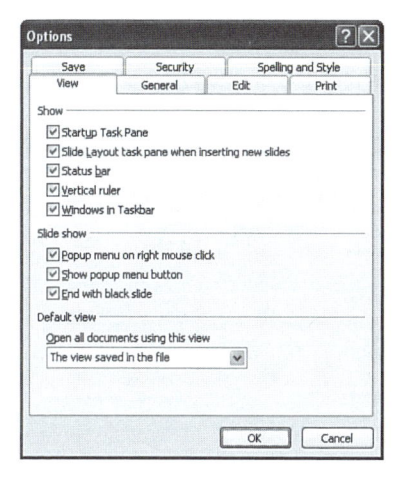

Figure 5.6 Set the default view that will be used when you open a saved presentation.

3 Click the **Open All Documents Using This View** drop-down list and select a view that you want to use whenever you open a saved presentation. The views range from **Normal-Outline**, **Notes**, and **Slide** to **Slide Sorter**.

4 Another option you might want to set is the default folder that is used when you first save a presentation. Click the **Save** tab on the Options dialog box.

5 In the Default File Location box, type the path that you want to use.

6 When you have finished changing your settings, click **OK** (or **Cancel** to reject any changes made).

→ Setting Special Options in Access

When you work in Access, you spend a lot of time in the Datasheet view, adding and manipulating records in a database table. Although forms can be used to handle some of the data entry and editing chores, you still will work a great deal with table datasheets. Therefore, you might want to customize the Datasheet view to make it easier to work with and provide an environment that is a little easier on your eyes.

Follow these steps to customize Access options:

1 In Access, select **Tools** and then select **Options**. The Options dialog box opens.

2 Click the **Datasheet** tab on the Options dialog box (see Figure 5.7).

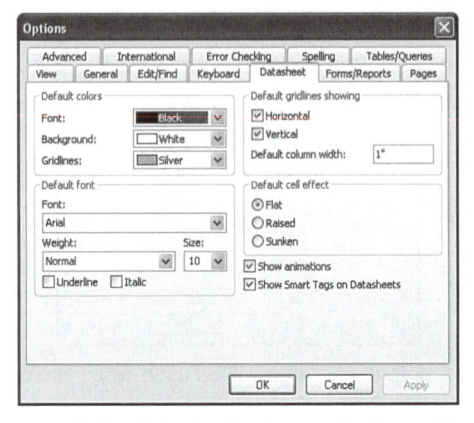

Figure 5.7 You can edit the datasheet colors and other settings on the Datasheet tab.

3 Use the Font drop-down box to select a color for the font used in the Datasheet view.

4 The Background and Gridlines drop-down boxes can be used to adjust the colors of these items to complement the Font color you select.

5 If you want to change the Default Cell Effect, select either the **Raised** or **Sunken** option buttons.

6 You can also specify a wider default column width for your datasheets in the Default Column Width box.

7 When you have finished making your changes, click **OK** (or **Cancel** to discard any changes made).

→ Customizing Toolbars

You might find as you use your Office applications that you would like to customize your toolbars. This enables you to add or remove buttons from the toolbars so that they provide you with quick access to the commands and features you use the most often.

For example, suppose you would like to add or remove buttons from a particular toolbar, such as the Formatting toolbar (which is common to a number of Office applications). Follow these steps:

1 In any application (such as Word), place the mouse on a toolbar's drop-down arrow (on the far right of the toolbar). Click the drop-down arrow to open a shortcut menu.

2 On the toolbar shortcut menu, point at **Add or Remove Buttons**, and then point at the toolbar's name on the pop-up menu that appears. A list of all the buttons available for that toolbar appears (see Figure 5.8). The buttons that are being used on the toolbar have a check mark to the left of them.

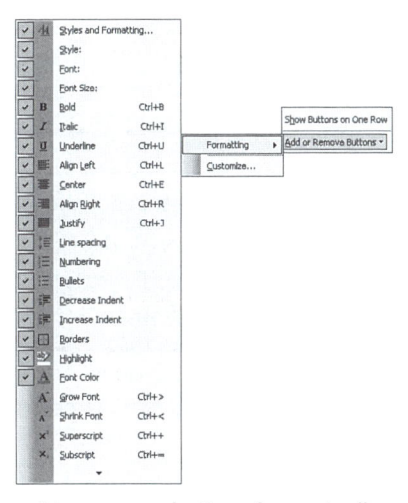

Figure 5.8 You can add or remove buttons from a toolbar.

3 Click a button to deselect it (remove it), or click one of the unselected buttons listed to add it.

4 Repeat step 4 until you have customized the buttons shown on the toolbar. Then, click anywhere in the application window to close the Button drop-down list.

> **Timesaver tip**
>
> **Resetting a Toolbar** If you want to reset a toolbar and start from scratch with the default buttons, open the Button drop-down list for a particular toolbar and then click **Reset Toolbar** at the very bottom of the Button drop-down list.

Another setting related to toolbars that you might want to adjust is for the Standard and Formatting toolbars in your Office applications, which are set up, by default, to share one line. This limits the number of buttons that can be shown on either of the toolbars at any one time. To place each of these toolbars on its own line, follow these steps:

1 In any application (such as Word or Excel), select the **Tools** menu and then select **Customize**.

2 The Customize dialog box opens. Click the **Options** tab, if necessary.

3 On the Options tab, click the **Show Standard and Formatting Toolbars on Two Rows** check box.

4 Click **Close**.

> **Timesaver tip**
>
> **Get Toolbars in Two Rows Quickly**   You can also quickly place the Standard and Formatting toolbars on two rows by clicking the **Toolbar Options** button on the Standard toolbar (when the toolbars are in a single row) and selecting **Show Buttons on Two Rows**.

6 Faxing and E-Mailing in Office 2003

In this lesson, you learn how to fax and e-mail documents from Office applications.

→ Understanding E-Mails and Faxes in Office

The capability to send e-mail and faxes directly from your Office applications enables you to quickly take the information on your screen and either fax it or e-mail it to a recipient. When you send an e-mail message directly from an Office application client, such as Word, Excel, Access, or PowerPoint, you are actually using your default e-mail client, such as Outlook, to send the message.

All the Office applications allow you to send the current document as an attachment. Word and Excel also provide the option of sending the document as part of the e-mail message.

There are two options for faxing documents from within an Office application. You can either send the fax using an Internet Fax Service, which allows you to actually fax the document over the Internet, or you can outfit your computer with a fax modem. Fax modems actually supply faxing capabilities as an extension of your computer's printing services.

> **Timesaver tip**
>
> **Sign Up for an Internet Fax Service** If you want to fax documents over the Internet, you need to sign up for an Internet Fax Service. Several Internet Fax Services exist, which not only allow you to fax information over the Internet but may also enable you to receive faxes over the Internet and have them sent to you as e-mail messages. The first time you attempt to use the Internet Fax Service to send a fax from a Microsoft Application, you are provided with the option of navigating to a Web page that lists Internet Fax Providers. The cost related to these services will vary.

Word makes the process of sending a fax easy and provides a Fax Wizard to walk you through the steps. The other Office applications send faxes in two different ways: either by "printing" to a fax modem or by using the Send To command on the File menu to send an Internet fax (Word also provides this option). Sending a fax from the Office applications via a fax modem is discussed later in the lesson.

To send a fax from any Office application using an Internet Fax Service, you click **File**, and then point at **Send To**. On the menu that appears, select **Recipient Using Internet Fax Service**. You can then complete the process by providing the recipient's fax number and other information required for a fax cover page.

Internet Fax Services provide their own cover page and set of instructions for sending a fax. The actual number of steps that you have to complete to send an Office document as a fax over the Internet depends on the actual service that you use.

→ Using the Word Fax Wizard

The Word Fax Wizard walks you through the steps of preparing your Word document. You can send your fax using a fax modem (attached to your computer) or using an Internet Fax Service.

Timesaver tip

Setting Up a Fax Modem and the Fax Service   Most "new" fax modems embrace plug-and-play technology as do Microsoft Windows XP and Microsoft Windows 2000. In most cases all you will have to do to get a fax modem up and running is to attach the modem to the computer (or install it internally) and then restart the PC. Windows XP requires that you add the Microsoft Fax Service to your computer to send and receive faxes. You add this service in the Printers and Faxes window of the Control Panel. When you open this window, click the Install Faxing link on the left side of the window and follow the prompts. Make sure you have your Windows XP CD available because files need to be copied to your system to enable the fax service.

To use the Word Fax Wizard and send a fax using a fax modem (in the Windows XP environment), follow these steps:

1 Select **File,** point to **Send To**, and then select **Recipient Using a Fax Modem** from the cascading menu. The Word Fax Wizard starts (see Figure 6.1).

Figure 6.1 The Fax Wizard walks you through the process of sending the current document as a fax.

2 The Fax Wizard starts to walk you through the process of sending the current document as a fax. Click **Next** to continue the process.

3 On the next wizard screen, a drop-down list enables you to select whether to send the current document or select another open document (see Figure 6.2). After making your selection, click **Next** to continue.

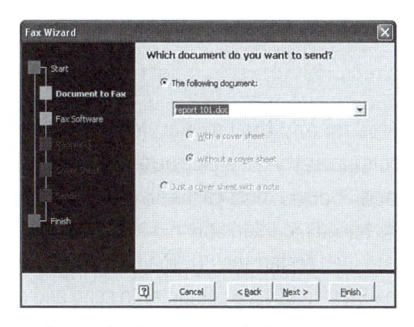

Figure 6.2 You can select whether to send the current document or select another open document.

4 On the next screen, you select your fax service. Microsoft Fax is the default. If you use a different fax program on your computer, select the option button labeled **A Different Fax Program Which Is Installed on This System**, and then select your fax program from the **Fax Service** drop-down list. Then click **Next** to continue.

5 At this point the Fax Wizard has completed the initial process of selecting the document and fax service. When you click **Finish**, the Send Fax Wizard appears. Click **Next** to bypass the initial Wizard screen.

6 On the next screen (see Figure 6.3), enter the recipient and the fax number into the appropriate boxes. If you have the recipient listed in your e-mail program's address book (such as the Outlook Contacts folder), click the **Address Book** button and select the person from the Address Book list. If a fax number is listed in the address book (as it is in Microsoft Outlook), all you have to do is select the recipients from the address book for your Word fax, and the fax numbers are entered for you automatically. When you have finished entering the recipient information for the fax, click **Next** to continue.

Figure 6.3 Enter the recipient (or recipients) information for the fax.

7 On this screen, select the cover page template you want to use for your fax cover page. Also provide a subject line and note (optional); click **Next** to continue.

8 On the next screen, you choose the schedule for when the fax should be sent. The default is Now, but you can also select a specific time. This screen also allows you to specify the priority for the fax: High, Normal (the default), or Low.

9 On the final screen of the Fax Wizard, you are can choose to preview the fax. Click the **Preview Fax** button to see the fax cover page and accompanying document. When you are ready to send the fax, click **Finish**.

Your fax modem will connect to your phone line and send the fax (if you chose to send the fax "Now"). If you want to view sent faxes or view a list of faxes waiting to be sent by the Microsoft Fax Service, you can open the Fax Console. Select **Start, All Programs, Accessories, Fax**, and then click on the **Fax Console**. The Fax Console operates much like an e-mail client. It provides an Inbox, Outbox, and Sent Items folders that store your received, pending, and sent faxes respectively.

→ Sending Faxes from Other Office Applications

You can also send faxes directly from other Office applications. You "print" the document to the fax service installed on your computer.

Follow these steps to send a fax from an Office application such as Excel or Access:

1 Select **File** and then select **Print** to open the Print dialog box.

2 In the Name box in the Print dialog box, select the fax service that you have installed on your computer (see Figure 6.4).

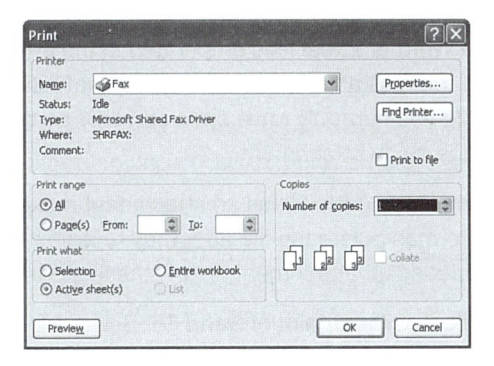

Figure 6.4 Select your fax service as the printer in the Print dialog box.

3 Click **OK**. Depending on the fax service you are using on your computer, a dialog box or wizard specific to the fax service opens. For example, if you have the Windows fax service installed on your computer, the Send Fax Wizard opens. You would then click **Next** to advance past the opening screen provided by the wizard.

4 Follow steps 5 through 8 in the preceding section if you are using the Windows Fax Service. At the completion of the process, click **Finish** to send your fax.

→ Sending E-Mails from Office Applications

If you have an e-mail client (software for sending and receiving e-mail) on your computer, such as Microsoft Outlook, you can send Office documents in e-mails. You can send a Word document, an Excel worksheet, or even an entire PowerPoint presentation with an e-mail message.

> **Jargon buster**
>
> **E-Mail Client** The e-mail program installed on your computer that you use to send and receive e-mail.

The process for sending e-mail from the different Office applications is the same for Word, Excel, PowerPoint, and Access. You use the Send To command on the File menu.

You can send Word or Excel files embedded in the e-mail message or you can send them as attachments. In the case of PowerPoint and Access, the file you currently have open can only be sent with the e-mail message as an attachment.

In most cases, sending the file as an attachment makes it easier for the recipient to manipulate the file after they receive it. To send an Excel worksheet as an attachment, follow these steps:

1 Select **File** and then point at **Send To**. Select **Mail Recipient (as Attachment)** from the cascading menu that appears. A new e-mail message opens (in your default e-mail client, such as Outlook) with the Excel file attached (see Figure 6.5).

2 Type the e-mail address of the recipient into the To box, or click the **To** icon and select an e-mail address from an address book, such as your Outlook Contacts list.

3 When you are ready to send the e-mail, click **Send**.

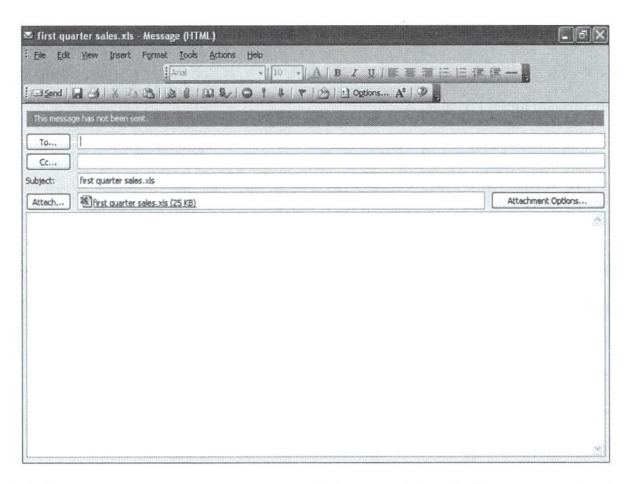

Figure 6.5 The new e-mail message contains the Excel file as an attachment.

Your e-mail is sent. You can view the sent e-mail by opening your e-mail client and then opening the Sent Items folder.

> **Timesaver tip**
>
> **Sending Word and Excel Files Using the Mail Recipient Command**
> As already mentioned, Word and Excel can send documents as the body of an e-mail. When you select **File, Send To** and then **Mail Recipient**, a mail window actually opens at the top of the Word or Excel document. You enter the recipient and other information required and then click the **Send This Sheet** button (in Excel) or **Send a Copy** button (in Word) that is provided on the Mail toolbar. For recipients to view this e-mail correctly they will need to be using Outlook. If they use another type of e-mail client, you are better off sending the file as an attachment.

One thing to remember when you are e-mailing documents directly from Office applications is that you must be connected to the Internet or your company's network to actually send the mail. If you use a dial-up connection to access the Internet (and Internet e-mail), connect to the Internet before sending the e-mail from the Office application.

Outlook

1 Getting Started in Outlook

In this lesson, you learn how to start and exit Outlook, identify parts of the Outlook window, and use the mouse to get around the program.

→ Starting Outlook

You start Outlook from the Windows desktop. After starting the program, you can leave it open, or you can minimize it to free up the desktop for other applications. Either way, you can access it at any time.

To start Microsoft Outlook, follow these steps:

1 From the Windows XP desktop, click the **Start** button, choose **All Programs**, point at **Microsoft Office**, and then select **Microsoft Office Outlook 2003**. (For Windows 2000, select **Start, Programs**, point at **Microsoft Office**, and then click **Microsoft Office Outlook 2003**.)

> **Timesaver tip**
>
> **Shortcut to Launching Outlook**   In Windows XP, you can click the **Outlook** icon, which is pinned to the Start menu or click the **Outlook** icon on the Quick Launch toolbar on the Windows taskbar (next to the Start button).

2 If your PC is set up for multiple users, the Choose Profile dialog box appears; click **OK** to accept the default profile or choose your profile and open Microsoft Outlook. Figure 1.1 shows the Outlook screen that appears.

Getting Started in Outlook   53

> **Jargon buster**
>
> **Profile** The profile includes information about you and your e-mail accounts and is created automatically when you install Outlook (the e-mail accounts are added to the profile when Outlook is set up for the first time). Multiple profiles become an issue only if you share your computer with other users.

[Figure: Screenshot of the Outlook Today window with labels pointing to: Title bar, Find a Contact box, Menu bar, Toolbar, Ask a Question box, Navigation pane, Folder list, Status bar.]

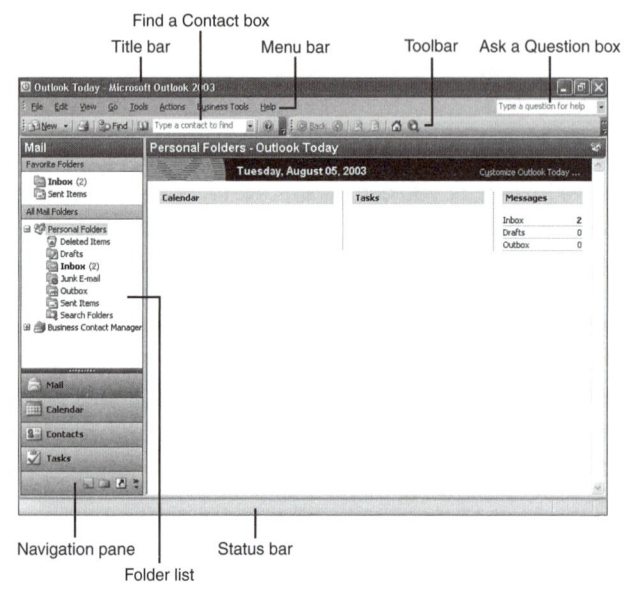

Figure 1.1 The Outlook window includes all the icons and items you need to access its various features.

If you connect to the Internet using a modem dial-up connection, the Connection Wizard attempts to make a dial-in connection as Outlook opens. This enables Outlook to check your e-mail server.

→ Understanding the Outlook Window

The Outlook window includes items you can use to navigate in and operate the program. If you do not see some of the items listed in Figure 1.1 on your screen, open the **View** menu and select the command for the appropriate element (such as **Toolbars**, **Status Bar**, or **Outlook Bar**). A check mark in front of an item means the item is currently showing.

Table 1.1 describes the elements you see in the opening screen.

Table 1.1 Elements of the Outlook Window

Element	Description
Title bar	Includes the name of the application and current folder, plus the Minimize, Maximize, and Close buttons.
Toolbar	Includes icons that serve as shortcuts for common commands, such as creating a new message or printing a message.
Navigation pane	Displays icons representing folders: Inbox, Calendar, Contacts, and so on. Click an icon to change to the folder it names. The Outlook Shortcuts, My Shortcuts, and Other Shortcuts buttons on the bar list specific groups of folders (for example, the My Shortcuts button lists icons related to your e-mail, such as the Drafts, Outbox, and Sent items).
Show Folder List	Displays the current folder. Click this to display a list of personal folders you can open. In this latest version of Outlook, the Folder List is now part of the Outlook bar.
Status bar	Displays information about the items currently shown in the Information Viewer.
Find a Contact box	This box allows you to search for a contact that you have entered in your Contacts folder.
Ask a Question box	This box allows you to quickly ask the Outlook Help system a question. It also allows you to forgo using the Office Assistant to access the Help system.

> **Timesaver tip**
>
> **Finding a Toolbar Button's Purpose** You can place the mouse pointer on any toolbar button to view a description of that tool's function.

> **Timesaver tip**
>
> **Keyboard Shortcuts**   Many shortcuts are provided that allow you to access Outlook features using the keyboard. For example, you can go to your mail by pressing Ctrl+1 or to the Calendar by pressing Ctrl+2. Check out the Outlook Go menu (on the Menu bar) for more keyboard shortcuts. You can also access Outlook menus by pressing the **Alt** key and then pressing the underlined letter in the menu name (press **Alt+F** to open the File menu, for instance). The Alt menu shortcuts are common to all the Office applications.

→ Working Offline

If you use a modem connection to access your e-mail server, you can close the connection while still working in Outlook. This allows you to free up your phone line or, if you pay for your connection based on the time you are connected, save on connection time. Working offline in Outlook does not affect any Outlook features or capabilities. E-mail that you create while working offline is held in the Outbox until you reconnect to your Internet connection.

To work offline, select the **File** menu and then select **Work Offline**. If you are prompted to confirm the closing of your dial-in connection, click **Yes**. To go back online, click **File** then **Work Online**.

→ Exiting Outlook

When you are finished working in Outlook, you can exit the application in several ways. You can use the File menu: select **File**, **Exit**. Or you can close Outlook by clicking the Outlook window's **Close (X)** button. If you are connected to the Internet using a dial-up connection, you are prompted as to whether you want to log off your connection. If you want to close the dial-up connection, select **Log Off** in the message box.

> **Timesaver tip**
>
> **Exiting Outlook Before Mail Is Sent or Received**   Outlook will complete any send or receive operations via your modem before it will actually allow you to exit the application.

2 Using Outlook's Tools

In this lesson, you learn how to change views in Outlook, how to use the Navigation pane, and how to use the Folder list.

→ Using the Navigation Pane

Microsoft Outlook 2003 has greatly enhanced the user environment in the Outlook workspace. The new Navigation pane replaces the Outlook bar and serves as the main navigational tool when you are working in Outlook. You will find that the Navigation pane has a button for each of the Outlook folders. Each Outlook organizational tool has its own folder. You have a folder for e-mail (Inbox), a folder for the calendar (Calendar), and so on.

To use the Navigation pane to switch to a different folder, select the appropriate button. Figure 2.1 shows the Navigation pane and some of the other areas of the Outlook window.

As already mentioned, the different Outlook folder buttons on the Navigation pane enable you to access your work in Outlook. This includes your e-mail messages, appointments, contact list, and so on. Table 2.1 describes each of the folders provided on the Navigation pane.

Table 2.1 Outlook Folders

Folder	Description
Mail	Includes messages you've sent and received by e-mail and fax.
Calendar	Contains your appointments, events, scheduled meetings, and so on.
Contacts	Lists names and addresses of the people with whom you communicate.
Tasks	Includes any tasks you have on your to-do list.
Notes	Lists notes you write to yourself or others.

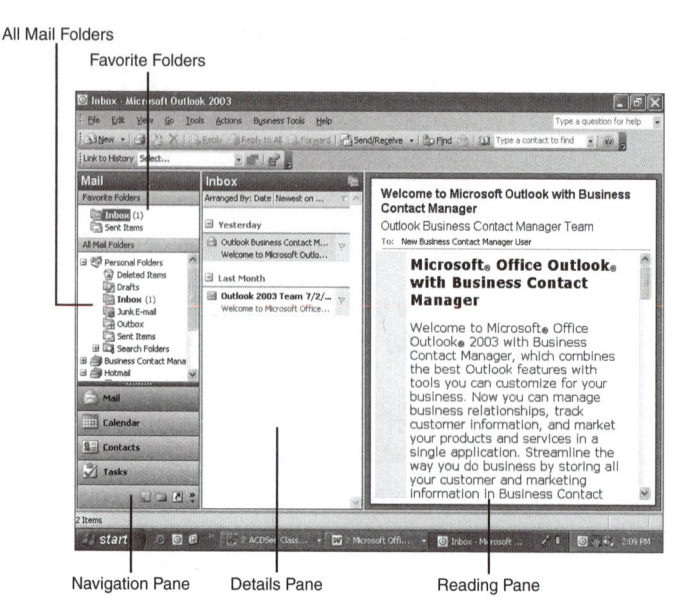

Figure 2.1 Use the Navigation pane to view your e-mail, appointments, and so on.

The Outlook 2003 Navigation pane also provides shortcuts that help you access the information in a particular folder. For example, when you access a Mail folder, you are also provided with two areas on the pane: Favorite Folders and All Mail Folders. These lists can be used to quickly access different mail-related folders found in Outlook.

The Navigation pane also allows you to control how the information is actually viewed in the Details pane of a particular folder. For example, you can choose from a number of current views to browse the records in your Contacts folder as shown in Figure 2.2.

The Navigation pane also makes it easy for you to quickly access the Folder list, custom shortcuts, and tools that allow you to configure the overall "feel" of the Navigation pane. Four buttons are provided along the bottom of the Navigation pane (see Figure 2.2) that allow you to access these features:

- **Notes**—This button opens the Notes pane and allows you to create reminder notes.
- **Folder list**—This button opens the Folder list in the Navigation pane (it is open by default when you start Outlook). The Folder list is used to view all your Outlook Personal folders.

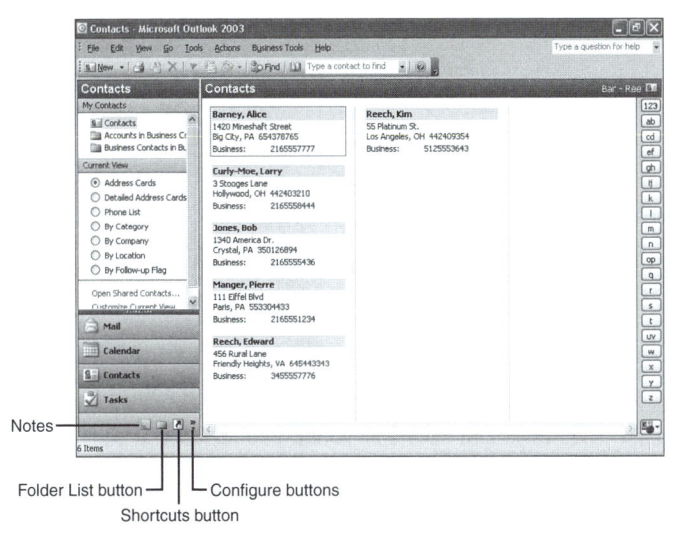

Figure 2.2 Different views can be quickly accessed from the Navigation pane.

- **Shortcuts**—This button allows you to access special shortcut icons such as those for Outlook Today (which provides an overview of current Calendar, mail, and tasks) and Outlook Update (which connects you to Microsoft and allows you to quickly update the Outlook software). You can also add custom shortcuts to the Shortcuts list by adding groups using the Add New Group link.
- **Configure Buttons**—This button opens a shortcut menu that allows you to change the size of the buttons on the Navigation pane, and change the order of the buttons that appear on the bar. You can also even add or remove buttons if you want to customize your Navigation pane further.

→ Using the Folder List

Although the Navigation pane provides quick access to your Outlook folders (such as Mail or the Calendar), you can view all your personal folders using the Folder List. To use the Folder List, click the **Folder List** button at the bottom of the Navigation pane (see Figure 2.3).

Choose any folder from the list, and the Outlook Details pane changes to reflect your selection. If you want to display another folder in the Details pane, click the folder to display its contents.

Complete list of folders

Figure 2.3 The Folder List shows all your personal folders.

→ Using Outlook Today

Outlook Today is a great way to get a snapshot view of your day. This feature provides a window that lists all your messages, appointments, and tasks associated with the current day.

To open the Outlook Today window, click **Personal Folders** in the folder list (or you can click the **Shortcuts** button at the bottom of the Navigation pane and then select the **Outlook Today** shortcut folder). Icons for your Calendar, Messages, and Tasks appear in the Outlook Today window, as shown in Figure 2.4. Items for the current day are listed below the icons.

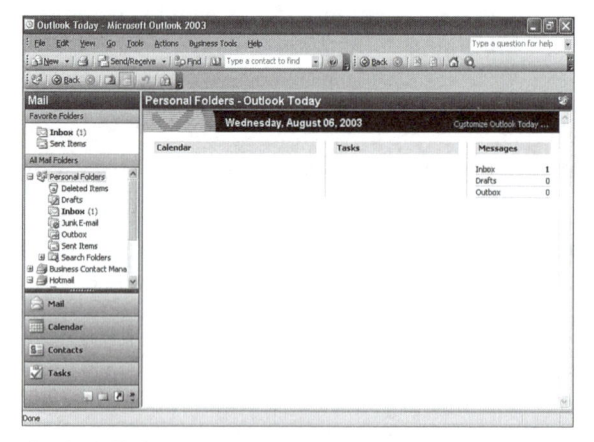

Figure 2.4 Outlook Today provides a list of all the items associated with the current day.

You can click any of the listed items (a particular appointment or task) to open the appropriate folder and view the details associated with the items. You can even update the items.

The Outlook Today Standard toolbar also provides the Type a Contact to Find box that you can use to quickly find people in your Contacts folder. Type a name into the Type a Contact to Find box (on the left of the Standard toolbar), and then press **Enter**. A Contact window appears for the person. You can edit the person's information or close the Contact box by clicking the **Close** button.

After you have viewed the items in the Outlook Today window, you can return to any of your folders by clicking their icons on the Navigation pane. Outlook Today is an excellent way to get a handle on what your day has in store for you.

3 Creating Mail

In this lesson, you learn how to compose a message, format text, check your spelling, and send e-mail. You also learn how to use different e-mail formats such as plain text and HTML.

→ Composing a Message

You can send an e-mail message to anyone for whom you have an e-mail address, whether that address is in your list of contacts or scribbled on a scrap of paper. In addition to sending a message to one or more recipients, in Outlook you can forward or copy messages to individuals in your Contacts list. You can even e-mail groups of people who are listed in your various distribution lists.

To open a new e-mail message while in the Outlook Inbox, select **File**, point at **New**, and then select **Mail Message** in the Outlook Inbox window (you can also click the **New** button on the Standard toolbar). A new message window appears (see Figure 3.1).

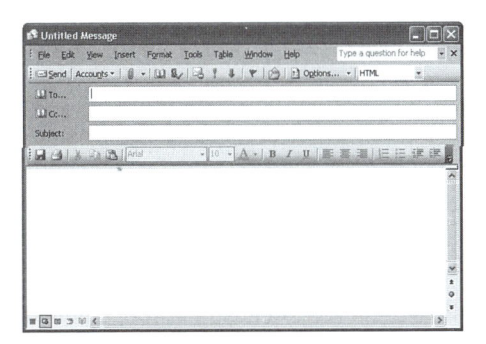

Figure 3.1 Compose a new message in the Untitled Message window.

E-mail addresses can be placed in the To box of a message that you want to send (a message you create from scratch or an existing message that you are forwarding) in several ways. You can

- Use your Outlook Contacts list
- Use your Outlook Address Book
- Type in an e-mail address that you don't currently have in any of your lists

In the case of e-mail messages that you reply to, the e-mail address of the person who sent you the message is automatically placed in the To box, making it ready to be sent.

Choosing from e-mail addresses listed in either your Contacts list or the Outlook Address Book is the easiest way to add an e-mail address to a message. It also helps you keep organized, and that is probably one of the reasons why you're using Outlook in the first place. You will also find that having e-mail addresses readily available in an Outlook list makes it easier to send carbon copies (duplicate e-mails) or blind carbon copies of messages when you are composing a particular message.

> **Jargon buster**
>
> **Blind Carbon Copy** A blind carbon copy (Bcc) of a message is a copy sent to someone in secret; the other recipients have no way of knowing that you are sending the message to someone as a blind carbon copy.

You can find more information on using Outlook's Personal Address Book in Lesson 7, "Using the Outlook Address Books."

To address a new e-mail message, follow these steps:

1 In the message window, click the **To** button to display the Select Names dialog box. Names that have been entered in your Contacts list appear on the left side of the dialog box. If you want to switch to a different list, such as the Outlook Address Book, click the drop-down list on the upper-right corner of the dialog box and make a new selection.

If the e-mail address you want isn't in your Contacts list, instead of clicking the **To** button, type the e-mail address directly into the To text box (if you do this, you can then skip steps 3 through 7).

2 From the list of addresses that appears on the left of the dialog box, choose the name of the intended recipient and select the **To**

button (or you can double-click the name). Outlook copies the name to the Message Recipients list. You can also add any distribution lists to the To box that appear in your address list. To send a carbon copy or blind carbon copy to a recipient, use the **Cc** or **Bcc** buttons.

Figure 3.2 shows a message that is addressed to an individual whose address was contained in the Contacts list and also to a group of people who are listed in a distribution list (you can enter as many addresses as you want).

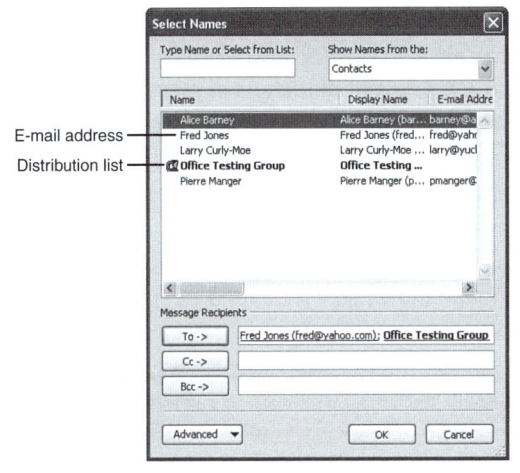

Figure 3.2 Add e-mail addresses or distribution list names quickly with the Select Names dialog box.

3 Click **OK** to return to the message window. Click in the Subject box and type the subject of your message.

4 Click in the text area, and then enter the text of the message. You do not have to press the Enter key at the end of a line; Outlook automatically wraps the text at the end of a line for you. You can use the Delete and Backspace keys to edit the text you enter.

5 When you finish typing the message, you can send the message, or you can format the message or check the spelling as detailed later in this lesson. To send the message, click the **Send** button on the message's Standard toolbar.

> **Important**
>
> **No Address** If you try to send a message without entering at least one address in the To, CC, or BCC address boxes, Outlook displays a message that you must include at least one e-mail address in one of those boxes. Make sure you provide an address; either type in an address or select an address from your Contacts list or Address Book.

→ Formatting Text

You can enhance the format of the text in your message to make it more attractive, to make it easier to read, or to add emphasis. Any formatting you do transfers to the recipient with the message if the recipient has Outlook or another e-mail client that can work with HTML or Rich Text Format messages. However, if the recipient doesn't have an e-mail client that can handle these special message formats, formatting might not transfer and the message will be received in plain text.

> **Jargon buster**
>
> **HTML** Hypertext Markup Language is used to design Web pages for the World Wide Web. Outlook can send messages in this format, providing you with several text formatting options. Graphics can even be pasted into an HTML message.

> **Jargon buster**
>
> **Rich Text Format** A special e-mail format developed by Microsoft for use with Microsoft mail systems. Outlook can send and receive messages in Rich Text Format. This enables you to send and receive messages with special formatting, such as bold, italic, various fonts, and other special characters and graphics.

You format text in two ways. You can format the text after you type it by selecting it and then choosing a font, size, or other attribute; or you can select the font, size, or other attribute to toggle it on, and then enter the text, which will be formatted as you type.

To format the text in your message, you use various formatting buttons that appear on the message's toolbar. If you are using Word as your e-mail editor, the formatting buttons will appear on the E-mail toolbar. If you are not using Word as your e-mail editor, the formatting buttons are provided on the Formatting toolbar. You can open either of these toolbars (as needed) by selecting the **View** menu on the message's menu bar and then pointing at **Toolbars**. Select the required toolbar from the list provided.

Figure 3.3 shows a message with the E-mail toolbar displayed (Word is being used as the e-mail editor, which is the default when you install Microsoft Office). Formatting options have also been applied to the text in the message. Table 3.1 explains the buttons found on the E-mail toolbar (these same buttons would be available on the Formatting toolbar).

> **Important**
>
> **The Formatting Buttons Don't Work** Only messages sent in HTML or Rich Text Format can be formatted using the formatting buttons. Plain-text messages don't supply you with any formatting options.

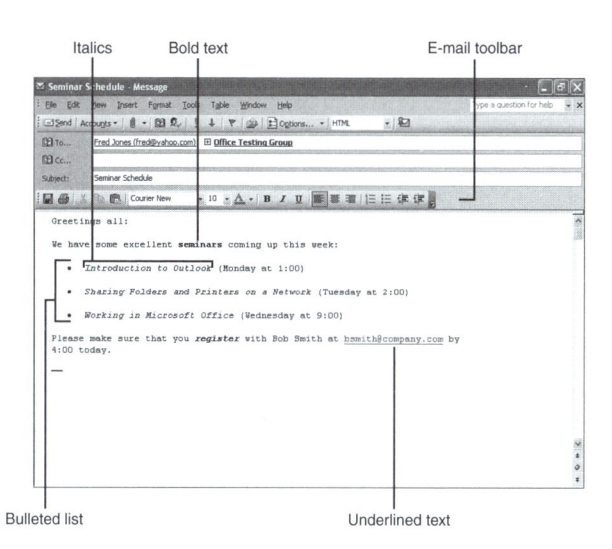

Figure 3.3 Use the formatting buttons to modify the format of your message text.

Table 3.1 Formatting Buttons

Button	Name
A	Font Color
B	Bold
I	Italic
U	Underline
	Align Left
	Center
	Align Right
	Numbering
	Bullets
	Decrease Indent
	Increase Indent

To change font attributes in a mail message, follow these steps:

1 To apply a new font to selected text, click the down arrow in the **Font** box. Scroll through the font list, if necessary, to view all fonts on the system, and then click the font you want to apply to the text. Make sure that you select an easy-to-read font such as Arial or Times New Roman. Using a highly stylized font such as Bauhaus 93 or Chiller can make the message difficult to read.

2 Assign a size by clicking the down arrow beside the **Font Size** drop-down list and choosing the size; alternatively, you can type a size into the Font Size text box (typically you should use a font size of 10 to 12 points).

3 To choose a color, click the **Color** button and select a color from the palette box that appears.

4 Choose a type style to apply to text by clicking the **Bold**, **Italic**, and/or **Underline** buttons.

5 Choose an alignment by selecting the **Align Left**, **Center**, or **Align Right** button from the toolbar.

6 Add bullets to a list by clicking the **Bullets** button on the toolbar. If you prefer a numbered list, click the **Numbering** button.

7 Create text indents or remove indents in half-inch increments by clicking the **Increase Indent** or **Decrease Indent** buttons (each time you click the Indent button, the indent changes by one-half inch).

Timesaver tip

Yuck, No Thanks! If you assign formatting to your text and don't particularly like it, click **Edit** and select **Undo** (or press Ctrl+Z) to remove the last formatting that you assigned the text.

→ Checking Spelling

If you send business-related e-mails, you will certainly want to check the spelling in your mail messages before you send them. Outlook includes a spelling checker you can use for that purpose. If you are using Word as your e-mail editor, you will use the Word Spelling and Grammar features. (Using Word as your e-mail editor also allows you to check for grammar errors.)

To check the spelling in a message, follow these steps:

1 In a message window, choose **Tools**, and then select **Spelling** or press **F7**. If the spelling checker finds a word whose spelling it questions, it displays the Spelling dialog box (shown in Figure 3.4). (If no words are misspelled, a dialog box appears saying that the spelling check is complete; choose **OK** to close the dialog box.)

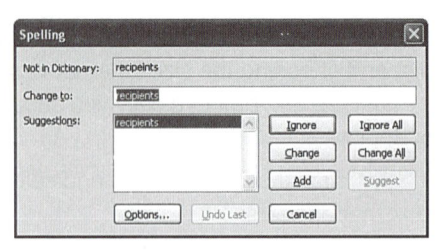

Figure 3.4 Check your spelling before sending a message.

2 Your response to the questions in the Spelling dialog box will vary. If you recognize that Outlook has correctly flagged a misspelled word, choose one of the following:

- **Suggestions**—Select the correct spelling in this text box, and it automatically appears in the Change To text box.
- **Change**—Click this button to change this particular occurrence of the word in question to the spelling in the Change To text box.
- **Change All**—Click this button to change the word in question to the spelling listed in the Change To text box every time the spelling checker finds the word in this message.

If Outlook checks a word that you know is already spelled correctly (such as a proper name), choose one of the following:

- **Not in Dictionary**—Enter the correct spelling into this text box.
- **Ignore**—Click this button to continue the spelling check without changing this occurrence of the selected word.
- **Ignore All**—Click this button to continue the spelling check without changing any occurrence of the word in question throughout this message.
- **Add**—Click this button to add the current spelling of the word in question to the dictionary so that Outlook will not question future occurrences of this spelling.
- **Undo Last**—Click this button to undo your last spelling change and return to that word.

3 Continue until the spelling check is complete (or click **Cancel** to quit the spelling check).

4 Outlook displays a message box telling you that the spell check is complete. Click **OK** to close the dialog box.

> **Timesaver tip**
>
> **Set Your Spelling Options** Click the **Options** button in the Spelling dialog box to set options that tell Outlook to do such things as ignore words with numbers, ignore original message text in forwarded messages or replies, always check spelling before sending, and so on.

→ Adding a Signature

You can further personalize your e-mails by adding a signature to the message. A signature can be as simple as just your name, or the signature can include your phone number or extension or other information. Some people even add a favorite quote to their signature. If you use HTML as your message format, you can even include signature files that contain graphics. Plain-text signatures (for use with plain-text messages) will consist only of text characters.

First, take a look at how you can create a signature. Then you can take a look at how you apply it to a message.

Creating a Signature

1 Choose **Tools**, **Options** to open the Options dialog box, and then select the **Mail Format** tab.

2 Click the **Signatures** button at the bottom of the dialog box. The Create Signature dialog box opens.

3 Click the **New** button; the Create New Signature dialog box opens as shown in Figure 3.5.

Figure 3.5 Outlook walks you through the steps of creating a signature.

Creating Mail   **71**

4 Type a name for your new signature, and then click **Next**.

5 The Edit Signature dialog box appears. Enter the text you want included in the signature. You can use the Paragraph or Font buttons to add formatting to the text in the signature.

6 When you have finished creating your signature, click the **Finish** button. Click **Close** to close the Create New Signature dialog box, and then click **OK** to close the Options dialog box.

> **Timesaver tip**
>
> **You Can Edit Signatures** To edit a signature, select the signature in the Create New Signature dialog box and then click **Edit**.

Inserting the Signature

After you've created a signature or signatures, you can quickly add it to any message by placing the insertion point where you want to place the signature, choosing **Insert**, and then choosing **Signature**; all the signatures that you have created appear on the menu. Select the signature from the list you want to use in the message you are currently composing.

You can also preview the signatures before inserting them; choose **Insert**, **Signature**, and then select **More** from the cascading menu. The Select a Signature dialog box opens. Select any of your signatures to view a preview of the signature. When you find the signature you want to use, click **OK**.

→ Sending Mail

You probably know that after you add recipient addresses, compose your message, format the text, spell check the message, and insert a signature in the e-mail, you are ready to send the message. But you can use a couple of ways to actually send the message on its way.

The fastest way to send the message using the mouse is to click the **Send** button on the Message toolbar. If you prefer, press **Ctrl+Enter**. In either case, your message is heading out to its destination. If you are working offline, the message is placed in the Outbox until you connect to the Internet and send and receive your messages.

→ Recalling a Message

If you use Outlook as an e-mail client in a Microsoft Exchange Server environment, you can actually recall or replace e-mail messages that you have sent. But you can only recall or replace messages that have not been opened by the recipient or moved to another folder by a recipient.

If the Folder List is not visible, click the **View** menu, and then click **Folder List**.

1 Click the **My Shortcuts** button on the Navigation pane, and then select the **Sent Items** folder.

2 Double-click to open the message that you want to recall.

3 In the message window, click the **Actions** menu, and then click **Recall This Message**. The Recall This Message dialog box opens as shown in Figure 3.6.

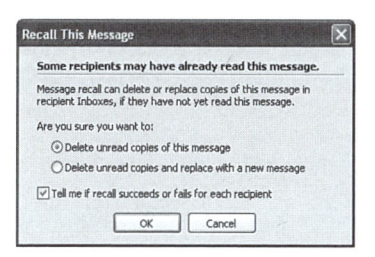

Figure 3.6 Messages that have not been read can be recalled or replaced.

4 To recall the message, click the **Delete Unread Copies of This Message** option button, and then click **OK**. A notice appears in the message window informing you that you attempted to recall this message on a particular date and at a particular time.

5 If you want to replace the message with a new message, click the **Delete Unread Copies and Replace with New Message** option button. When you click **OK**, a new message window opens with a copy of the message you want to recall in it. Just change the message text or address and then send the message.

6 You eventually receive a notification in your Inbox (as new mail) notifying you whether the recall was successful.

Creating Mail

Although you can't recall messages that are sent as Internet e-mail, you can use this feature to notify the recipients of a particular e-mail message that you want them to ignore the message. Use the message recall feature as detailed in the steps in this section. When you "recall" the message, a new message is sent to the original recipient (or recipients) that states you would like to recall the previous message. This doesn't remove the original message from their inbox but it at least provides them with a follow-up message that lets them know that the original message is essentially invalid.

4 Working with Received Mail

In this lesson, you learn how to read your mail, save an attachment, answer mail, and close a message.

→ Reading Mail

When you open Outlook, the Outlook Today window appears by default (unless you have specified that your Inbox should open; see the Tip that follows for how to open the Inbox by default). To switch to your Inbox, select the **Mail** button on the Navigation pane.

> **Timesaver tip**
>
> **Change the Startup View to Your Inbox** To have the inbox open by default in Outlook, select **Tools** and then **Options**. In the Options dialog box, select the **Other** tab and then select the **Advanced Options** button. In the Advanced Options dialog box, set the **Startup in This Folder** option to the **Inbox**.

New e-mail is downloaded when you open Outlook and connect to your mail server; this is either accomplished automatically if you have a persistent connection to the Internet (such as through network, DSL, or cable modem connections) or when you connect to your Internet service provider via your modem. You can check if any new mail is available on your mail server as you are working in Outlook by clicking the Send/Receive button on the Outlook toolbar.

No matter what the connection situation, after you download any new e-mail to your computer, the new mail appears in the Outlook Inbox (see Figure 4.1). The Inbox list and the Reading pane (formerly the Preview pane) have been enhanced in Outlook 2003.

As you can see in Figure 4.1, the Inbox provides a list of messages that you have received. Outlook 2003 lists your e-mails in logical groupings. By default, messages are listed in subsets according to when they were received, such as Today, Yesterday, Last Week, and so on. Notice that at the top of the Inbox, it says: "Arranged By: Date." You can change how the e-mails are grouped by clicking on **Arrange By: Date** and selecting another grouping from the menu that appears. You can group the messages in the Inbox by sender (From), subject (Subject), and even by e-mails from different senders that were part of an overall conversation (Conversation).

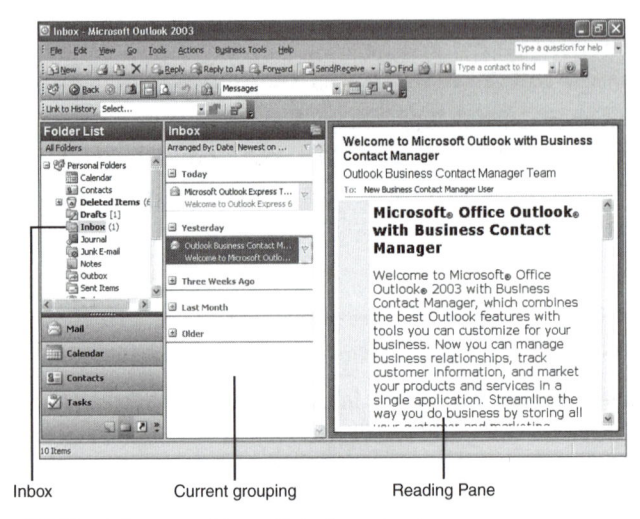

Figure 4.1 The Inbox provides a list of received messages.

To expand one of the groups that appear in the Inbox, click the **Expand** button (the plus sign) to the left of the group name. If you want to expand all the groups shown in the Inbox, select **View**, then point at **Expand/Collapse Groups**, and then select **Expand All Groups**.

> **Timesaver tip**
>
> **Use the Expand/Collapse Groups Menu to Expand or Collapse a Specific Group** If you have a message selected in the Inbox that is in a particular group (such as Today), you can expand or collapse the group using the Expand/Collapse menu or the Expand/Collapse icon on the group itself.

Additional information about a particular message, such as the actual date sent, the message subject, and the message size can be viewed by placing the mouse pointer on the message. The message statistics will appear. To read a message, you can select it, and its contents appear in the Reading pane (see Figure 4.1). The Reading pane is a vertical window (by default) that replaces the Outlook Preview pane found in earlier versions of Outlook.

You can also open a message in its own window; double-click a mail message to open it. Figure 4.2 shows an open message.

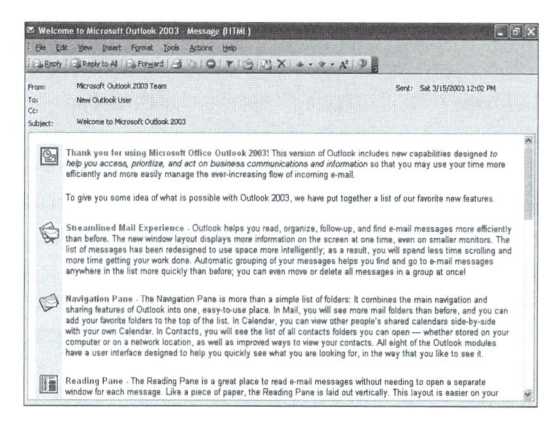

Figure 4.2 The message window displays the message and tools for responding to the message or moving to the previous or next message in the Inbox.

To read the next or previous mail message in the Inbox when you have opened a mail message, click either the **Previous Item** or the **Next Item** button on the message window toolbar.

To access more view choices, click the drop-down arrow next to either the Previous Item or Next Item button; submenu choices are provided for each of these buttons that allow you to jump to another item, an unread item, or to an item found under a particular conversation topic.

Jargon buster

Item Outlook uses the word *item* to describe a mail message, an attached file, an appointment or meeting, a task, and so on. Item is a generic term in Outlook that describes the currently selected element.

Working with Received Mail

→ Saving an Attachment

You often receive messages that have files or other items attached to them, such as documents or pictures. In the Inbox list of messages, a paper clip icon beside the message subject represents the presence of an attachment. You can save any attachments sent to you so that you can open, modify, print, or otherwise use the attached document or image. Messages can contain multiple attachments.

> **Important**
>
> **What About Viruses?** Unfortunately, there is a chance that an attachment to a message can be a virus or other malicious software. Computer viruses can really wreak havoc on your computer system. When you receive an e-mail message from someone you don't know and that message has an attachment, the best thing to do is delete the message without opening it or the attachment. Detecting questionable mail is difficult; mail with no body text or a vague subject can be good indicators that a mail message contains a malicious attachment. You can also check questionable attachments with an antivirus program before you open the file.

To save an attachment, follow these steps:

1 Open the message containing an attachment by double-clicking the message. The attachment appears as an icon below the subject area of the message (see Figure 4.3).

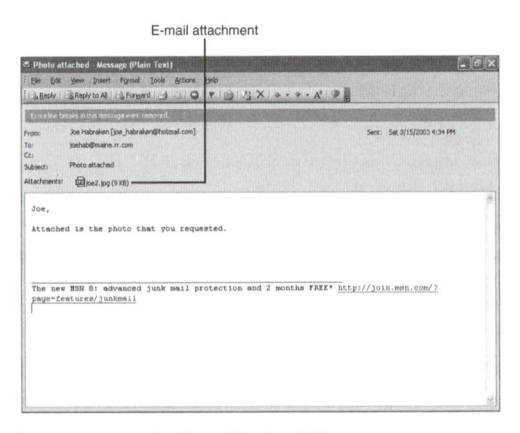

Figure 4.3 An icon represents the attached file.

78 Brilliant Microsoft Office 2003 Pocket Book

2 (Optional) You can open the attachment from within the message by double-clicking the attachment icon. A message appears, as shown in Figure 4.4, warning you that you should only open attachments received from reliable sources. To open the file, click the **Open** button. The attachment will be opened in the application in which it was created (such as Word or Excel) or the default application assigned to that particular file type (such as an image editor that you have installed on our computer). When you have finished looking at the attachment, you can return to the e-mail message by closing the open application.

Figure 4.4 You can open or save an attachment by double-clicking its icon.

3 If you choose **Save** in the Opening Mail Attachment dialog box, a Save As dialog box appears (as shown in Figure 4.5).

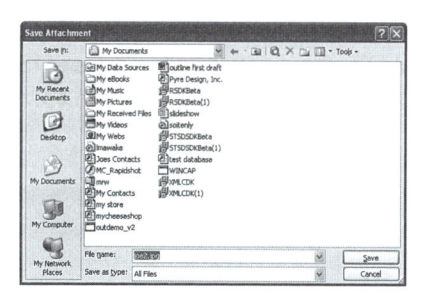

Figure 4.5 Save the attachment to a convenient folder.

4 (Optional) There is also an additional option for saving an attachment (other than the option provided in step 2). This method makes it easier to save multiple attachments. In the message window, select **File**, **Save Attachments**. The Save Attachment dialog box appears (see Figure 4.5).

5 Choose the folder in which you want to save the attachment or attachments and click **Save**. The dialog box closes and returns to the message window. You can change the name of the file in the

Working with Received Mail   **79**

File Name box, if you want. After you save the attachment, you can open the attachment, which is now like any other saved file on your computer, at any time from the application in which it was created.

> **Timesaver tip**
>
> **Use the Right Mouse Button** You can also quickly save an attachment by right-clicking the attachment icon. On the shortcut menu that appears, click **Save As**, and then save the attachment to an appropriate folder.

→ Answering Mail

You might want to reply to a message after you read it. The message window enables you to answer a message immediately as you read it. To reply to any given message, follow these steps:

1 Select the message in the Inbox window, and then click the **Reply** button on the Inbox toolbar.

If you have the message open, click the **Reply** button in the message window. The Reply message window appears, with the original message in the message text area and the sender of the message already filled in for you (see Figure 4.6).

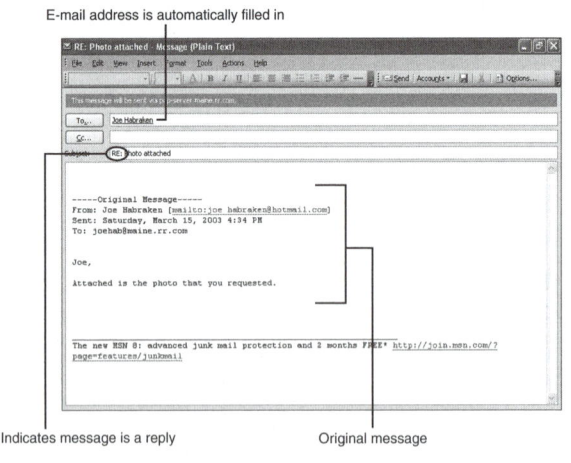

Figure 4.6 You can reply to a message quickly and easily.

80 Brilliant Microsoft Office 2003 Pocket Book

> **Timesaver tip**
>
> **Reply to All** If you receive a message that has also been sent to others—as either a message or a carbon copy (Cc)—you can click the **Reply to All** button to send your reply to each person who received the original message.

2 The insertion point is automatically place above the message text that you are replying to. Enter your reply text.

3 When you finish your reply, click the **Send** button. Outlook sends the message.

The next time you open a message to which you've replied, there is a reminder at the top of the message window telling you the date and time you sent your reply. Don't forget that the purple arrow next to a message in the Inbox window shows that the message has been replied to.

→ Printing Mail

You can print mail messages, either directly from the Inbox when they have been selected or from a message window when you have opened a particular message. To print an unopened message, select the message in the message list of the Inbox or other folder and choose **File, Print**. The Print dialog box opens; click **OK** to send the message to the printer. If the message is already open, you can follow these steps:

1 Open the message in Outlook.

2 Choose **File** and then select **Print**, to open the Print dialog box.

3 In the Print dialog box, click **OK** to print one copy of the entire message using the printer's default settings.

> **Timesaver tip**
>
> **Print a Message from the Inbox** You can also print a message or messages from the Inbox. Select the message or messages in the Inbox list and then click the **Print** button on the Outlook toolbar.

When you finish reading or printing a message, click the **Close** button on the message window.

5 Managing Mail

In this lesson, you learn how to delete and undelete messages, forward messages, and create folders. You also learn how to move messages to these folders.

→ Deleting Mail

You will want to delete a number of the messages that you receive, read, and respond to (or ignore). You can easily delete messages in Outlook. Messages that you want to save can actually be organized into folders that you create so that they don't clutter your Inbox.

The easiest way to delete a selected message, such as a message selected in the Inbox, is to click the **Delete** button on the Outlook toolbar. If the message is open, just click the **Delete** button on the message window toolbar instead.

If you want to delete several messages in the Inbox, just select the messages using the mouse. To select several contiguous messages, click the first message, and then hold down the **Shift** key when you click the last message in the series. To select noncontiguous messages, hold down the **Ctrl** key and click each message. When you have all the messages selected that you want to delete, click the **Delete** button (or you can select the **Edit** menu and then select **Delete**).

Undeleting Items

If you change your mind and want to get back items you've deleted, you can usually retrieve them from the Deleted Items folder. By default, when you delete an item, it doesn't disappear from your computer; it is moved to the Deleted Items folder. Items stay in the Deleted Items folder until you delete them from that folder—at which point they are unrecoverable. Typically, when you exit Outlook, the Deleted Items folder is emptied automatically.

> **Timesaver tip**
>
> **Determining When the Deleted Items Folder Should Be Emptied** You can choose whether or not the Deleted Items folder should be emptied when you close Outlook. Select Tools, Options. In the Options dialog box select the Other tab and then select Empty the Deleted Items Folder Upon Exiting. Then click OK. If you are using Outlook on an Exchange Server network, see your system manager for information related to discarding deleted items.

To retrieve a deleted item from the Deleted Items folder, follow these steps:

1 With the Inbox selected in the Navigation pane, click the **Deleted Items** folder in the All Mail Folders group.

2 Select the items you want to retrieve; you can then drag them back to the Inbox by dragging them and dropping them onto the Inbox icon in the Navigation pane. Or if you don't like dragging messages, select the files you want to move from the Deleted Items folder, and then select **Edit, Move to Folder**. The Move Items dialog box appears as shown in Figure 5.1.

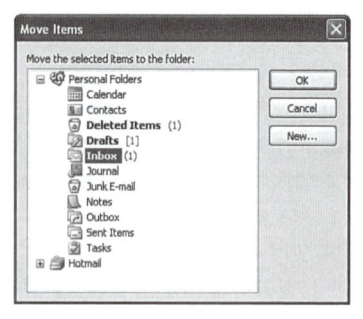

Figure 5.1 Deleted messages can be moved out of the Deleted Items folder back into the Inbox.

3 Select the folder you want to move the items into (such as the Inbox) and then click the **OK** button.

> **Timesaver tip**
>
> **Use Undo Immediately** If you want to undelete a message or messages that you just deleted, select the **Edit** menu, and then select **Undo Delete** (or type Ctrl+Z).

Emptying the Deleted Items Folder

If you're sure you no longer need them, you can completely discard the item or items in the Deleted Items folder. To "completely delete" items in the Deleted Items folder, follow these steps:

1 On the Navigation pane, choose the **Mail** icon. In the All Mail Folders group, expand the Personal Folders icon. The Deleted Items folder will appear in the All Mail Folders group. Select the Deleted Items folder; deleted items in that folder appear in the message list, as shown in Figure 5.2.

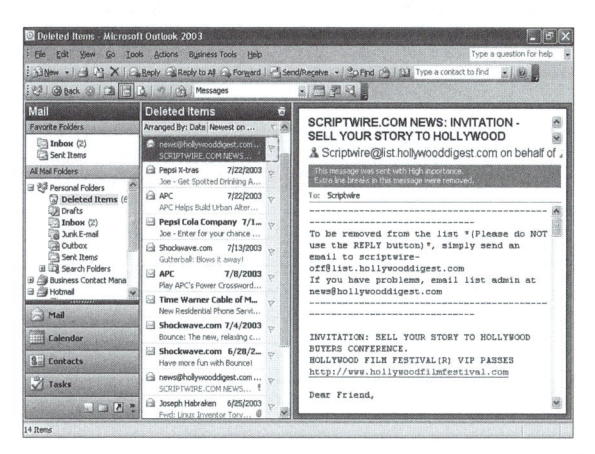

Figure 5.2 Deleted messages remain in the Deleted Items folder until you permanently delete them or empty the folder.

2 To permanently delete an item or items, select it (or them) in the Deleted Items folder.

3 Click the **Delete** button. Outlook displays a confirmation dialog box asking whether you're sure you want to permanently delete the message. Choose **Yes** to delete the selected item.

If you typically are pretty confident about the status of messages that you delete (you know you won't want to undelete them), you can empty all the messages out of the Deleted Items folder (rather than emptying it piecemeal, message by message). Right-click on the **Deleted Items** folder icon in the All Mail Folders group on the Navigation bar.

On the shortcut menu that appears, select **Empty "Deleted Items" Folder**. You will be asked to confirm the emptying of the folder; click **Yes**. The Deleted Items folder will be emptied. All messages or other items in the folder can no longer be retrieved.

> **Timesaver tip**
>
> **Automatic Permanent Delete** You can set Outlook to empty the contents of the Deleted Items folder every time you exit the program. To do so, in the Outlook window choose **Tools**, and then click **Options**. Select the **Other** tab of the Options dialog box and click the **Empty the Deleted Items Folder Upon Exiting** check box. Then click **OK**.

→ Forwarding Mail

You can forward mail that you receive to a co-worker or anyone else with an e-mail address. When you forward a message, you can also add your own comments (or even attachments) to the message if you want.

> **Jargon buster**
>
> **Forward Mail** When you forward mail, you send a copy of a message you have received to another person; you can add your own comments to the forwarded mail, if you want.

You can forward an open message or a message selected in the message list in the Inbox in the same way. To forward mail, follow these steps:

1 Select or open the message you want to forward. Then click the **Forward** button. The FW Message window appears (see Figure 5.3).

"FW:" indicates a forwarded message

Contents of forwarded message

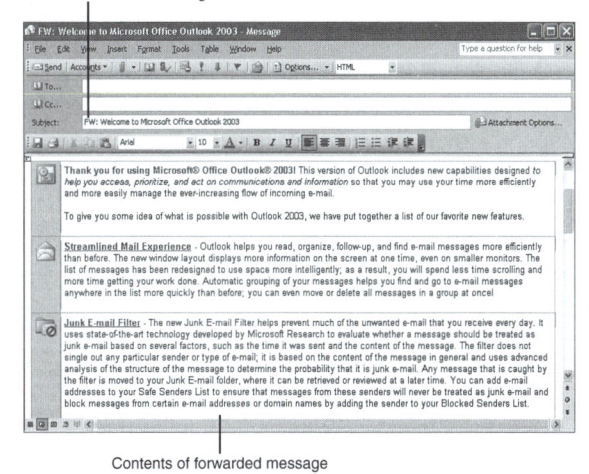

Figure 5.3 When you forward a message, the original message appears at the bottom of the message window.

2 In the To text box, enter the addresses of the people to whom you want to forward the mail. If you want to choose an address or addresses from a list, click the To button to display the Select Names dialog box, and then select the address or addresses from your Contacts list.

3 (Optional) In the Cc text box, enter the addresses of anyone to whom you want to forward copies of the message.

4 In the message area of the window, enter any message you want to send with the forwarded text.

> **Timesaver tip**
>
> **Attachments Are Forwarded, Too** If the message that you forward contains attached files, the attachments are also forwarded.

5 When you are ready to send the message, click the **Send** button.

Managing Mail **87**

→ Creating Folders

Although Outlook provides you with an Inbox, an Outbox, a Sent Items folder, an Unread Mail folder, and a Deleted Items folder, you might find it advantageous to create your own folders. This provides you with alternative places to store items and can make finding them in the future easier (rather than just having all your messages languish in the Inbox). Folders can also be used to store items other than messages, so you could even create subfolders for your Contacts folder or Calendar.

> **Timesaver tip**
>
> **Folders Aren't the Only Way to Get Organized** Although the creation of folders can help you organize messages and other items that you want to store in Outlook, another tool called the Organizer has been designed to help you move, delete, and even color-code received e-mail messages.

To create a folder, follow these steps:

1 Click the **Folder List** button at the bottom of the Navigation pane. The Folder List appears in the Navigation pane.

2 To create a folder in the Folder List, right-click the Personal Folders icon.

3 On the shortcut menu that appears (see Figure 5.4), select **New Folder**. The Create New Folder dialog box appears.

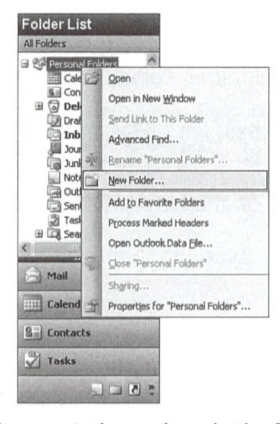

Figure 5.4 Folders can be created anywhere in the Folder List.

> **Timesaver tip**
>
> **Create Folders from the File Menu** You can also open the Create New Folder dialog box from the File menu. Just select **File**, point at **New**, and then select **Folder**.

4 In the Create New Folder dialog box, type a name for the folder into the Name box.

5 Use the Folder Contains drop-down list in the New Folder dialog box to select the type of folder that you want to create. For example, if you want to hold mail messages in the folder, select **Mail and Post Items** from the list (see Figure 5.5).

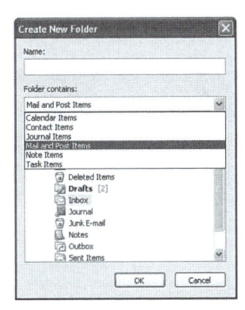

Figure 5.5 Folders can be created to hold mail messages, contacts, and even calendar appointments.

6 Use the folder locations provided in the Select Where to Place Your Folder list to select the location for the new folder. If you want to nest the new folder in an existing folder, such as the Inbox, select that folder on the list. If you want to create the new folder as a first-level folder, select **Personal Folders**.

7 When you have finished making your entries and selections in the New Folder dialog box, click **OK** to create the folder.

The new folder appears on the Navigation pane in the Folder List.

> **Important**
>
> **I Want to Delete a Folder** If you add a folder and then decide you don't want it, right-click the folder in the Folder List and select **Delete** from the shortcut menu. You then must verify the deletion; click **Yes**.

→ Moving and Copying Items to Another Folder

You can move items from one folder in Outlook to another; for example, you can create a folder to store all messages pertaining to a specific account or just make a folder that holds personal messages instead of business-related messages. You can easily move any messages to a new folder and then open them later to read them or to reply to them.

To move an item to another folder, follow these steps:

1 From the Inbox or any Outlook folder, select the message or messages you want to move.

2 Select **Edit, Move to Folder**. The Move Items dialog box appears (see Figure 5.6).

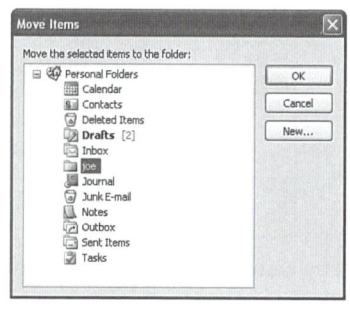

Figure 5.6 Choose the folder in which you want to store the message or messages.

3 In the Move Items dialog box, select the folder to which you want to move the message or messages.

4 Click **OK**. The message or messages are moved to the destination folder.

Timesaver tip

Quickly Move Items You can quickly move any message or other Outlook item by dragging it from the open folder in which it resides to any folder icon in the Outlook bar.

You can also copy items from one folder to another (rather than moving them). Select the items you want to copy. Then select **Edit, Copy to Folder**. Specify the location that you want to copy the items to in the Copy Items dialog box (which is similar to the Move Items dialog box shown in Figure 5.6) and then click **OK**.

6 Attaching Files and Items to a Message

In this lesson, you learn how to attach a file and Outlook items to an e-mail message.

→ Attaching a File

You can attach any type of file to an Outlook message, which makes for a convenient way of sending your files to your co-workers or sending pictures to anyone (anywhere in the world) who has access to Internet e-mail. You can send Word documents, Excel spreadsheets, a family photo (taken from a digital camera or scanned from a photograph), or any other file you have on your hard drive.

When you attach a file, it appears as an icon in an attachment box that resides in the message window right below the Subject box, as shown in Figure 6.1. A button to the left of the attached file can be used to quickly access the Insert File dialog box if you want to change the attached file or add additional attachments before sending the message.

You can also open or view any files that you attach to your e-mail messages (before or after you send them) by double-clicking the file. Next, you take a look at attaching and viewing attachments, such as files created in other applications and picture files. Then, you can take a look at attaching an Outlook item such as a contact or appointment to an e-mail message.

Timesaver tip

E-mail Attachments and E-mail Clients Depending on the e-mail client they are using, the way recipients of your file attachments retrieve them will vary. For example, some e-mail packages do not show the attachment as an icon, but save the attachment directly to a specific folder on the recipient's computer after the e-mail message is received.

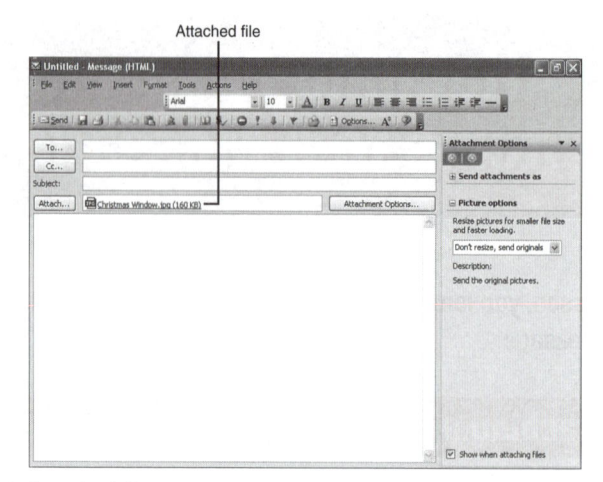

Figure 6.1 Attached files appear as an icon in the Attach box.

To attach a file to a message, follow these steps:

1 In the new message window, choose **Insert** and then select **File**, or click the **Insert File** button on the toolbar. The Insert File dialog box appears (see Figure 6.2).

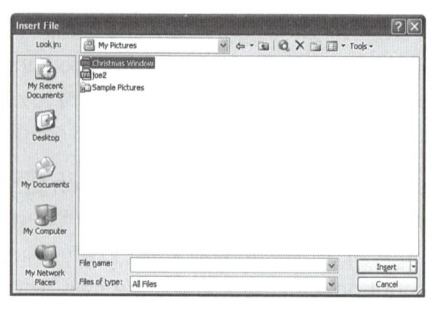

Figure 6.2 Select the file you want to attach to a message.

2 From the **Look In** drop-down list, choose the drive and folder that contain the file you want to attach.

3 Select the file you want to attach.

4 Click **Insert** to insert the file into the message.

An Attach box appears below the Subject box on the message, and an icon and the filename are inserted. If you attached a photo file to your Outlook message, the Attachment Options Task Pane also appears (see Figure 6.3).

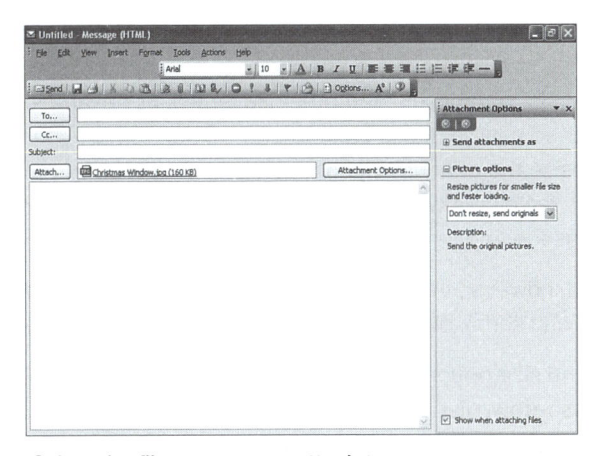

Figure 6.3 Select the file you want to attach to a message.

> **Timesaver tip**
>
> **Where Is the Attachment Options Task Pane?** If you don't see the Attachment Options Task Pane, click the **Attachment Options** button to the right of the Attachment box on the e-mail message.

The Attachment Options Task Pane allows you to control how the attachments are sent and also allows you to change the size of an image attachment.

To control how the attachments are sent, click the **Send Attachments As** heading. You are provided with two possibilities:

- **Regular Attachments:** The default setting for attachments sends a set of attachments to each recipient of the e-mail.

- **Shared Attachments:** This option allows you to provide each recipient with a copy of the attachments and also to place the attachments on a Document Workspace located on the Web (you must have access to a Web server for this feature to work). You must supply a Web address (URL) that is the address of the Web server that will hold the file attachments.

Select the option that is appropriate to your needs. All file attachments including documents, databases, and images can be configured so that they are shared attachments available on a particular Website.

Attaching Files and Items to a Message   **95**

The Attachments Options Task Pane also allows you the option of changing the size of image file attachments (this option is not available for documents, databases, and other file types). For example, if you have attached a large digital camera photo to an e-mail, you can have Outlook resize the attachment so that it is sent as a smaller file size. This allows recipients with slow Internet connections to download the e-mail message and its attachments faster.

Be advised, however, that this feature can't be used to make a small file larger. You can shrink picture attachments but you can't enlarge them.

To select the size options for the image attachment, click the Picture options drop-down list and select one of the following:

- **Don't Resize, Send Originals**—The default setting, the images are sent as attached (the original file size).

- **Small (448×336)**—This option lowers the resolution of the image making the file smaller.

- **Medium (640×480)**—This option lowers the resolution less drastically than the Small option but also gives you a slightly small file size.

- **Large (1024×768)**—This option provides a higher resolution file that may actually increase the file size of the image you are sending.

After making your selections in the Attachments Options Task Pane, you can complete your e-mail message (address it, add a message text). When you send the message, the options you selected in the Task Pane will be used in relation to the attached file.

Timesaver tip

Large Files Take Time   Sending an extremely large file can take a great deal of time, depending on your connection speed. Some ISPs and Web-based e-mail providers, such as America Online and Yahoo! Mail, set a limit for attachment file size for sent or received attachments.

→ Attaching Outlook Items

In addition to attaching files from other programs, you can also attach an Outlook item to a message. An Outlook item can be any item saved in one of your personal folders, including an appointment, a contact, a note, and so on. You can attach an Outlook item in the same manner you attach a file.

Follow these steps to attach an Outlook item:

1 In the message window, choose **Insert, Item** (or click the drop-down arrow next to the Insert File icon and select **Item**). The Insert Item dialog box appears (see Figure 6.4).

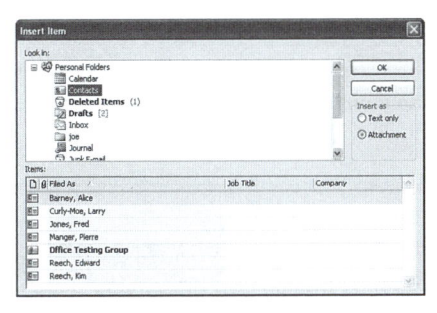

Figure 6.4 Select items from any folder in Outlook, such as a contact's information from the Contacts folder.

2 From the **Look In** list, choose the folder containing the item you want to include in the message.

3 Select from the items that appear in the **Items** list when you have the appropriate folder selected. To select multiple adjacent items, hold down the **Shift** key and click the first and last desired items; to select multiple nonadjacent items, hold down the **Ctrl** key and click the items.

4 In the Insert As area, choose from the following option buttons:

- **Text Only**—Inserts the file as text into the message, such as the contact's information or the text in an e-mail message.

- **Attachment**—Attaches the e-mail message or Contact record as an attachment to the current e-mail message.

5 Click **OK**, and Outlook inserts the selected items into your message (either as an attachment or as inserted text).

Figure 6.5 shows an attached contact record in an Outlook e-mail message. When the e-mail recipient receives the message, he or she can access the contact information by double-clicking the attachment icon. The recipient can then save the contact information to their Contacts folder.

An attached contact item

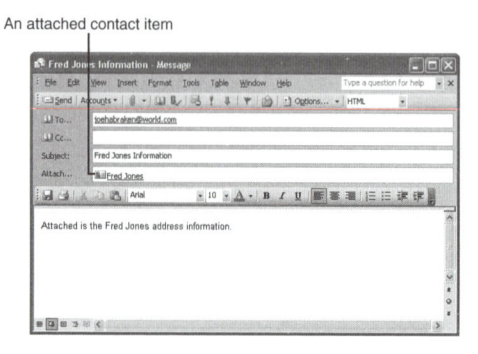

Figure 6.5 Select an item from any folder in Outlook, such as a contact's information, and attach it to your e-mail message.

> **Timesaver tip**
>
> **It Doesn't Work Without Outlook** If recipients don't have Outlook on their computers, they will not be able to view the attached item, such as an Outlook contact record. If you know that a recipient doesn't have Outlook, insert the contact information into the message as text using the Text Only option in the Insert Item dialog box.

7 Using the Outlook Address Books

In this lesson, you learn about different Outlook address books and how to import lists to Outlook from other applications.

→ Understanding the Outlook Address Books

Outlook has the capability to access different stores or lists of information that can provide you with people's e-mail addresses and other contact information, such as phone numbers and addresses. The address books that you can access include the Personal Address Book, your Contacts list, and other directory lists that are provided by other e-mail systems and communication servers. For example, in a corporate network, a Microsoft Exchange Server can provide you with a Global Address list that is shared by all users on the Exchange network. The e-mail addresses of any users on the network are then easily found in one resource.

> **Jargon buster**
>
> **The Contacts List** You might notice contacts in the list of address books; this list contains entries you create in your Contacts list.

Where your e-mail addresses and other contact information are stored depends on whether you are using Outlook on a corporate network that uses Active Directory (a network that deploys Microsoft Windows network servers), a network that uses Exchange Server, or as a standalone product where you use an Internet e-mail account. However, no matter where your contact information is kept, Outlook makes it easy for you to access your different address books using the Address Book feature.

> **Timesaver tip**
>
> **Using Address Books** On a home computer Outlook provides the Contacts List as the primary location for contact information and e-mail addresses (although you may also have access to the Outlook Address Book, depending on your Outlook configuration). If you imported settings from another e-mail client such as Outlook Express, you may also have Personal Address Book or other directory. On a network using Exchange Server, corporate contact information is supplied by the Windows Active Directory, which is a database of all users on the network. In most cases it is a best practice to place your new contacts in the Contacts List instead of the Address Book.

→ Using the Address Book

The Address Book is basically a launch pad that allows you to access information lists (they are all considered address books) that contain e-mail addresses and other contact information. Because you create your own Contacts list, you always have this resource available, even if you aren't connected to a special network server and you access your e-mail by connecting to the Internet.

As already mentioned, Outlook also has the capability to access a number of different address lists. If Outlook is used as a mail client for the Microsoft Exchange Server mail system, Outlook will be able to access distribution lists as well as the entire Exchange Server e-mail catalog.

You can open the Address Book feature by clicking the **To** button or **Cc** button on a new message or by clicking the **Address Book** icon on the Outlook toolbar. After the Address Book dialog box is open (see Figure 7.1), you can use the **Show Names** from the drop-down list to select the specific address book (such as your Outlook Address Book or Contacts list) that you want to view.

Figure 7.1 The Address Book provides access to your various e-mail address and contacts lists.

Finding Records in an Address Book

The Address Book dialog box also makes it easy for you to search through a particular address book for a particular person. In the Type Name box, begin to type the name of a contact you want to find in the list; as soon as you type enough of the contact's name for Outlook to find that particular contact, it will be highlighted in the list provided.

For cases where you want to search for a record or records by a particular character string (such as all records in the address book that have the last name of Smith), the Address Book provides you with a Find dialog box.

Click the **Find Items** button on the Address Book toolbar. The Find dialog box appears as shown in Figure 7.2.

Figure 7.2 You can search a particular address book by keywords or text strings using the Find dialog box.

Using the Outlook Address Books   **101**

Type your search string into the Find Names Containing box. Then, click **OK** to run the search. The search results appear in the Address Book dialog box. Only the records that match your search parameters appear in the list.

Adding Records to an Address Book

You can also add records to any of the address books that you have access to. For example, you can add records to your Personal Address book or to your Contacts list directly in the Address Book window. Keep in mind that in a corporate environment, your network administrator probably controls some address books, such as the Global Address Book. This means that you won't be able to add information to these address books; you can use them only as resources to find information such as e-mail addresses.

To add a record to an address book that you do control:

1 In the Address Book dialog box, make sure that you have the address book selected that you want to add the new record to.

2 Click the **New Entry** button on the Address Book toolbar. The New Entry dialog box appears (see Figure 7.3).

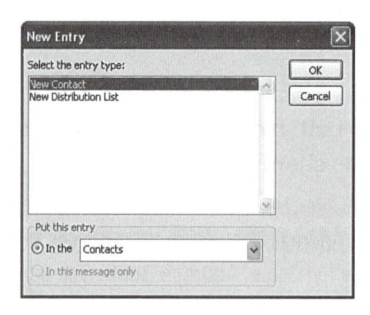

Figure 7.3 You can add new records to address books using the New Entry dialog box.

3 Use the **Put This Entry In the** drop-down box at the bottom of the New Entry dialog box to make sure that your new record ends up in the correct address book. To add a new record (a new contact, for example), click **New Contact** and then click **OK**.

Swindon Libraries
01793 707120
Thank you for using
North Swindon Library

Borrowed Items 29/07/2007
XXXXX40006

Item Details	Due Date
Excel 2003	19/08/2007
Brilliant Office 2003 poc	19/08/2007

Alan Simpson's Windows Vista Bible 005.446
9/8/07

Teach yourself visually Windows Vista. 005.446
9/8/07

Jargon buster

Distribution List A distribution list allows you to create a record that includes the e-mail addresses for several people. This makes it easy to send e-mails to a group of people. You can create distribution lists in the New Entry dialog box. You will learn how to create distribution lists in the next lesson.

4 A blank record appears for your new entry. Enter the appropriate information for the new record, such as the person's name, e-mail address, and so on into the appropriate text boxes. When you have finished entering the information, click **OK** to save the new entry. In the case of new contacts added to the Contacts list, click the **Save and Close** button.

The blank records that open for your new entries look slightly different, depending on the address book in which you are creating the new record. In the case of new contacts (which is discussed in the next chapter), you can enter information for the new entry that includes the person's address, phone number, fax number, and even a Web page address. Some address books may allow you to enter only the name and e-mail address of the person.

Timesaver tip

Create a New Message from the Address Book Dialog Box If you opened the Address Book using the **Address Book** icon on the Outlook toolbar (or selected **Tools, Address Book**), you can open a new message for any of the contacts listed in one of the address books. Select the particular person, and then click the **New Message** icon on the Address Book icon. A new message opens addressed to that particular person.

8 Using the Calendar

In this lesson, you learn how to navigate the Calendar, create appointments, and save appointments. You also learn how to insert an Office object, such as an Excel workbook, in an appointment.

→ Navigating the Calendar

You can use Outlook's Calendar to schedule appointments and create a task list. If necessary, Outlook can also remind you of appointments and daily or weekly tasks. You can schedule appointments months in advance, move appointments, cancel appointments, and so on. The Calendar makes it very easy to identify the days on which you have appointments.

To open the Outlook Calendar, click the **Calendar** button on the Navigation pane, or select the **Calendar** folder from the Folder List. Figure 8.1 shows the Calendar in Outlook.

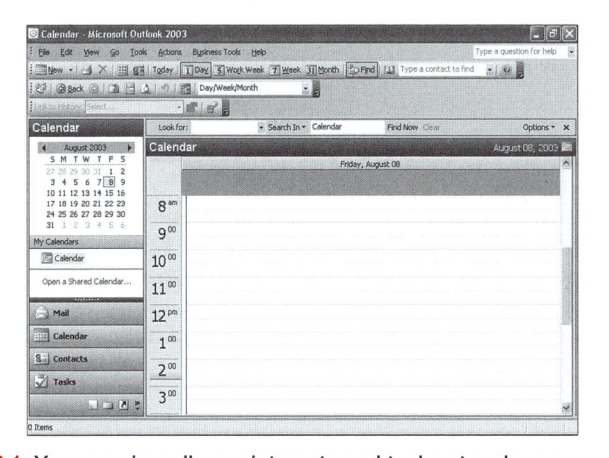

Figure 8.1 You can view all appointments and tasks at a glance.

By default the Calendar shows the current day and will list all the appointments that you have scheduled for that day. You can scroll through the hours of the day to view scheduled appointments.

On the Navigation pane, the current month is shown. To see the appointments for a day in the current month, click that day on the Calendar. If you want to see multiple days in the Appointment pane, select the first date on the Calendar and then hold down the Control key as you select other days. A column will appear for each day in the Appointment pane. If you want to move to a different month, use the navigation arrows on either side of the current month shown.

Timesaver tip

Changing Calendar Views   You can change to different views of the Calendar by clicking the **Current View** drop-down arrow on the Advanced toolbar. Views including Active Appointments, Recurring Appointments, and By Category are available.

Another aspect of tracking activities in the Calendar is to be able to view tasks that you assigned to yourself or tasks that have been assigned to you by other users. By default, tasks are not shown in the Calendar. To view the Task pane along with the Calendar, select the **View** menu, then select **Taskpad**. The Taskpad will be added to the Calendar. You can now track your appointments and tasks for a particular day (or days) simultaneously.

Timesaver tip

Change the Date Quickly   To quickly go to today's date or to a specific date without searching through the Monthly Calendar pane, right-click in the Schedule pane and choose either **Today** or **Go to Date**.

→ Creating an Appointment

You can create an appointment on any day in the Outlook Calendar. When you create an appointment, you can add the subject, location, starting time, category, and even an alarm to remind you ahead of time.

Follow these steps to create an appointment:

1 On the Calendar in the Navigation pane, select the month and the date for which you want to create an appointment.

2 In the Schedule pane, double-click next to the time at which the appointment is scheduled to begin. The Untitled - Appointment dialog box appears, with the Appointment tab displayed (see Figure 8.2).

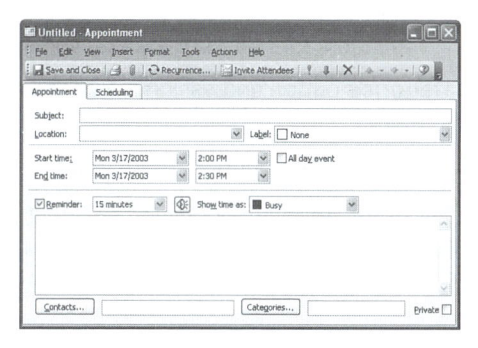

Figure 8.2 Enter all the details you need when scheduling an appointment.

3 Enter the subject of the appointment in the **Subject** text box (you can use a person's name, a topic, or other information).

4 In the **Location** text box, enter the meeting place or other text that will help you identify the meeting when you see it in your calendar.

5 Enter dates and times in the **Start Time** and **End Time** boxes (or click the drop-down arrows and select the dates and times).

Timesaver tip

Autodate It! You can use Outlook's Autodate feature: Enter a text phrase such as **next Friday** into the Start time or End time box, and then press **Enter**; Outlook figures out the date for you and places it into the appropriate box.

Using the Calendar

6 If you want your PC to let you know when you're due for the appointment, select the **Reminder** check box and enter the amount of time before the appointment occurs that you want to be notified. If you want to set an audio alarm, click the **Alarm Bell** button and browse your hard drive to select a specific sound file for Outlook to play as your reminder.

7 From the **Show Time As** drop-down list, you can select how the appointment time block should be marked on the calendar. The default is Busy. But you can also block out the specified time as Free, Tentative, or Out of Office. The drop-down list uses different colors and patterns to specify each of the different appointment types.

8 In the large text box near the bottom of the Appointment tab, enter any text that you want to include, such as text to identify the appointment, reminders for materials to take, and so on.

9 Click the **Categories** button and assign a category (or categories) to the appointment.

10 Click the **Save and Close** button to return to the Calendar.

The Scheduling tab of the Appointment dialog box enables you to schedule a meeting with co-workers and enter the meeting on your calendar.

Word

1 Working in Word

In this lesson, you learn how to start Microsoft Word and navigate the Word window. You also learn how to use common tools such as menus, toolbars, and dialog boxes.

→ Starting Word

Microsoft Word is an efficient and full-featured word processor that provides you with all the tools you need to produce a wide variety of document types—everything from simple documents, such as memos and outlines, to complex documents, such as newsletters and Internet-ready HTML pages. You create your Word documents in the Word window, which provides easy access to all the tools you need to create all your documents.

Before you can take advantage of Word's proficient document processing features, you must open the Word application window. To start the Word program, follow these steps:

1 From the Windows XP desktop, click **Start**, **All Programs** (on Windows 2000, click **Start**, then **Programs**). The Programs menu appears (see Figure 1.1).

2 To start Word, point at the Microsoft Office icon and then click the **Word** icon. The Word application window appears.

> **Timesaver tip**
>
> **Pin a Program to the Windows XP Start Menu** For quick access to an application such as Word, right-click on the program icon when accessing the Programs menu. On the shortcut menu that appears, select **Pin to Start menu**. The application icon will now be available on the main Start menu, when you click **Start**.

Figure 1.1 Open the Programs menu and click the Word icon to start Word.

→ Understanding the Word Environment

When you start Word, the Word application window opens (see Figure 1.2). You create your documents in the Word window. The Word window also provides items that help you navigate and operate the application itself.

> **Timesaver tip**
>
> **Control the View** If your view differs from the view shown in Figure 1.2 (the Normal view), or if you don't see all the Word window elements shown in the figure (particularly the ruler), you can easily change your view. Select **View**, and then choose the menu selection (such as **Normal** or **Ruler**) that matches your view to the figure.

Notice that the largest area of the window is blank; this is where you create your new document. All the other areas—the menu bar, the toolbar, and the status bar—either provide a fast way to access the various commands and features that you use in Word, or they supply you with information concerning your document, such as what page you are on and where the insertion point is currently located in your document.

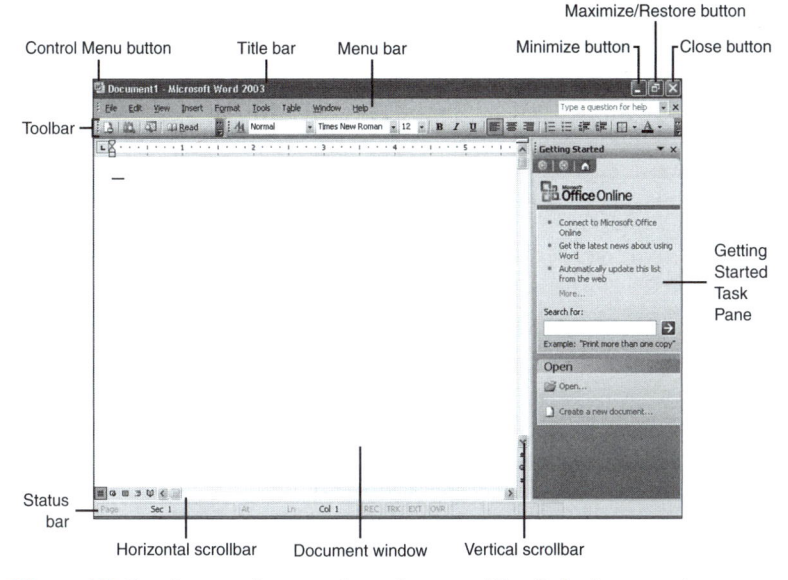

Figure 1.2 Create your documents and access Word's features and commands in the Word window.

Table 1.1 describes the elements you see called out in the Word application window.

Table 1.1 Elements of the Word Window

Element	Description
Title bar	Includes the name of the application and the current document, as well as the Minimize, Maximize, and Close buttons.
Control Menu button	Opens the Control menu, which provides such commands as Restore, Minimize, and Close.
Minimize button	Reduces the Word window to a button on the taskbar; to restore the window to its original size, click the button on the taskbar.
Maximize/Restore button	Enlarges the Word window to cover the Windows desktop. When the window is maximized, the Maximize button changes to a Restore button that you can click to return the window to its previous size.
Close (X) button	Closes the Word program. "X" is the icon for closing any window.

Table 1.1 continued

Element	Description
Menu bar	Contains menus of commands you can use to perform tasks in the program, such as Edit, Format, and Tools.
Toolbar	Includes icons that serve as shortcuts for common commands, such as Save, Print, and Spelling.
Status bar	Displays information about the current document, including page number, the section in which you are located, and the current location of the insertion point (inches, line, and column). The status bar also shows you other information, such as whether you have turned on the Typeover (OVR) mode or turned on Word's track changes (TRK) feature.
Document window	This window is where you type and format your documents.
Scrollbars	The horizontal scrollbar is used to scroll your view of the current document in a left-to-right motion. The vertical scrollbar is used to scroll up and down through the current document.
Task pane	The column of information on the right side of the document is the task pane. This is where you can access features such as the Clipboard, styles, and formatting; you can also open another document or mail merge.

→ Using Menus and Toolbars

Word provides several ways to access the commands and features you use as you create your documents. You can access these commands by using the menus on the menu bar and the buttons on the various toolbars.

You can also access many Word commands using shortcut menus. Right-clicking a particular document element (a word or a paragraph, for example) opens these menus, which contain a list of commands related to the item on which you are currently working.

The Word Menu Bar

The Word menu bar gives you access to all the commands and features that Word provides. As in all Windows applications, Word's menus reside below the title bar and are activated by clicking a particular menu name. The menu then drops open, providing you with a set of command options.

Word (and the other Office applications) uses a menu system called personalized menus that enables you to quickly access the commands you use most often (while hiding those that you use less frequently). When you first choose a particular menu, you find only a short list of Word's most commonly used menu commands. When you've spent some time using Word, this list of commands will actually be the ones that you have used most recently on that particular menu.

If a menu has a small double arrow at the bottom of its command list, you can click that to gain access to other, less commonly needed, commands. As you use hidden commands, Word adds them to the normal menu list. This means that you are basically building the list of commands available on the menu as you use Word.

This personalized strategy is also employed by the toolbar system. As you use commands, they are added to the toolbar (this personalized toolbar feature is available only when you have the Standard toolbar and the Formatting toolbar on the same line in an application window). This provides you with customized menus and toolbars that are, in effect, personalized for you.

To access a particular menu, follow these steps:

1 Select the menu by clicking its title (such as **View**), as shown in Figure 1.3. The most recently used commands appear; wait just a moment for all the commands on a particular menu to appear (if the commands do not appear, click the down arrow at the bottom of the menu).

2 Select the command on the menu that invokes a particular feature (such as **Header and Footer**).

You will find that many of the commands found on Word's menus are followed by an ellipsis (…). These commands, when selected, open a dialog box that requires you to provide Word with additional information before the particular feature or command can be used. More information about understanding dialog boxes is included later in this lesson.

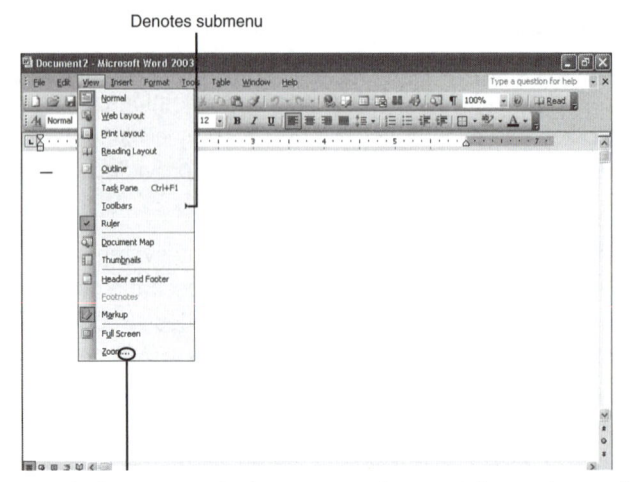

Figure 1.3 Select a particular menu to view, and then point to a Word command.

Some of the menus also contain a submenu or cascading menu from which you make choices. The menu commands that produce a submenu are indicated by an arrow to the right of the menu choice. When a submenu is present, you point at the command (marked with the arrow) on the main menu to open the submenu.

The menu system itself provides a logical grouping of the Word commands and features. For example, commands related to files, such as Open, Save, and Print, are all found on the File menu.

> **Timesaver tip**
>
> **Activating Menus with the Keyboard** You can activate a particular menu by holding down the **Alt** key and then pressing the keyboard key that matches the underscored letter in the menu's name. This underscored letter is called the hotkey. For example, to activate the File menu in Word, press **Alt+F**.

you find that you would rather have access to all the menu commands (rather than accessing only those you've used recently), you can turn off the personalized menu system. To do this, follow these steps:

1 Click the **Tools** menu, and then click **Customize**.

2 In the Customize dialog box, click the **Options** tab.

3 To show all the commands on the menus, click the **Always Show Full Menus** check box.

4 Click **OK** to close the dialog box.

Shortcut Menus

A fast way to access commands related to a particular document element is to select that document object and then right-click. This opens a shortcut menu that contains commands related to the particular object with which you are working.

> **Jargon buster**
>
> **Object** Any element found in a document, such as text, a graphic, a hyperlink, or other inserted item.

For example, if you select a line of text in a document, right-clicking the selected text (see Figure 1.4) opens a shortcut menu with commands such as Cut, Copy, and Paste, or it provides you with quick access to formatting commands, such as Font and Paragraph.

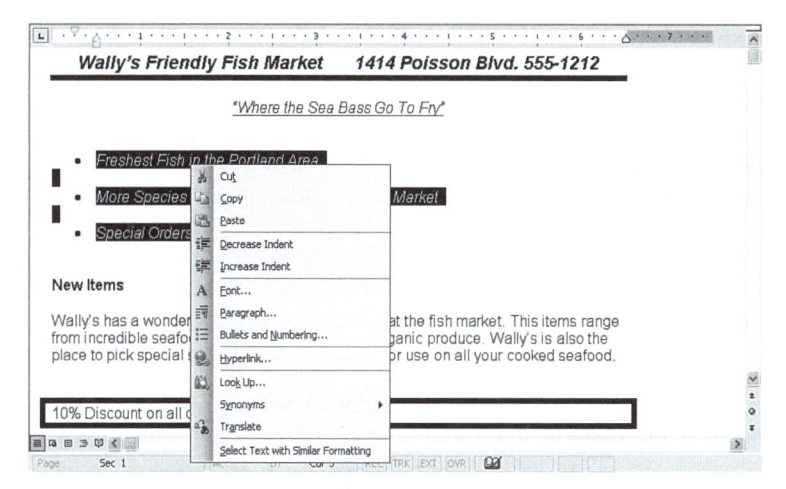

Figure 1.4 By right-clicking areas in Word, you can use shortcut menus to quickly access Word commands related to the item that was clicked.

Word Toolbars

The Word toolbars provide a very quick and straightforward way to access often-used commands and features. When you first start Word, the Standard and Formatting toolbars reside as one continuous toolbar found directly below the menu bar (as shown in Figure 1.2). You can quickly place the Standard and Formatting toolbars in their own row by selecting the Toolbar Options button on either toolbar, and then selecting Show Buttons on Two Rows (as shown in Figures 1.3 and 1.4).

To access a particular command using a toolbar button, click the button. Depending on the command, you see either an immediate result in your document (such as the removal of selected text when you click the Cut button) or the appearance of a dialog box requesting additional information from you.

> **Timesaver tip**
>
> **Finding a Toolbar Button's Purpose**   You can place (hover but do not click) the mouse pointer on any toolbar button to view a description of that tool's function. If you also want to see the shortcut keys associated with a toolbar button, select **Show Shortcut Keys in ScreenTips** on the Options tab of the Customize dialog box.

Word offers several toolbars; many of them contain buttons for a specific group of tasks. For example, the Drawing toolbar provides buttons that give you access to tools that enable you to draw graphical elements in your documents (such as text boxes, lines, and rectangles).

To place additional toolbars in the Word window, right-click any toolbar currently shown and select from the list that appears. Specific toolbars exist for working with tables, pictures, other Word features, and the World Wide Web.

You can also easily add or remove buttons from any of the toolbars present in the Word window. Each toolbar is equipped with a Toolbar Options button that you can use to modify the buttons shown on that particular toolbar.

To add or remove buttons from a specific toolbar, follow these steps:

1 Click the **Toolbar Options** button on any toolbar; a drop-down area appears.

2 Click **Add or Remove Buttons** and then select the name of the toolbar that appears on the pop-up menu. A list of all the buttons for the current toolbar appears, as shown in Figure 1.5.

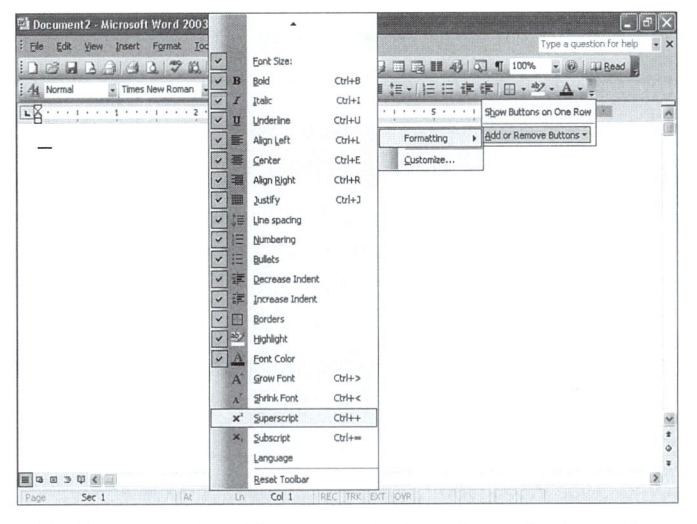

Figure 1.5 You can easily add or remove buttons from a toolbar using the button list.

3 For a button to appear on the toolbar, a check mark must appear to the left of the button in this list. For buttons without a check mark next to them, clicking this space puts the button on the toolbar. These buttons work as toggle switches; one click adds the check mark, another click removes it.

4 When you have completed your changes to the current toolbar, click outside the button list to close it.

The Word toolbars provide fast access to the commands you need most often. Buttons exist for all the commands that are available on the Word menu system.

> **Timesaver tip**
>
> **Moving Toolbars in the Word Window**   You can rearrange toolbars in the Word window. Place the mouse on the dotted vertical handle on the left side of a toolbar and drag it to a new position. You can change the relative position of toolbars below the menu bar and you can also drag toolbars and nest them on the left side of the Word window. Toolbars dragged onto the document window will float and can be positioned as needed.

→ Exiting Word

When you have completed your initial survey of the Word application window or whenever you have completed your work in the program, you will want to exit the software. More than one way exists to close the Word window, which is the same as exiting the program.

You can exit Word by selecting the **File** menu and then **Exit**. Or you can close Word with one click of the mouse by clicking the Word **Close** (**X**) button in the upper-right corner of the application window.

When you close Word, you might be prompted to save any work that you have done in the application window. If you were just experimenting as you read through this lesson, you can click **No**. The current document will not be saved, and the Word application window closes. All the ins and outs of saving your documents are covered in Lesson 2, "Working with Documents."

2 Working with Documents

In this lesson, you learn how to start a new document and enter text. You also learn how to take advantage of Word document templates and Word document wizards.

→ Starting a New Document

When you choose to start a new document in Word, you can take three routes. You can

- Create a blank new document using Word's default *template*.
- Create a document using one of Word's many other templates or a custom one you created yourself.
- Create a document using one of the Word *wizards*, such as the Fax or Envelope Wizard.
- Create a document based on an existing document; using this method you are essentially opening a copy of an existing document, and you can then save it using a new filename.

Templates and wizards allow you to create more complex documents such as newsletters or Web sites. When you want to create a simple document, your best bet is to open a new blank document.

> **Jargon buster**
>
> **Template** A blueprint for a document that may already contain certain formatting options and text.

> **Jargon buster**
>
> **Wizard** A feature that guides you step by step through a particular process in Word, such as creating a new document.

When you create a new document from scratch, you are actually using a template—the Blank Document template. Documents based on the Blank Document template do not contain any premade text (as some of the other templates do), and the formatting contained in the document reflects Word's default settings for margins, fonts, and other document attributes (including any you customized specifically to your needs or preferences).

As covered in Lesson 1, Word automatically opens a new blank document for you when you open the Word application window. You can also open a new document when you are already working in Word.

To open a new document, follow these steps:

1 Select **File**, **New**. The New Document task pane opens on the right side of your screen. The task pane makes it easy for you to quickly create a new blank document, XML document (a document in the eXtensible Markup Language), Web page, or Email. For our purposes, let's look at available templates: under **Other templates**, select **On My Computer**. Word opens the Templates dialog box with a range of templates from which to choose (see Figure 2.1).

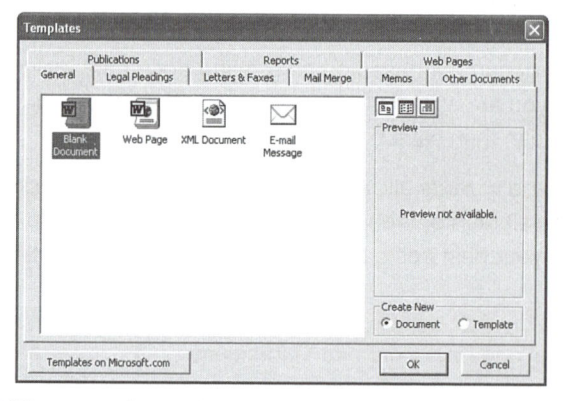

Figure 2.1 When you choose New on the File menu, the task pane opens and you can choose to open templates on your computer.

2 Make sure that the General tab is selected in the Templates dialog box, and then double-click the Word **Blank Document** icon. A new document appears in the Word application window.

Although the steps shown here are designed for you to create a new blank document, you could have chosen any of the templates available in the Templates dialog box to create a new document. The fastest way to create a new blank document is to click the **New Blank Document** icon on the Word Standard toolbar.

> **Important**
>
> **What Happened to My Previous Document?** If you were already working on a document, the new document will, in effect, open on top of the document you were previously working on. You can get back to the previous document by clicking the appropriately named document icon on the Windows taskbar (if you haven't yet named the first document, it might appear as Document1 on the taskbar). You can also select the **Windows** menu to see a list of currently opened documents. Click any document in the list to switch to it.

> **Timesaver tip**
>
> **Multiple Document Icons Are Grouped** When you open a number of Word documents that exceed the number of single buttons that can be shown on the Windows Taskbar (which depends on your screen resolution), the document buttons are grouped under one Microsoft Word icon on the Taskbar. Click the single Word icon and a list of the currently open documents appears. As you close documents, the open documents remain grouped under the one icon until you close all but one of the documents (or all the documents by right-clicking on the Word icon and then selecting **Close Group**).

Using Document Templates

You don't have to base your new documents on a blank template. Instead, you can take advantage of one of the special document templates that Word provides. These templates make it easy for you to create everything from memos to newsletters.

Templates contain special text and document attributes; therefore, the look and layout of the document you create using a template are predetermined by the options contained in the template. This can include margins, fonts, graphics, and other document layout attributes.

To base a new document on a Word template, follow these steps:

1 Select the **File** menu, and then click **New**. The task pane opens in your current document window.

2 Several templates such as the Blank Document, Web Page, and XML Document templates, appear at the top of the New Document task pane. You can select any of these templates. Or you can use the Search box under Templates on Microsoft.com to search for online templates that Microsoft stores on the Office Web site. You can also select templates on your computer or templates held on other Web sites. To create a new memo from a template stored on your computer, click the **On My Computer** link under the Other Templates heading.

3 In the Templates dialog box that appears, choose the **Memos** tab (see Figure 2.2). Select your favorite style of memo and click **OK** (or double-click the icon of choice).

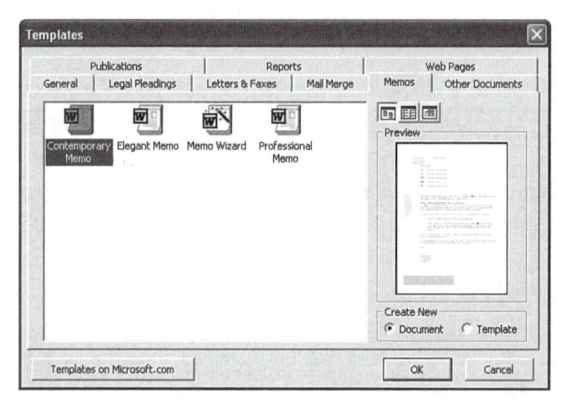

Figure 2.2 The document category tabs in the Templates dialog box contain templates for different document types.

4 The new document based on the template appears as shown in Figure 2.3.

Most new documents based on templates already contain text, such as headings, and a variety of document layouts and text attributes, such as a particular font. For example, the document based on the Contemporary Memo template already contains the layout for a memo, and it automatically enters the current date in the memo for you.

You can easily enter text into the document using the Click Here and Type boxes that are placed in the document. Just click anywhere on the bracketed boxes provided and type the text you want to enter.

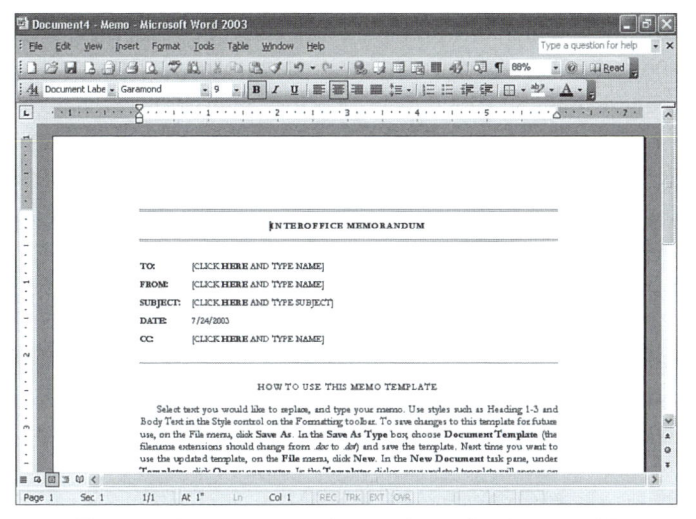

Figure 2.3 The new document contains predetermined text and formatting attributes derived from the template.

Many templates (the Contemporary Memo template, for example) contain text that gives you advice on how to use the template. Any of this explanatory text can be selected and removed or replaced with your own text (for more about selecting and editing text, see Lesson 3, "Editing Documents").

Using Word Wizards

If you find that you would like even more help as you create a new document, you can use any of a number of Word document wizards. These wizards actually walk you through the document creation process, and in many cases, they make sure that you enter the appropriate text in the proper place in the new document.

The wizards are found on the same tabs that housed the templates located in the Templates dialog box (reached through the task pane). The wizards can be differentiated from standard templates by a small wizard's wand that appears over the top right-hand corner of a template's icon.

To create a new document using one of the wizards, follow these steps:

1 Select the **File** menu, and then click **New** to open the New Document task pane.

2 Under the **Other Templates** heading, select the **On My Computer** link. In the Templates dialog box that appears, choose the new document tab of your choice (only the Legal Pleadings, Letterhead & Faxes, Memos, and other Documents tabs provide wizards).

3 To start the document creation process using the wizard, double-click the appropriate wizard icon (for example, the Memo Wizard on the Memos tab).

When you double-click the wizard icon, the wizard dialog box opens with an introductory screen and outlines the document creation process for the type of document you want to create. For example, the Memo Wizard shown in Figure 2.4 details the memo creation process on the left side of the wizard dialog box.

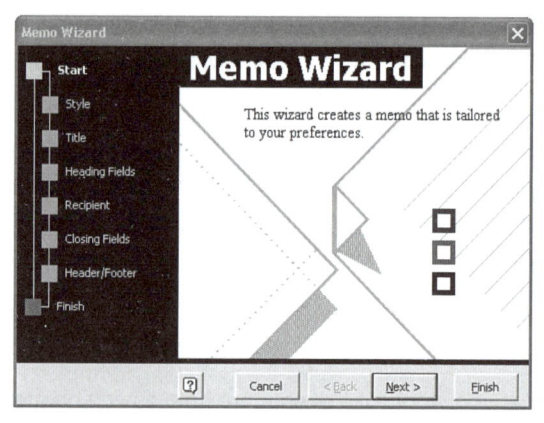

Figure 2.4 The various document wizards, such as the Memo Wizard, outline the new creation process and then walk you through the steps of creating the document.

If you find that you need help as you work with a wizard, you can click the **Office Assistant** button on the wizard dialog box. The Office Assistant, which appears as an animated paper clip by default, appears with context-sensitive help related to the wizard screen on which you are currently working. If the button is not available, cancel the wizard, select the **Help** menu, and then **Show the Office Assistant**; then repeat the steps necessary to open the particular document wizard.

To move to the next step in the document creation process, click the **Next** button at the bottom of the wizard screen.

The various document wizards walk you through the entire document creation process. After completing the steps for document creation, click the **Finish** button to close the wizard. A new document appears in the Word window based on the choices you made as you worked with the wizard. Figure 2.5 shows a new document created using the Memo Wizard.

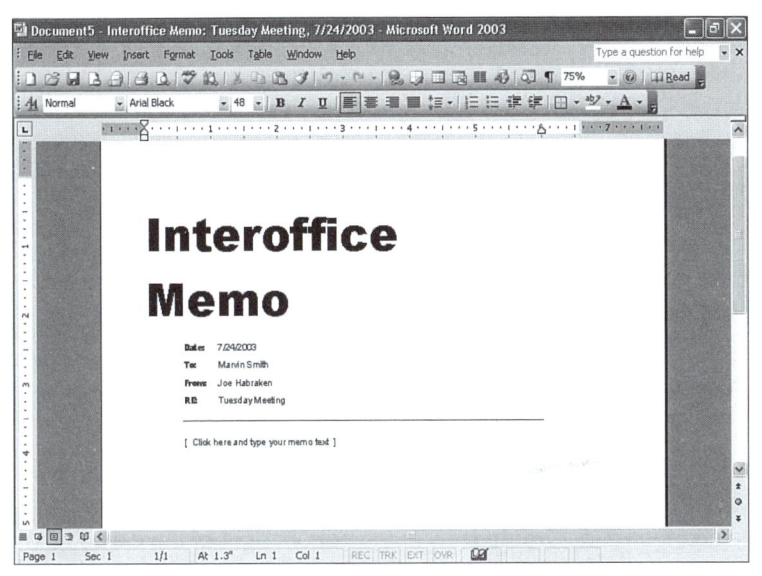

Figure 2.5 The Memo Wizard prompts you to input the appropriate information for a memo and provides the formatting for the new document.

The wizards you use vary in look and feel, depending on the type of document you are trying to create. For example, the Resume Wizard produces a decidedly different product than the Envelope Wizard does. A good rule to follow is to read each wizard screen carefully. Remember that you can always back up a step by clicking the **Back** button if you find that you've made an inappropriate choice (or you can close the unwanted document and start over).

Creating a New Document From an Existing Document

A new option that Word provides is the ability to quickly create a copy of an existing document. This allows you to open the existing document but have Word treat it as a new document without a filename. You can then edit the text and other items in the document as needed.

To create a new document from an existing document, click **File**, then **New**. The New Document task pane opens. Select the **From Existing Document** link under the New heading. The New from Existing Document dialog box opens (see Figure 2.6).

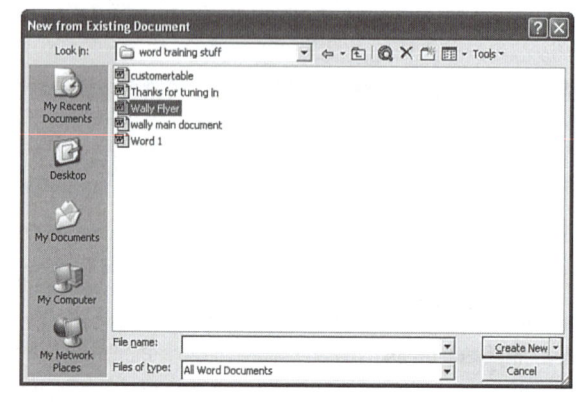

Figure 2.6 The New from Existing Document dialog box allows you to create a new document from an existing one.

Use the **Look In** drop-down box to specify the drive where the file is located. Then double-click to open the appropriate folder. Select the file and then click **Create New** in the bottom right of the dialog box. A new document will open, which is a copy of the document you specified in the New from Existing Document dialog box. After making changes to the new document, you will want to save it under a new document name. The next section discusses saving a new document.

→ Entering Text

After you have opened a new document, you are ready to start entering text. Notice that a blinking vertical element called the *insertion point* appears in the upper-left corner of your new document. This is where new text will be entered.

Begin typing text from the keyboard. The insertion point moves to the right as you type. As soon as you reach the end of the line, the text automatically wraps to the next line for you using word wrap.

When you reach the end of a paragraph in Word, you must press the **Enter** key to manually insert a paragraph break. If you want to view the manually placed paragraph breaks (called paragraph marks) in your document, click the **Show/Hide** button on the Word Standard toolbar.

If the Show/Hide button is not visible on the Word Standard toolbar, click the **Toolbar Options** button located at the end of the Standard toolbar. From the shortcut menu that appears, select **Add or Remove Buttons** and then **Standard**. A drop-down box of other buttons, including the Show/Hide button, appears. Clicking this button adds it to the Standard toolbar. When you are finished, click outside the drop-down box to return to your document. Now you can turn the Show/Hide option on and off as previously described.

> **Timesaver tip**
>
> **How Word Views Paragraphs** Word considers any line or series of lines followed by a paragraph break (created when you press the Enter key) a separate paragraph. This concept becomes very important when you deal with paragraph formatting issues, such as line spacing, indents, and paragraph borders.

→ Saving a Document

Whether you create your new document using the Blank Document template, a Word template, a document wizard, or from an existing document, at some point you will want to save the new document. Saving your work is one of the most important aspects of working with any software application. If you don't save your Word documents, you could lose them.

> **Important**
>
> **Save and Save Often** You don't want to lose your valuable documents as you create them in Word. Power failures, an accidentally kicked-out power cord, or your computer locking up as you work can all lead to lost work. If you are really absent-minded about periodically saving your work, use the AutoSave feature. Select the **Tools** menu, then **Options**. Click the **Save** tab on the dialog box. Make sure the **Save AutoRecover Info Every** check box is selected. Use the minutes box to set the time interval between autosaves. This feature doesn't replace periodically saving your document using the Save command, but it will help you recover more of your document if there is a problem such as a power failure. I suggest setting AutoRecover to 10 or 15 minutes.

To save a document, follow these steps:

1 Click the **Save** button on the Word toolbar, or select the **File** menu and then **Save**. The first time you save your new document, the Save As dialog box appears.

2 Type a filename into the File Name box. If you want to save the file in a format other than a Word document (.doc), such as a text file (.txt), click the **Save As Type** drop-down arrow and select a different file type.

3 To save the file to a different location (the default location is My Documents), click the **Save In** drop-down arrow. After you select a particular drive, all the folders on that drive appear.

4 Double-click the desired folder in the Save In box to open that folder.

5 After you have specified a name and a location for your new document, select the **Save** button to save the file. Word then returns you to the document window.

As you edit and enhance your new document, you should make a habit of frequently saving any changes that you make. To save changes to a document that has already been saved under a filename, just click the **Save** button.

If you would like to keep a backup of a document (the version as it appeared the last time you saved it) each time you save changes to it, you need to set the backup option.

1 Click the **Tools** command on the toolbar, and then select **Options**.

2 In the Options dialog box, click the **Save** tab and then the **Always Create Backup Copy** check box. Click **OK** to return to the document.

3 Name your file and save it for the first time to an appropriate location such as My Documents or another folder on your computer or your network.

Now, when you use the Save command to save changes you've made to the document, a backup copy of the file (with the extension .wbk) is also saved. This backup copy is the previous version of the document before you made the changes. Each subsequent saving of the document replaces the backup file with the previous version of the document.

Occasionally, rather than using the backup option, you might want to save the current document under a new filename or drive location. You can do this using the Save As command. To save your document with a new filename, follow these steps:

1 Select **File**, **Save As**.

2 In the Save As dialog box, type the new filename into the File Name box (make sure that you are saving the document in the desired path).

3 Click **Save**. The file is saved under the new name.

→ Closing a Document

When you have finished working with a document, you need to save your changes and then close the document. To close a document, select the **File** menu and then select **Close**. You can also close a document by clicking the **Close** (**X**) button on the right side of the document window. If you are working with multiple documents, closing one of the documents does not close the Word application. If you want to completely end your Word session, select the **File** menu, and then select **Exit**. Before closing a document, Word checks to see whether it has changed since it was last saved. If it has, Word asks whether you want to save these changes before closing. If you don't want to lose any recent changes, click **Yes** to save the document.

→ Opening a Document

Opening an existing document is a straightforward process. You will find that the Open dialog box shares many of the attributes that you saw in the Save As dialog box.

To open an existing Word file, follow these steps:

1 Select the **File** menu, and then **Open** (or click the Open button on the Standard toolbar). The Open dialog box appears.

2 By default, Word begins showing the files and folders in your My Documents folder. If the document you need is located elsewhere on your computer, click the **Look In** drop-down arrow to select the drive on which the file is located, and navigate to the folder containing the document you need.

3 To open the file, click the file, and then click the **Open** button (you can also double-click the file). The file appears in a Word document window.

If you are working with text files or documents that have been saved in a format other than the Word document format (.doc), you must select the file type in the **Files of Type** drop-down box to see them.

3 Editing Documents

In this lesson, you learn how to do basic text editing in Word, including moving and copying text; you work with the mouse and keyboard to move your document, and you learn how to save existing documents under a new filename.

→ Adding or Replacing Text and Moving in the Document

After you have completed a draft of your document, you will find yourself in a situation where you want to add and delete text in the document as you edit your work. Word makes it very easy for you to add new text and delete text that you don't want. You also will find that, whether you use the mouse or the keyboard to move around in your document as you edit, Word offers a number of special keystrokes and other tricks that make moving within the document a breeze.

The primary tool for placing the insertion point into a document that already contains text using the mouse is the *I-beam*. It looks like an uppercase "I." Place it anywhere in the document and click the left mouse button. This places the insertion point in the document at the I-beam's current position.

> **Jargon buster**
>
> **I-beam** This is the shape that the mouse pointer takes when you place it over any text in a Word document. Use it to place the insertion point at a particular position in a document.

Adding New Text

You actually have two possibilities for adding text to the document: *insert* and *typeover*. To insert text into the document and adjust the position of the existing text, place the I-beam where you want to insert the new text. Click the mouse to place the insertion point at the chosen position. Make sure that the OVR indicator on the Status bar near the bottom of the screen is not active (it will be gray rather than bolded). This means that you are in the insert mode.

> **Jargon buster**
>
> **Insert Mode** The default text mode in Word. New text is added at the insertion point and existing text is pushed forward in the document so that it remains as part of the document.

Type your new text. It is added at the insertion point, and existing text (the text to the right of the inserted text) is pushed forward in the document.

Replacing Text with Typeover

If you want to add new text to a document and simultaneously delete text to the right of the insertion point, use the mouse to place the insertion point where you want to start typing over the existing text. Press the **Insert** key on the keyboard and add your new text. The added text types over the existing text, deleting it (see Figure 3.1). When you switch to Typeover mode using the **Insert** key, the Word status bar displays the message OVR. This means that you are currently in Typeover mode.

Appears in black text when in Typeover mode

Figure 3.1 When you are in Typeover mode, existing text is overwritten by the new text.

> **Jargon buster**
>
> **Typeover Mode** Press the **Insert** key to enter this mode; new text is added at the insertion point and types over the existing text, deleting it.

If you want to return to Insert mode, press the **Insert** key again (it toggles Word between the Insert and Typeover modes) and the OVR message on the status bar is dimmed (you can also double-click **OVR** on the status bar to toggle this feature on and off).

> **Important**
>
> **Undo That Typeover** If you inadvertently type over text in a document because you are in the Typeover mode, click the **Undo** button (it might take several clicks in cases where you have added several words to the document) on the toolbar to return the deleted text to the document (or press **Ctrl+Z**).

Moving Around the Document

Whether you are a mouse aficionado or prefer to stick close to your keyboard, Word provides several shortcuts and tools for moving around a document that you are trying to edit.

When you use the mouse, you can move to a different position on the current page by using the I-beam. You also can use the mouse to move through your document using the vertical and horizontal scrollbars. For example, clicking the up scroll arrow on the vertical scrollbar moves you up through the document. Clicking the down scroll arrow moves you down through the document. If you want to quickly move to a particular page in the document, you can drag the scroll box to a particular place on the vertical scrollbar. As soon as you click on the scroll box, a page indicator box appears that you can use to keep track of what page you are on as you drag the scroll box up or down on the vertical scrollbar.

The vertical scrollbar also provides Previous Page and Next Page buttons (the double-up arrow and double-down arrow buttons on the bottom of the scrollbar) that can be used to move to the previous page and next page, respectively. Use the mouse to click the appropriate button to move in the direction that you want to go in your document.

The horizontal scrollbar operates much the same as the vertical scrollbar; however, it offers the capability to scroll only to the left and the right of a document page. This is particularly useful when you have zoomed in on a document and want to scrutinize an area of the page in great detail.

You should be aware that clicking the mouse on the vertical scrollbar to change your position in a document allows you to view a different portion of a page or a different part of the document; however, it does not move the insertion point to that position on the page. To actually place the insertion point, you must move to a specific place or position in the document, and then click the mouse I-beam where you want to place the insertion point.

When you're typing or editing text, you might find that the fastest way to move through the document is with the help of the keyboard shortcuts shown in Table 3.1. Keeping your hands on the keyboard, rather than reaching out for the mouse, can be a more efficient way to move in a document while you compose or edit.

> **Timesaver tip**
>
> **Scroll Quickly with a Wheel Mouse** You might want to purchase a wheel mouse, such as Microsoft's IntelliMouse, which provides a rolling device on the top of the mouse (between the click buttons). With your finger on the wheel device, you can literally "roll" the vertical scrollbar through the document at the pace of your choice—rapidly or slowly.

Table 3.1 Using the Keyboard to Move Through the

Key Combination	Movement
Home	Move to the beginning of a line
End	Move to the end of a line
Ctrl+Right arrow	Move one word to the right
Ctrl+Left arrow	Move one word to the left
Ctrl+Up arrow	Move to the previous paragraph
Ctrl+Down arrow	Move to the next paragraph
PgUp	Move up one window
PgDn	Move down one window
Ctrl+PgUp	Move up one page
Ctrl+PgDn	Move down one page
Ctrl+Home	Move to the top of a document
Ctrl+End	document

→ Selecting Text

Having a good handle on the different methods for selecting text in a document makes it easy for you to take advantage of many features, including deleting, moving, and formatting text. You can select text with either the mouse or the keyboard. Both methods have their own advantages and disadvantages as you work on your documents.

Selecting Text with the Mouse

The mouse is an excellent tool for selecting text in your document during the editing process. You can double-click a word to select it and also use different numbers of mouse clicks (quickly pressing the left mouse button) or the mouse in combination with the Shift key to select sentences, paragraphs, or other blocks of text. You also can hold the left mouse button down and drag it across a block of text that you want to select.

How you use the mouse to select the text depends on whether the mouse pointer is in the document itself or along the left side of the document in the *selection bar*. The selection bar is the white space on the left edge of your document window, just in front of your text paragraphs. When you place the mouse in the selection bar, the mouse pointer becomes an arrow (in contrast to placing the mouse in the document where the pointer appears as an I-beam).

Selecting text lines and paragraphs from the selection bar makes it easy for you to quickly select either a single line or the entire document. Table 3.2 shows you how to select different text items using the mouse. Figure 3.2 shows the mouse pointer in the selection bar with a selected sentence.

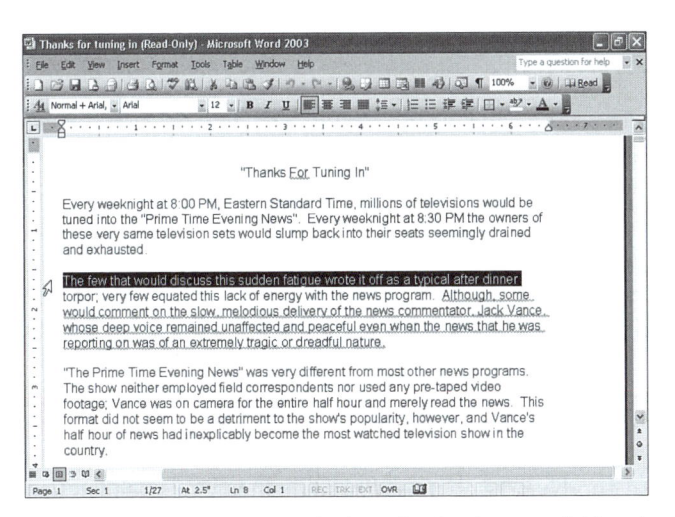

Figure 3.2 Place the mouse pointer in the selection bar to quickly select a line, a paragraph, or other text block.

Editing Documents

Table 3.2 Using the Mouse to Quickly Select Text in the Document

Text Selection	Mouse Action
Selects the word	Double-click a word
Selects text block	Click and drag
	or
	Click at beginning of text, and then hold down the Shift key and click at the end of text block
Selects line	Click in selection bar next to line
Selects multiple lines	Click in selection bar and drag down through multiple lines
Selects the sentence	Hold Ctrl and click a sentence
Selects paragraph	Double-click in selection bar next to paragraph
	or
	Triple-click in the paragraph
Selects entire document	Hold down Ctrl and click in selection bar

You will find these mouse manipulations are particularly useful when you are editing the document. Selected text can be quickly deleted, moved, or copied.

Selecting Text with the Keyboard

You can also select text using only the keyboard. Press the F8 function key to turn on the extend (or select) feature; the EXT indicator becomes active on the Word status bar as soon as you press one of the arrow keys on the keyboard (meaning it is no longer "grayed" out).

To select text using the extend feature, use the arrow keys to move over and highlight characters, words, or sentences you want to select. You can quickly select entire words by placing the insertion point at the beginning of a word, pressing **F8** and then pressing the spacebar. To select an entire sentence, turn on the extend feature, and then press the period (**.**) key. You can select entire paragraphs using this method by pressing the **Enter** key. To turn off the extend feature, press the **Esc** key.

Finally, you can select text by pressing only the F8 function key. Press **F8** once to turn on the select feature where you want it, press it twice to select a word, three times to highlight an entire sentence, four times to select a paragraph, and five times to select your entire document.

→ Deleting, Copying, and Moving Text

Another important aspect of editing is being able to delete, move, or copy text in your document. Each of these tasks can be easily accomplished in Word and uses the mouse or the keyboard to select the text that you want to delete, move, or copy. Then, it's just a matter of invoking the correct command to delete, move, or copy the selected text.

Deleting Text

Deleting text can be accomplished in more than one way. The simplest way to remove characters as you type is with the Backspace key or the Delete key. If no text is selected, these keys work like this:

- **Delete**—Deletes the character to the right of the insertion point.
- **Backspace**—Deletes the character to the left of the insertion point.

You will probably find, however, that when you delete text you want to remove more than just one character, so use the keyboard or the mouse to select the text you want to delete. After the text is selected, press the **Delete** key. The text is then removed from the document.

You can also delete text and replace it with new text in one step. After the text is selected, type the new text. It replaces the entire existing, selected text.

> **Important**
>
> **Delete and Cut Are Different** When you want to erase a text block forever, use the **Delete** key. When you want to remove text from a particular place in the document but want to have access to it again to place it somewhere else, use the **Cut** command on the **Edit** menu. When you cut an item, it is automatically placed on the Office Clipboard. These steps are covered later in this lesson.

Copying, Cutting, and Pasting Text

Copying or cutting text and then pasting the copied or cut item to a new location is very straightforward. All you have to do is select the text as we discussed earlier in this lesson and then invoke the appropriate commands. Use the following steps to copy and paste text in your document:

1 Using the mouse or the keyboard, select the text that you want to copy.

2 Select the **Edit** menu, and then select **Copy**, or press **Ctrl+C** to copy the text.

3 Place the insertion point in the document where you want to place a copy of the copied text.

4 Select the **Edit** menu and then select **Paste**, or press **Ctrl+V**. A copy of the text is inserted at the insertion point.

> **Timesaver tip**
>
> **Use the Copy, Cut, and Paste Icons** To quickly access the copy, cut, and paste features, use the Copy, Cut, and Paste icons on the Word toolbar, respectively.

After you paste your selected text, the Paste Smart Tag icon appears just below the text that you have pasted. When you click this icon, it provides a shortcut menu that allows you to keep the formatting that was applied to the source text that you copied, match the formatting supplied by the destination for the text (the paragraph you are placing the text in), or just paste the text into the new location with no formatting at all (which means it will assume the formatting that is provided at the current location). Figure 3.3 shows the Paste Smart Tag provided for pasted text.

> **Timesaver tip**
>
> **What Are Smart Tags?** Smart Tags are shortcuts that are assigned to particular types of information in a Word document. For example, you will see that people's names are labeled with a smart tag (a purple dotted line below the text) that makes it easy to add a person to your Outlook Contact folder. Text that has been pasted to a new location is also flagged with a smart tag that makes it easy to format the pasted text.

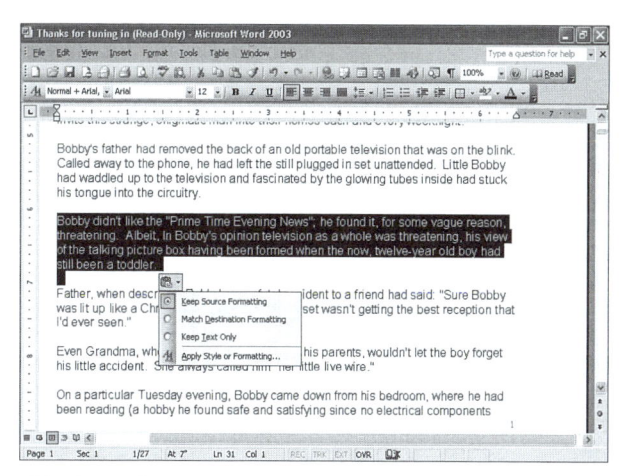

Figure 3.3 The Paste Smart Tag allows you to choose how the text is pasted into the new location.

Cutting text from the document and then pasting it to a new location is every bit as straightforward as using copy and paste. Select the text, and then press Ctrl+X or click the **Cut** button on the Standard toolbar. Click the I-beam to place the insertion point on the document, and then you can use Ctrl+V or the **Paste** button on the Standard toolbar to place the text in a new location. A Paste Smart Tag will appear below the pasted text as shown in Figure 3.3.

Using the Office Clipboard to Copy and Move Multiple Items

The Office Clipboard feature now resides in the task pane of your Office application windows as discussed in "Using Office Task Panes," which is found on page 19 of this book. If you want to copy or cut more than one item and then be able to paste them into different places in the document, you must use the Office Clipboard. Follow these steps:

1. To open the Clipboard task pane, select the **Edit** menu and select **Office Clipboard**. The Clipboard appears in the task pane.

2. As shown in Figure 3.4, select and copy each item to the Clipboard.

3. After you have copied your items onto the Clipboard, place the insertion point where you want the first item to be pasted. Then, return to the Clipboard and with the mouse, point to your first item and click; Word automatically inserts the item into the document.

Figure 3.4 The Clipboard can hold up to 24 separate items.

4 Repeat step 3 as needed to paste other items from the Clipboard into your document.

If you want to cut and paste (or move) multiple items, you must use the Office Clipboard. Follow these steps:

1 To open the Clipboard, select the **Edit** menu and select **Clipboard**. The Clipboard appears in the task pane.

2 Select and cut each item to the Clipboard.

3 After you have your cut items on the Clipboard, place the insertion point where you want the first item to be pasted. Then, return to the Clipboard and with the mouse, point to your first item and click; it will automatically be inserted into the document.

4 Repeat step 3 as needed to paste other items from the Clipboard into your document.

Timesaver tip

Open the Task Pane from the View Menu You can also open the task pane by selecting View and then Task Pane. Then use the Other Task Panes drop-down list to select the task pane you want to use such as the Clipboard.

Using Drag and Drop

One other way to move text is by selecting it and dragging it to a new location. This is called *drag and drop*. After the text is selected, place the mouse on the text block and hold down the left mouse button. A Move pointer appears, as shown in Figure 3.5.

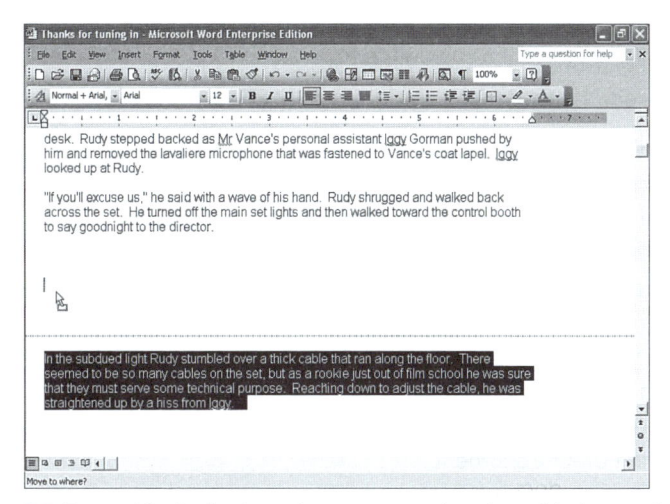

Figure 3.5 Drag a block of selected text to a new location with drag and drop.

Drag the Move pointer to the new location for the text. A dotted insertion point appears in the text. Place this insertion point in the appropriate position and release the mouse button. The text is moved to the new location.

→ Copying and Moving Text Between Documents

You can copy text easily between documents. All you have to do is open the appropriate documents and then use the methods already discussed for copying or moving text. You can even use drag and drop to move information from one document to another.

To copy information from one document to another, follow these steps:

1 Open the document you want to copy information from and the one you want to copy that information to (see Lesson 2, "Working with Documents," for more information on opening documents).

2 Switch to the document that contains the text you want to copy by clicking the document's button on the **Taskbar** or selecting the **Windows** menu and then the name of the document.

3 Select the text you want to copy, select the **Edit** menu, and then select the **Copy** command.

4 Using the instructions in step 2, switch to the document into which you want to paste the text.

5 Select the **Edit** menu, and then select **Paste**. The text is pasted into your document.

You can also use the preceding steps to move text from one document to another by substituting the Cut command for the Copy command. You can also use drag and drop to move text from one document to another. Working with multiple document windows can be tricky. You probably won't want to have more than two documents open if you want to use drag and drop, because you won't have enough space in the Word workspace to scroll through the documents and find the text you want to move or the final resting place for the text in the other document.

To view multiple document windows (all the documents you currently have open), select the **Window** menu and then select **Arrange All**. Each document is placed in a separate window in the Word workspace. The windows might be small if you have several documents open. Locate the text you want to move and select it. Drag it from the current document window to the document window and position where you want to place it.

4 Using Proofreading and Research Tools

In this lesson, you learn to check your documents for errors such as misspellings and improper grammar. You work with the spell checker and grammar checker and learn how to find synonyms with the thesaurus, how to proof your document as you type, and how to use the AutoCorrect feature. You learn how to add a service to the Research task pane.

→ Proofing As You Type

Word offers several excellent features for helping you to create error-free documents. Each of these features—the spell checker, the grammar checker, and the thesaurus—are explored in this lesson. Word also gives you the option of checking your spelling and grammar automatically as you type. You can also use the AutoCorrect feature to automatically make some proofing changes for you (for more about AutoCorrect, see "Working with AutoCorrect" in this lesson).

Proofing as you type simply means that errors in spelling and grammar can be automatically flagged as you enter text into your document. This enables you to quickly and immediately correct errors as you build your document.

When you proof as you type, spelling errors—words not found in the Word dictionary file or in your custom dictionary file—are flagged with a wavy red underline. Errors in grammar are underlined with a wavy green line. Spelling and grammar errors marked in this way can be corrected immediately, or you can correct them collectively by running the spelling and grammar checking features after you have finished entering all the text. For information on using the Spelling and Grammar Checker on a completed document, see the section "Using the Spelling and Grammar Checker," later in this lesson.

The check-as-you-type features are turned on in Word by default. To change the defaults associated with the automatic spelling and grammar checking features (or to turn them off completely), follow these steps:

1 Select the **Tools** menu, and then choose **Options**. The Options dialog box opens.

2 Make sure the **Spelling and Grammar** tab is selected, as shown in Figure 4.1.

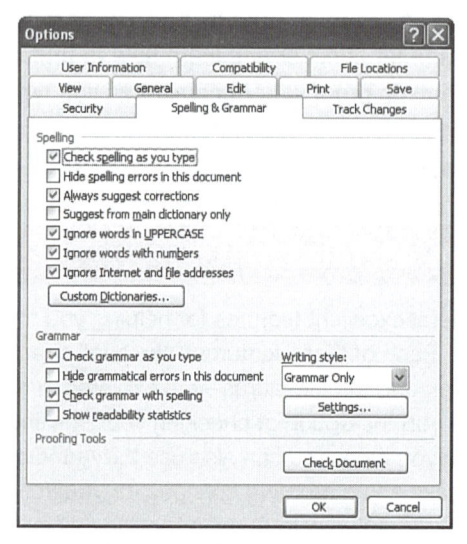

Figure 4.1 You can turn the automatic spelling and grammar checking options on or off in the Options dialog box.

3 To toggle the automatic spelling checker on or off, click the **Check Spelling As You Type** check box in the Spelling area of the dialog box.

4 To toggle the automatic grammar checker on or off, click the **Check Grammar As You Type** check box in the Grammar area of the dialog box (near the bottom).

Several other options are also available in this dialog box that relate to how the Spelling and Grammar features operate when you use them in Word.

- **Hide Spelling Errors in This Document**—This option hides the wavy red lines that flag misspellings in the document.

- **Always Suggest Corrections**—This option provides a list of suggested corrections for each misspelled word when the spell checker is used.
- **Suggest from Main Dictionary Only**—This option uses only the main dictionary for spell checking the document. Any customized dictionaries that have been created are ignored.
- **Ignore Words in UPPERCASE**—This option ignores uppercase words in the document.
- **Ignore Words with Numbers**—This option ignores combinations of text and numbers in the document.
- **Ignore Internet and File Addresses**—This option ignores Web addresses and filenames (such as C:\my documents\joe.doc).
- **Hide Grammatical Errors in the Document**—This option hides the wavy green line that marks potential grammar errors in the document.
- **Check Grammar with Spelling**—This option is used to have Word also check the grammar in the document when you run the spell checker.
- **Show Readability Statistics**—This option is used to display different readability statistics that show you the readability level and grade level of your text.

After you have finished making your selections in the Options dialog box, click **OK**.

Timesaver tip

Understanding Readability Statistics   Readability statistics provide you with a way to assess the reading level of a document. Two scales that are based on the average syllables per word and the number of words per sentence are provided: Flesch Reading Ease score and Flesch-Kincaid Grade Level score. Flesch Reading Ease uses a 100-point scale; the higher the number the easier the document is to read (you should aim for documents with a score of 60 to 70). Flesch-Kincaid Grade Level uses U.S. school grade levels. For example, a rating of 8.0 would be equivalent to an eighth grade reading level (aim for scores between 7.0 to 8.0).

With the check–as-you-type options enabled, suspected misspellings and grammatical errors are flagged with the appropriate colored wavy line.

Correcting Individual Spelling Errors

As mentioned, Word marks all words not found in its dictionary with a wavy red line. Because Word's dictionary isn't entirely complete, you might find that it marks correct words as misspelled. To correct words flagged as misspelled (whether they are or not), follow these steps:

1 Place the mouse pointer on the flagged word and click the right mouse button. A shortcut menu appears, as shown in Figure 4.2.

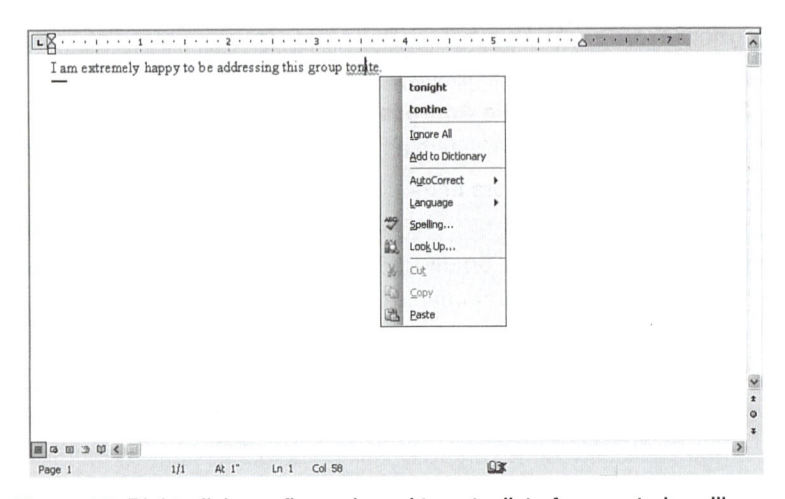

Figure 4.2 Right-click any flagged word to get a list of suggested spellings.

2 Word provides a list of possible correct spellings when it encounters a word not in its dictionary. If the correct spelling for the word you want appears in the list, simply click it, and Word replaces the incorrect spelling with the correct one.

If the flagged word is correctly spelled (and just not in Word's dictionary) or the correct spelling is not in the suggestions list, you have two other options:

- If the word is correct and you don't want it flagged at all in the current document, you can click **Ignore All** and the wavy red line will be removed from all occurrences of the word.

- If the word is correct and you don't want it flagged in this or any other document, you can add the word to the dictionary file; click **Add to Dictionary**.

> **Timesaver tip**
>
> **Take Advantage of AutoCorrect** If you find that you constantly misspell the word as it currently appears in your document, you can add the word to the AutoCorrect list (discussed later in this chapter). Right-click on the misspelled word and then point to AutoCorrect on the shortcut menu. Suggested spellings will be listed. Select a spelling from the list; the incorrect spelling and the correct spelling are entered into the AutoCorrect list. The word in your document is corrected, and the next time you type the word incorrectly, it is automatically corrected.

Correcting Individual Grammatical Errors

Correcting grammatical errors as you type is similar to correcting spelling errors that are flagged in the document. Suspected grammatical errors are marked with a green wavy line.

To correct a suspected grammatical error, follow these steps:

1. Right-click text blocks marked with the green wavy line.
2. The shortcut menu that appears might offer you a list of grammatically correct phrases. Select the phrase that corrects your text entry. In most cases, however, rather than providing a correct solution, the Grammar Checker provides the nature of the error such as passive voice or fragment. You will have to correct the error yourself, but Word at least provides information on why it was flagged.
3. If your text is not incorrect grammatically or requires that you manually make any necessary changes, click **Ignore Once**.
4. If you select Grammar on the shortcut menu, the Grammar dialog box will open. It offers suggestions related to the error and also gives you the option of ignoring the grammar rule that flagged the error in the document.

As soon as you make a selection from the shortcut menu or click **Ignore Once**, the shortcut menu closes. You can then either use the Grammar dialog box to fix the error or continue working on your document (the Spelling and Grammar features are discussed in the next section).

> **Timesaver tip**
>
> **How Good is the Grammar Checker?** Although the Grammar Checker is useful, you will find that it will miss grammar errors and even flag correct sentences. The Grammar Checker does not have the ability to interpret the context of the words you use in a sentence. So, use it as an aid to writing, not necessarily the final word, however.

→ Using the Spelling and Grammar Checker

You might prefer not to correct spelling and grammatical errors as you type. If you're a touch typist, you might not even notice Word has flagged a word or sentence as incorrect. Waiting to correct the document until you have finished composing enables you to concentrate on getting your thoughts down without interruption. Then, you can check the entire document upon completion.

To use the Word Spelling and Grammar feature, follow these steps:

1. Select **Tools**, **Spelling and Grammar**, or click the **Spelling and Grammar** button on the toolbar. The Spelling and Grammar dialog box appears as shown in Figure 4.3.

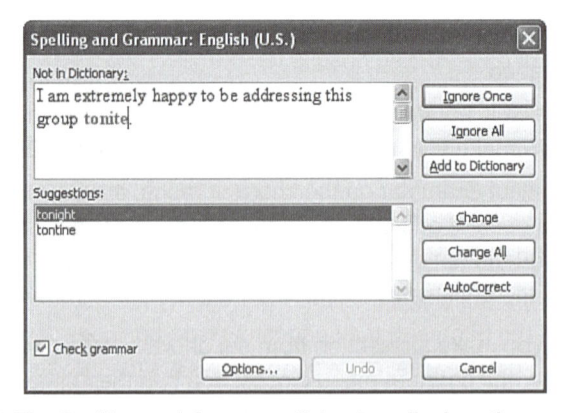

Figure 4.3 The Spelling and Grammar dialog box displays the suspected spelling and grammar errors in your document and offers you options for correcting them.

2 Words not found in the dictionary are flagged, and the text in which the word is contained is displayed in the Not in Dictionary box. You can manually correct the highlighted word in the box and then click **Change** to correct the word in the document. The following are other options available for the flagged word:

- Select the appropriate selection for the flagged word from the Suggestion box and click **Change**. If you want to correct all occurrences of the misspelled word (assuming you have consistently and knowingly misspelled it), click **Change All**.

- Ignore the flagged word if it is correctly spelled. Click **Ignore Once** to ignore this occurrence of the word, or click **Ignore All** to ignore all occurrences of the word in the document.

- You can also add the word to the dictionary; just click **Add**.

- If you would rather add the misspelled word and an appropriate correct spelling to the AutoCorrect feature, click **AutoCorrect**; the word is corrected, and future insertions of the word (even in other documents when they're opened) with the incorrect spelling are automatically corrected.

Regardless of which selection you make, the word is dealt with appropriately and the spelling checker moves on to the next flagged word. Make your selection either to correct or to ignore the word, as previously outlined.

If the Check Grammar check box in the Spelling and Grammar dialog box is selected, Word also checks the grammar in your document.

When the Spelling and Grammar dialog box flags a grammatical error in the document, the suspected error appears in the text box at the top of the Spelling and Grammar dialog box with a heading that describes the type of error. Figure 4.4 shows an error in subject-verb agreement that has been caught by the grammar checker.

Suggested corrections, if available, appear in the Suggestions box. In the case of the fragment, the suggestion is to consider revising the fragment. In other cases, more suggestions with actual sentence revisions might appear in this box. If the appropriate revision is present, select it and click **Change**.

You are also presented with different ignore options for flagged grammatical errors:

Text specifies the nature of the problem

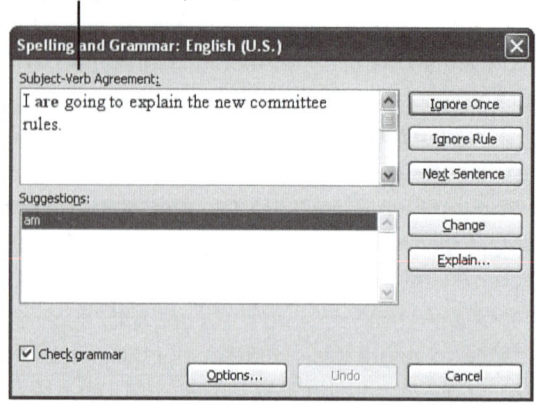

Figure 4.4 The grammar checker flags suspected grammar errors and offers suggestions and possible fixes for the problem.

- You can choose to ignore the suspected grammatical error by clicking **Ignore**. This ignores only the currently flagged error.
- In some cases, **Ignore All** is also an option. If you click **Ignore All**, the grammar checker ignores all occurrences of this same grammatical error in the rest of the document.
- Word also provides you with the option of ignoring the actual grammar rule that was used to flag the current grammatical error; click **Ignore Rule** to do this throughout the document. This means that any error (not just the current error) that is flagged because of that particular rule (fragment or long sentence, for example) is not flagged as a grammatical error.

Use the Grammar feature to check the entire document using the options discussed in this section. When you reach the end of the document and the Grammar check is complete, a dialog box will appear letting you know that the spelling and grammar check has been completed.

→ Finding Synonyms Using the Thesaurus

The Word thesaurus provides you with a tool that can be used to find synonyms for the words in your document. Synonyms are words that mean the same thing. Because the thesaurus can generate a list of synonyms for nearly any word in your document, you can avoid the constant use of a particular descriptive adjective (such as "excellent") and actually add some depth to the vocabulary that appears in your document.

The thesaurus is now part of a new Research tool that has been added to Microsoft Office. Research tools like the Word thesaurus are accessed in the Research task pane, which you can open by clicking the Research button. The Research task pane can be used to search local resources such as the thesaurus and custom data sources specifically created by a company or institution. For example, a data source could be created that would allow a user to find information about a particular product they are writing about by accessing the custom data resource through the Research task pane.

The Research task pane also allows you to access remote data sources such as resources on the Internet. Although it is beyond the scope of this book to discuss the creation of custom data sources, we will look at how you can add additional resources to the Research task pane later in the lesson. We will get our feet wet using the new Research task pane by using the Word thesaurus.

> **Timesaver tip**
>
> **The Thesaurus Also Lists Antonyms** Depending on the word you select to find synonyms, you might find that a list of antonyms—words that mean the opposite—are also provided. Antonyms are marked with (antonym) to the right of the suggested word.

To use the thesaurus, follow these steps:

1 To select the word for which you want to find a synonym, double-click it.

2 Select the **Tools** menu, point at **Language**, and then select **Thesaurus**. (You can also click the **Research** button on the Standard toolbar.) The Research task pane appears as shown in Figure 4.5. By default the English (U.S.) thesaurus is used to find a list of synonyms for the selected word.

3 To replace the word with a synonym, place the mouse on the synonym in the synonym list, and then click on the drop-down arrow that appears to the right of the synonym. Click Insert from the menu that appears.

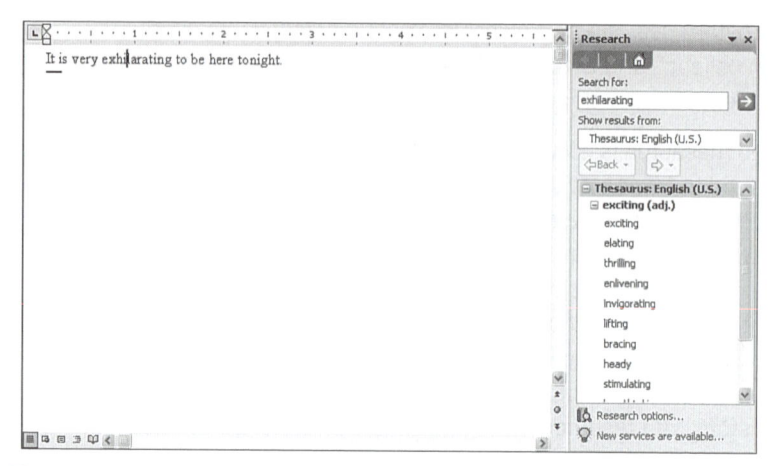

Figure 4.5 The Research task pane provides a list of synonyms for the selected word.

4 You can also choose to see a list of synonyms for any of the words listed in the synonym list. Double-click on the synonym. This can provide a greater number of possible words to use when you replace the particular word in your document. Synonyms provided for a word in the synonym list might be less close in meaning, however, to the word in your document. If you want to return to the original lists of synonyms (for the word you originally selected), click the **Back** button.

After you have selected a synonym and clicked **Replace**, the word is replaced in the document. If you want to close the Research task pane, click the Close button in the upper-right corner of the task pane.

Timesaver tip

Right-Click for Synonyms A quick way to check for a list of synonyms for a word is to right-click that word in your document and then select **Synonyms** from the shortcut menu. A list of synonyms (if available for that word) appears. Select the appropriate word on the list to replace the currently selected word. Words flagged as misspelled or in a sentence marked as a grammar error will not provide a list of synonyms when you right-click them.

→ Adding Research Services

As we already discussed briefly, the new Research task pane provides a tool that can be used to access all sorts of information related to a selection in a document. These tools can be standard tools such as the thesaurus and can also consist of specialized data sources created to find specific kinds of information.

In the case of the Word thesaurus, you can actually access different thesaurus files. For example, by default you use the English (U.S.) thesaurus (if you installed the U.S. version of Office). But you can also access other thesaurus files such as the English (U.K.) or French (Canada or France). To access these additional reference books click the **Show Results From** drop-down list in the Research task pane.

You can also add new reference services to the Research task pane. These can be custom resources or resources provided by Microsoft. To add a new reference service, follow these steps:

1 Select **Tools**, and then select **Research** to open the Research task pane.

2 Select the Research options link at the bottom of the Research task pane. The Research Options dialog box will open as shown in Figure 4.6.

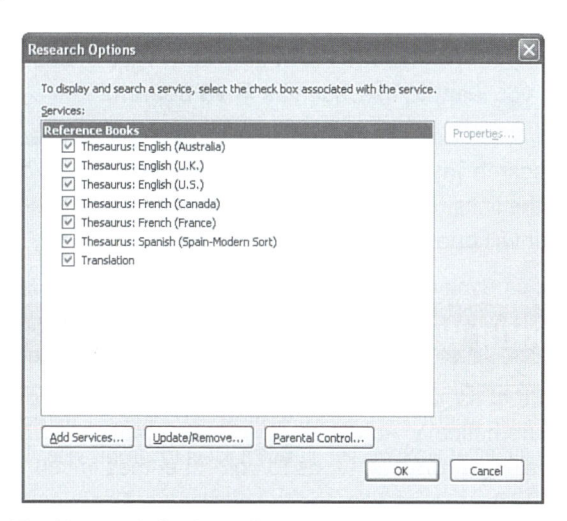

Figure 4.6 The Research Options dialog box allows you to view installed Research services and add new services.

3 Click **Add Services**. The Add Services dialog box appears. It will contain a list of services that are available for addition (this will typically consist of only Microsoft services).

4 To add a service, either click a service in the Available services list or provide the URL (the Web address) of the new service.

5 When you select a Microsoft service that is listed, an additional dialog box will open with service options. For example, you may be able to add Encarta dictionaries or other services such as MSN search to your Research services.

6 Select the specific services you want to add from the list and then click Install. The services will be added.

Now when you use the Research task pane the additional services will be available in the **Show Results From** drop-down list. You can use these new services for a variety of purposes. For example, if I have referenced a company name in a document, I can use the Research task pane to automatically search the Web for information on that company using an added service such as the MSN search tool from Microsoft. Follow these steps:

1 Click at the end of the company name or other information in the document.

2 Select **Tools**, and then select **Research** to open the Research task pane.

3 Select the **Show Results From** drop-down list and select the service you want to use (such as **MNS Search**).

4 A list of links or other information will appear in the results area of the Research Task pane. In the case of Web links you can click any of the links to open the referenced Web page. Internet Explorer will open to the referenced page.

→ Working with AutoCorrect

You will find that as you type some of your misspelled words are corrected automatically. AutoCorrect, a feature that uses a list of common spelling errors and typos to correct entries in your documents, is the tool making these corrections. For example, Word has already arranged to have the incorrect spelling of "t-e-h" to be replaced with "the." You can also add your own words to the

AutoCorrect feature. For example, if you always spell aardvark as ardvark, you can set up AutoCorrect to correct this spelling error every time you type it.

You've already seen that the Spelling feature provides you with the option of placing misspelled words into the AutoCorrect library. You can also manually enter pairs of words (the incorrect and correct spellings) into the AutoCorrect dialog box.

To place words in the AutoCorrect list, follow these steps:

1 Click the **Tools** menu, and then click **AutoCorrect Options**. The AutoCorrect dialog box appears as shown in Figure 4.7.

2 In the **Replace** box, enter the word as you misspell it. In the **With** box, enter the correct spelling of the word.

3 Click **Add** to add the entry to the AutoCorrect list.

4 When you have completed adding entries, click **OK** to close the dialog box.

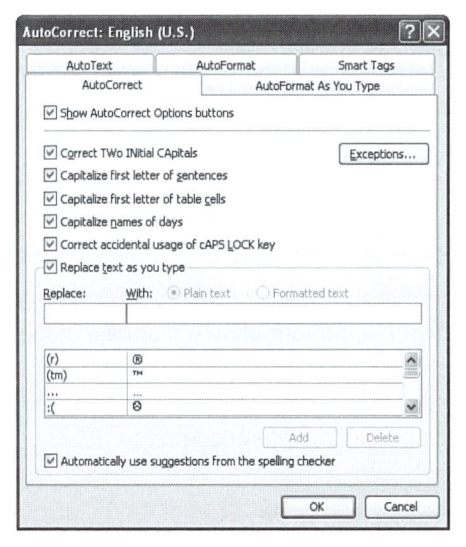

Figure 4.7 The AutoCorrect feature enables you to build a list of commonly misspelled words for automatic correction.

Now when you misspell the word, Word corrects it for you automatically. You can also use the AutoCorrect dialog box to delete AutoCorrect entries that you do not use (highlight the entry and click

Delete) or that inadvertently correct items that you want to have in your document (clear the applicable check box).

This feature can also be used to help speed your typing along. For example, suppose that you are writing a technical paper that includes a long organizational name, such as the National Museum of American Art. If you tell the AutoCorrect feature to replace "nmaa" with "National Museum of American Art," it saves you a lot of typing.

> **Timesaver tip**
>
> **Override the AutoCorrect Feature** If you type a text entry that is automatically changed by the AutoCorrect feature but you want it spelled your original way, immediately place your mouse on the corrected text. The AutoCorrect Smart Tag (it has a lightning bolt symbol on it) appears. When you click this Smart Tag's arrow, you can choose to return the word to its original text, among other options.

5 Changing How Text Looks

In this lesson, you learn basic ways to change the look of your text. You work with fonts and learn how to change font attributes. You also work with text alignment, such as centering and right justification.

→ Understanding Fonts

When you work in Word, you want to be able to control the look of the text in the documents that you create. The size and appearance of the text is controlled for the most part by the font or fonts you choose to use in the document. Each available font has a particular style or typeface. A variety of fonts exists, with names such as Arial, Courier, Times New Roman, CG Times, Bookman Old Style, and so on; the fonts you can choose depend on the fonts that have been installed on your computer (Windows offers a large number of default fonts; other font families are added when you install Office, and you can purchase software for special lettering and printing projects). Each font has a particular look and feel that makes it unique.

> **Timesaver tip**
>
> **Keep Your Business Documents Standard** The standard point size for most business documents is 12 points, which is 1/6 of an inch tall. So, when selecting a new font, it's generally a good idea to make sure that you use 12 points for documents such as business letters and memos.

You can change the font or fonts used in a document whenever you need to, and you can also manipulate the size of the characters and their attributes, including bold, underlining, and italic. You can select a new font before you begin typing your document, or you can select text and change its fonts and text attributes at any time.

→ Changing Font Attributes

The easiest way to change font attributes is through the use of the buttons provided on the Word Formatting toolbar. Figure 5.1 shows the Word Formatting toolbar with some of the most common font attribute buttons displayed.

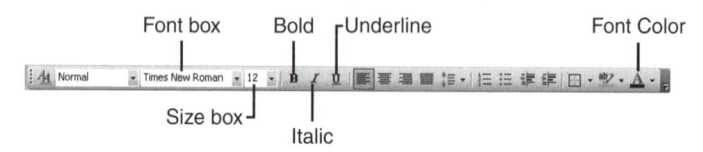

Figure 5.1 The Word Formatting toolbar gives you quick access to control the font attributes in your documents.

You can quickly change the font of selected text by clicking the **Font** box and selecting a new font from the list that appears. Other attributes, such as bold, italic, and underline, require that you select the text and then click the appropriate button once to add that attribute to the text. For example, you might want to apply special formatting to a heading so that it stands out from the rest of the text. You can do that by adding bold to the text.

To add bold to text in a document, follow these steps:

1. Select the word or other text to be bold.
2. Click the **Bold** button on the Formatting toolbar. The text appears in bold.
3. Click any other part of the document to deselect the text and view the results of your formatting.

You can use this same technique to underline and italicize text in your documents.

You can also use the various font buttons to select font attributes for the new text you type into a new document or insert into an existing document. Select the appropriate font attributes on the Formatting toolbar, and then type the text. To turn off a particular attribute, such as bold or italic, click the appropriate button a second time. To change to a new font or size, use the appropriate drop-down box.

> **Timesaver tip**
>
> **I Don't Have Those Buttons on My Toolbar** Click the **Toolbar Options** drop-down arrow, point at **Add or Remove Buttons**, and then select the name of the toolbar you want to add the buttons to (such as the Formatting toolbar). From the drop-down list, select the buttons that you want to add to the Formatting toolbar. If you don't see the Formatting toolbar at all, right-click any of the toolbars and select **Formatting** on the menu that appears.

When you are typing in a document, you might find that selecting font attributes from the toolbar actually slows you down because you must remove one hand from the keyboard to use the mouse to make your selection. You can also turn on or off a number of the formatting attributes using shortcut keys on the keyboard. Table 5.1 shows some of the common keyboard shortcuts for formatting attributes.

Table 5.1 Font Attribute Shortcut Keys

Attribute	Shortcut Keys
Bold	Ctrl+B
Italic	Ctrl+I
Underline	Ctrl+U
Double underline	Ctrl+Shift+D
Subscript	Ctrl+equal sign (=)
Superscript	Ctrl+Shift+plus sign (+)

To use any of the shortcut key combinations, press the keys shown simultaneously to turn the attribute on, and then repeat the key sequence to turn the attribute off. For example, to turn on bold while you are typing, press the **Ctrl** key and the **B** key at the same time. Press these keys again to turn the bold off.

→ Working in the Font Dialog Box

Although the Formatting toolbar certainly provides the quickest avenue for controlling various font attributes, such as the font and the font size, you can access several more font attributes in the Font dialog box. The Font dialog box gives you control over common attributes, such as font, font size, bold, and so on, and it also provides you with control over special font attributes, such as superscript, subscript, and strikethrough.

To open the Font dialog box, click the **Format** menu, and then select **Font**. The Font dialog box appears, as shown in Figure 5.2.

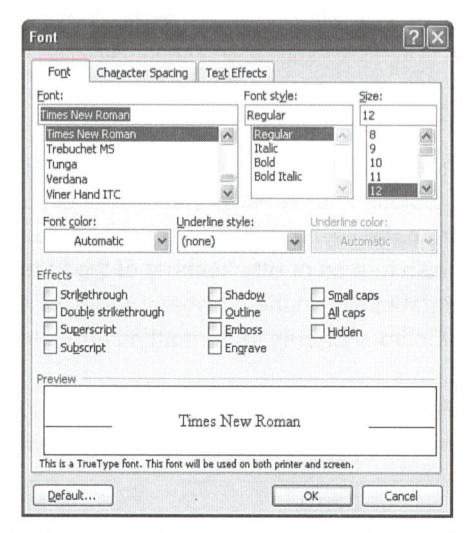

Figure 5.2 The Font dialog box provides you with control over several font attributes not found on the Formatting toolbar.

As you can see, the Font dialog box enables you to choose from several font attributes. You can control the font, the font style, and other character attributes such as strikethrough, superscript, and shadow.

- To change the font, click the **Font** drop-down box and select the new font by name.
- To change the font style to italic, bold, or bold italic, make the appropriate selection in the **Font Style** box.
- To change the size of the font, select the appropriate size in the **Size** scroll box.
- For underlining, click the **Underline Style** drop-down box and select an underlining style.
- To change the color of the font, click the **Font Color** drop-down box and select a new color.

- To select any special effects, such as strikethrough, superscript, or shadow, select the appropriate check box in the lower half of the dialog box.

As you make the various selections in the Font dialog box, a sample of what the text will look like appears in the Preview box at the bottom of the dialog box. After you have made all your selections in the Font dialog box, click **OK**.

> **Timesaver tip**
>
> **Change the Default Font** To change the default font that you use for your documents (those created using the current or desired template), select the font attributes in the Font dialog box and then click the **Default** button at the lower left of the dialog box. Click **Yes** when Word asks for a confirmation of the change.

→ Aligning Text

Another important basic attribute of the text in your documents is how that text is oriented on the page. When you first start typing in a new document, all the text begins at the left margin and moves to the right as you type; this means the text is left-justified using the default align left feature. Left-justified text is characterized by text that is straight or unvarying on the left margin but has a ragged right-edged margin.

Text that serves a special function in a document, such as a heading, would probably stand out better in the document if it is placed differently than the rest of the text. Word makes it easy for you to change the alignment of any text paragraph. Several alignment possibilities are available:

- **Align Left**—The default margin placement for normal text, aligned on the left.
- **Align Right**—Text is aligned at the right margin and text lines show a ragged left edge.
- **Center**—The text is centered between the left and right margins of the page (with both margins having irregular edges).

- **Justify**—The text is spaced irregularly across each line so that both the left and the right margins are straight edged and uniform (often used in printed publications such as the daily newspapers).

> **Important**
>
> **Remember How Word Sees a Paragraph** Any text followed by a paragraph mark—created when you press the Enter key—is considered a separate paragraph in Word. This means that when you use alignment features, such as those discussed in this section, only the paragraph that currently holds the insertion point will be affected by the alignment command that you select (such as Center). If you need to align multiple lines that are in separate paragraphs, select that text before selecting the alignment command.

Figure 5.3 shows examples of each of the alignment possibilities.

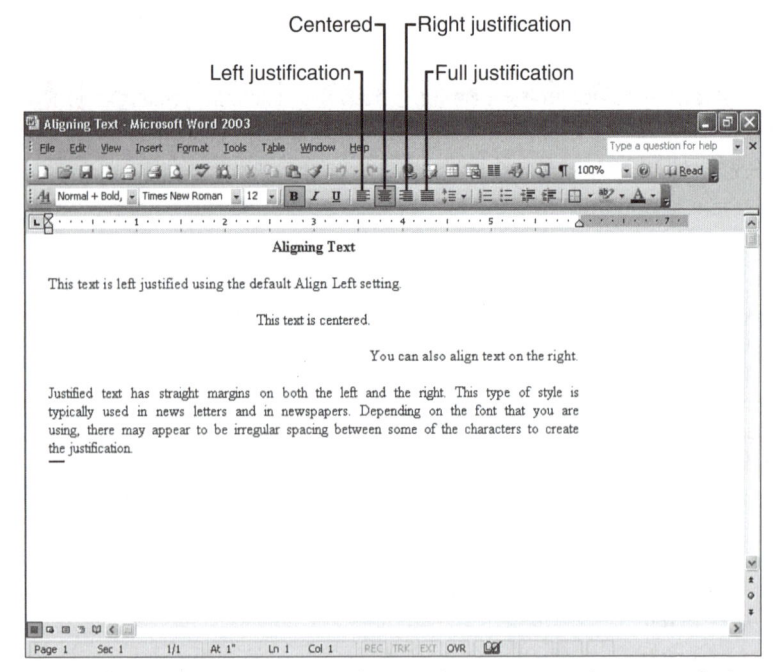

Figure 5.3 You can align the text in your document to suit your particular needs on a document page.

The easiest way to change the alignment of text in the document is to use the alignment buttons on the Formatting toolbar. Also, a button exists in the Paragraph dialog box for each of the alignment possibilities.

164 Brilliant Microsoft Office 2003 Pocket Book

These justification buttons can be used to align new text or selected text. Again, if you are typing new text with a particular justification, your selected justification will still be in force even after you press Enter. You must change the justification as needed.

→ Aligning Text with Click and Type

Word offers a unique and quick way to insert and align text or to insert graphics, tables, and other items in a blank area of a document. Before entering text or another item, place the mouse pointer on a blank line on the page. As you move the mouse pointer from right to left on the blank line, the pointer (or I-beam, in this case) changes shape as you move it, denoting a particular line alignment. This makes it very easy to center or right-align the insertion point before you insert the text or other item.

> **Important**
>
> **Click and Type Option Must Be On**   To use Click and Type, you must also make sure that the **Enable Click and Type** box is selected on the **Edit** tab of the Options dialog box (select **Tools**, **Options** to open this dialog box).

To use the Click and Type feature, you must be in the Print Layout or Web Layout view. The feature is not available in the Normal view. To switch to the Print Layout or Web Layout view, select **View**, and then select the appropriate view from the View menu.

Then, to use Click and Type to align your new text, follow these steps:

1. Move the mouse pointer toward the area of the page where you want to place the insertion point. The pointer icon changes to

   - Center (the centering pointer appears)

   - Right (the align-right pointer appears)

2. After the mouse pointer shows the centering or right-align icon, double-click in the document. The insertion point moves to the selected justification. In the case of the align-right pointer, the insertion point is placed at the mouse position and the text is right aligned from that position.

3. Type your new text.

After you've typed the centered or right-aligned text and you've pressed **Enter** to create a new line, you can return to left justification by placing the mouse on the left of the line (the align-left icon appears on the mouse pointer) and double-clicking.

→ Automatically Detecting Formatting Inconsistencies

Word can help you out as you work with formatting by marking formatting inconsistencies in your document. This allows you to make sure that the text in your document is formatted as you intended. The Detect Formatting feature keeps track of the formatting in your document and can also be configured to flag any formatting inconsistencies.

To configure the Detect Formatting feature to flag formatting inconsistencies, follow these steps:

1. Select **Tools**, and then select **Options**. The Options dialog box opens.
2. On the Options dialog box, select the **Edit** tab.
3. Under Editing options, select the **Keep Track of Formatting** check box, if it is not already selected. Also select the **Mark Formatting Inconsistencies** check box.
4. Click **OK** to close the Options dialog box.

Now, formatting inconsistencies will be marked with a wavy blue line as you type. When you find a word or paragraph that has been flagged with the wavy blue line, right-click the word or paragraph. A shortcut menu appears as shown in Figure 5.4.

Use the menu choices on the shortcut menu to either replace the direct formatting with an available style or ignore the direct formatting occurrence. To ignore this occurrence of the formatting, click **Ignore Once**. If you want all occurrences of the formatting that has been flagged by the Detect Formatting feature to be ignored in the document, click the **Ignore Rule** choice on the shortcut menu.

Be advised that the Detect Formatting feature doesn't always catch formatting errors. For example, if you have most of your text in a 12-point font, some font that you might have inadvertently formatted for

14 points won't necessarily be flagged. Word assumes you might be using the 14 points for a heading or other special text.

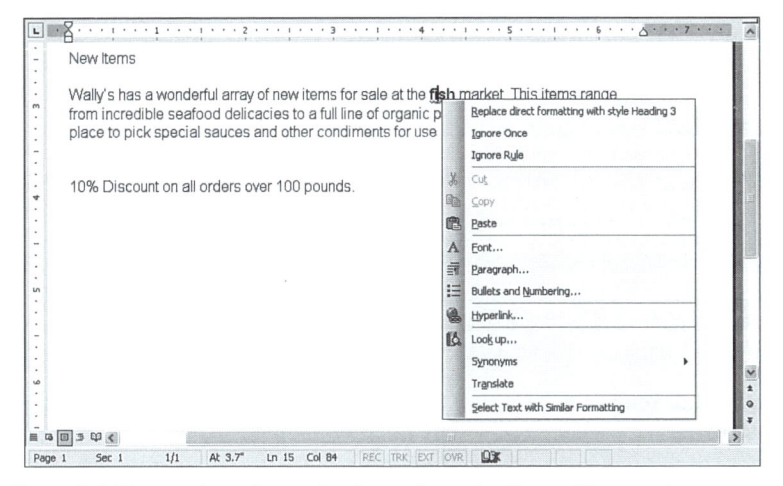

Figure 5.4 You can have formatting inconsistencies flagged in your documents.

The Detect Formatting feature is best at detecting direct formatting changes that you have made to text in a document (such as directly adding bold to text, as shown in Figure 5.4), where other text that has been bolded has been formatted using a "bold" style that you created. The inconsistency that Word picks up on is that you didn't use the style to bold the item as you had done in the rest of the document.

→ Reveal Formatting

Another useful feature in relation to text formatting is the Reveal Formatting feature. This feature allows you to quickly review the font and paragraph formatting used on your text.

To use Reveal Formatting, select the text for which you want to view the formatting information. Select the **Format** menu and then select **Reveal Formatting**. The Reveal Formatting task pane will open as shown in Figure 5.5. To view the formatting on a word, click on the word. To view the formatting on more than one word of text, select the text.

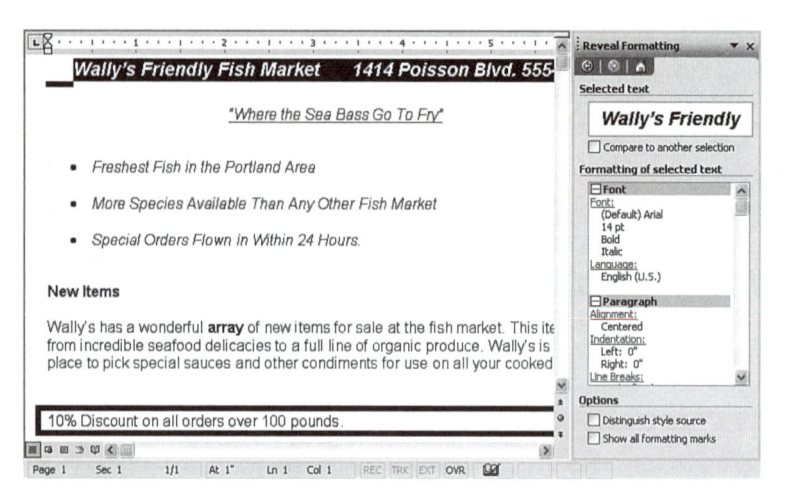

Figure 5.5 You can quickly view text formatting using the Reveal Formatting task pane.

6 Printing Documents

In this lesson, you learn how to preview your documents and then print them.

→ Sending Your Document to the Printer

When you have finished a particular document and are ready to generate a hard copy, Word makes it easy for you to get your document to the printer. In fact, you have three choices:

- You can send the document directly to the printer (no questions asked) by clicking the **Print** button on the Standard toolbar.

- You can open the Print dialog box (select **File**, **Print**) and set any print options that you want, such as printing a particular range of pages or printing multiple copies of the same document.

- You also have the option of previewing your hard copy before printing. This enables you to view your document exactly as it will appear on the printed page.

To preview your document before printing, click the **Print Preview** button on the Word Standard toolbar. The Print Preview window opens for the current document (see Figure 6.1).

You will find that the Print Preview window provides several viewing tools that you can use to examine your document before printing.

- **Zoom In or Out**—In the Print Preview window, the mouse pointer appears as a magnifying glass. Click once on your document to zoom in, and then click a second time to zoom out. To turn this feature off (or on again), click the **Magnifier** button.

- **Zoom by Percentage**—You can change to different zoom levels on the current document by using the **Zoom** drop-down arrow.

- **View Multiple Pages**—You can also zoom out and view several pages at once in the Preview window. Click **Multiple Pages**, and then drag to select the number of pages to be shown at once.

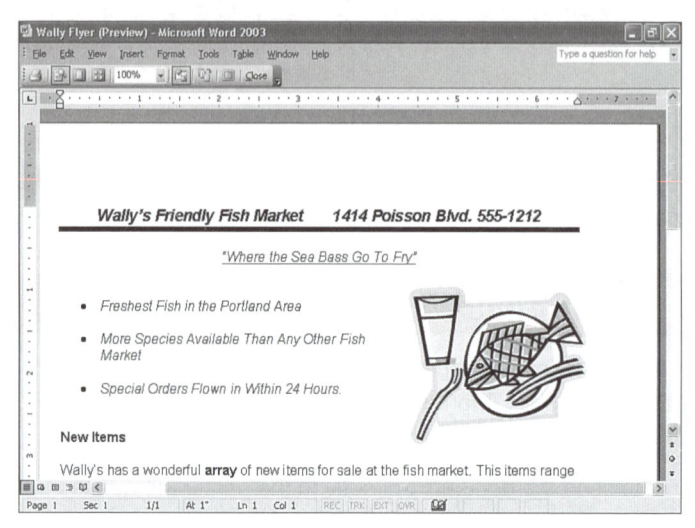

Figure 6.1 The Print Preview mode enables you to view your document the way it will print.

- **Shrink to Fit**—If you have a two-page document and only a small amount of text appears on the second page, you can condense all the text to fit on the first page only; click the **Shrink to Fit** button.

When you have completed viewing your document in the Print Preview mode, you can click the **Print** button to print the document, or if you want to edit the document before printing, click the **Close** button on the toolbar.

→ Changing Print Settings

In some situations, you might want to print only the current page or a certain range of pages. These options are controlled in the Print dialog box. The Print dialog box supplies you with several options, including the printer to which you send the print job, the number of copies, and the page range to be printed.

To open the Print dialog box, select **File**, then **Print**. The Print dialog box is shown in Figure 6.2.

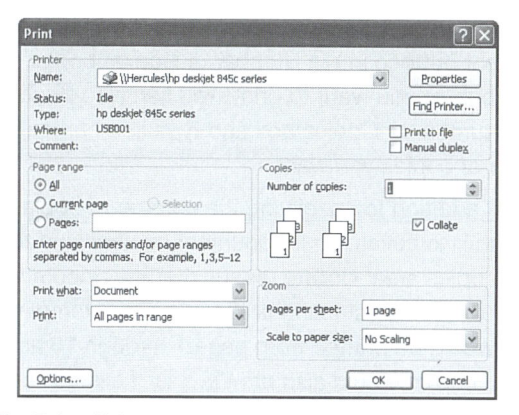

Figure 6.2 The Print dialog box gives you control over the options for your document.

Depending on your home or office situation, you might have your computer connected to more than one printer (especially if you are on a network). The Print dialog box has a drop-down box that lists all the printers to which you have access. To select a printer other than the current printer, click the drop-down arrow in the **Name** box and choose your printer from the list.

The Print dialog box also enables you to select the range to be printed. This range can consist of a page, a group of specific pages in a sequence, or all the pages in the document.

- **All Pages**—To print all the pages in the document, make sure the **All** option button is selected.
- **Current Page**—To print a single page, click the **Current Page** option button (this prints the page that the insertion point is parked on).
- **Page Range**—To designate a range of pages, click the **Pages** option button and type the page numbers into the Pages box.

> **Timesaver tip**
>
> **Specifying Page Ranges** To print a continuous range of pages, use the 1–5 format (where 1 is the start and 5 is the end of the range). For pages not in a continuous range, use the 5,9,13 format (where each distinct page number to be printed is separated by a comma). You can also mix the two formats. For example, you could specify 1–5,9,13.

- **Number of Copies**—In the Copies area of the Print dialog box, use the increment buttons in the Number of Copies box to select the number of copies you want to print. You can also double-click inside the Number of Copies box and type in a particular value for the number of copies you want.

- **Collate**—In addition to specifying the number of copies, you can select whether to collate your document by checking the Collate box in the copies area. *Collate* means that the document is printed in the proper order for stapling or binding. For example, a 10-page document would be printed from page 1 through 10 and then the subsequent copies would also print in this "collated" arrangement. If you do not choose to collate, all the copies of page 1 will be printed, then page 2, and so on.

You can also choose to print all the pages in a chosen range or print only the odd or even pages. Click the **Print** drop-down box (near the bottom left of the dialog box) and select **All Pages in Range**, **Odd Pages**, or **Even Pages**, as required.

Another print option worth mentioning is the Zoom print option in the Print dialog box. This feature enables you to place several document pages on one sheet of paper. To use Zoom print, click the **Pages per Sheet** drop-down box in the **Zoom** area of the Print dialog box and select the number of document pages you want to place on a sheet of paper. To select a scale for the print job (the scale is the relative size of the mini-pages on the printout page, such as 8.5 by 11 inches or legal size), click the **Scale to Paper Size** drop-down box.

After you select these two options, proceed with your print job. Be advised, however, that the more pages you place on a single sheet, the smaller the text appears.

Finally, you can print special items that you have placed in your document, such as comments, styles, and AutoText entries. When you choose to print one of these items, you are supplied with a page or pages separate from the main document that lists the comments, styles, or other items you've selected.

Select the **Print What** drop-down arrow and select from the list of items as follows:

- **Document**—Prints the document.
- **Document Properties**—Prints a summary of the information found in the document properties dialog (click File, Properties).

- **Document Showing Markup**—Shows the document with markup from tracking changes by multiple authors.
- **List of Markup**—Prints a list of changes added to a document involving multiple authors.
- **Styles**—Lists the styles in the document.
- **AutoText Entries**—Provides a list of the AutoText entries in the document.
- **Key Assignments**—Shows the shortcut key assignments for the document.

If you want to print more than one of these optional items with the document printout, you must select them in the Print options dialog box.

→ Selecting Paper Trays, Draft Quality, and Other Options

Several additional print options are also available from the Print dialog box. Each printer, depending on the features it provides, will have its own set of unique options. To access these options, click the **Options** button on the bottom left of the Print dialog box (see Figure 6.3).

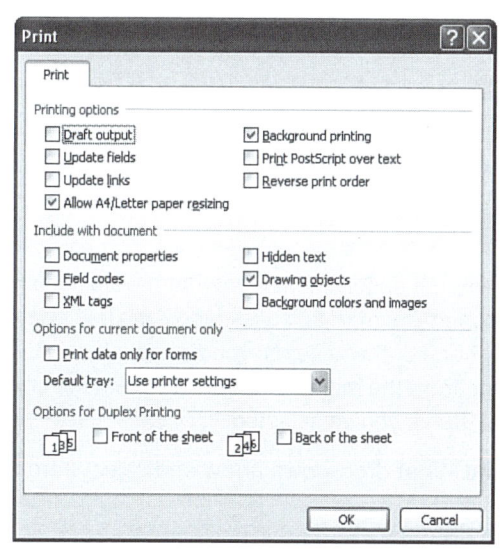

Figure 6.3 In the Print options dialog box, you can select or deselect certain options associated with your print job.

The Print options dialog box, using a series of check boxes, gives you control over the output of the print job as well as other options. You can also select the paper tray in your printer that you want to use for the print job (this is very useful in cases where you have a specific tray for letterhead, envelopes, and so on). Several of these options are described in Table 6.1.

Table 6.1 Print Options on the Print Dialog Box

Option	Purpose
Draft Output	Prints the document faster with less resolution
Reverse Print Order	Prints pages last to first, collating your document on printers that output documents face up
Background Printing	Prints the document quickly to a memory buffer so that you can work while the output is actually sent out to the printer
Document Properties	Prints the document properties

When you have finished selecting the various options for the printing of your document, click the **OK** button. You are returned to the Print dialog box. When you are ready to print the document, click **OK**.

Excel

1 Creating a New Workbook

In this lesson, you learn how to start and exit Excel and you become familiar with the Excel window. You also learn how to create new workbooks and open existing workbook files.

→ Starting Excel

Excel is a spreadsheet program that can help you create worksheets and invoices and do simple and sophisticated number crunching; it is designed to help you calculate the results of formulas and help you organize and analyze numerical data.

To start Excel from the Windows desktop, follow these steps:

1. Click the **Start** button, and the Start menu appears.
2. Point at **All Programs** (in Windows XP; in Windows 2000 select **Programs**), and the Programs menu appears.
3. Select the **Microsoft Office** program group and then **Microsoft Office Excel 2003** to start the program.

→ Understanding the Excel Window

When you click the Microsoft Excel icon, the Excel application window appears, displaying a blank workbook labeled Book1 (see Figure 1.1). On the right side of the Excel window is the Getting Started task pane. This task pane enables you to connect to Microsoft online. It also allows you to open existing Excel workbooks or create new workbooks (which is discussed later in the lesson).

> **Timesaver tip**
>
> **Close the Task Pane** If you would like a little more room in the Excel window to work on the current workbook sheet, click the **Close** (**X**) button on the task pane.

When you work in Excel, you use workbook files to hold your numerical data, formulas, and other objects, such as Excel charts. Each Excel workbook can consist of several sheets; each sheet is called a worksheet.

> **Jargon buster**
>
> **Workbook** An Excel file is called a workbook. Each workbook consists of several worksheets made up of rows and columns of information.

You enter your numbers and formulas on one of the workbook's worksheets. Each worksheet consists of 256 columns. The columns begin with column A and proceed through the alphabet. The 27th column is AA, followed by AB, AC, and this convention for naming subsequent columns continues through the entire alphabet until you end up with the last column (column 256), which is designated IV.

Each worksheet also consists of 65,536 rows. The intersection of a column and a row on the worksheet is called a cell. Each cell has an address that consists of the column and row that intersect to make the cell. For example, the very first cell on a worksheet is in column A and row 1, so the cell's address is A1.

> **Jargon buster**
>
> **Worksheet** One sheet in an Excel workbook. Each worksheet consists of 256 columns and 65,536 rows (plenty of space to create even the most enormous spreadsheets).

Jargon buster

Cell Where a row and column intersect, each cell has an address that consists of the column letter and row number (A1, B3, C4, and so on). You enter data and formulas in the cells to create your worksheets.

Figure 1.1 shows cell A1 highlighted in worksheet 1 (designated as Sheet1 on its tab) of Workbook 1 (designated in the title bar as Book1; this will change to a particular filename after you name the workbook using the Save function).

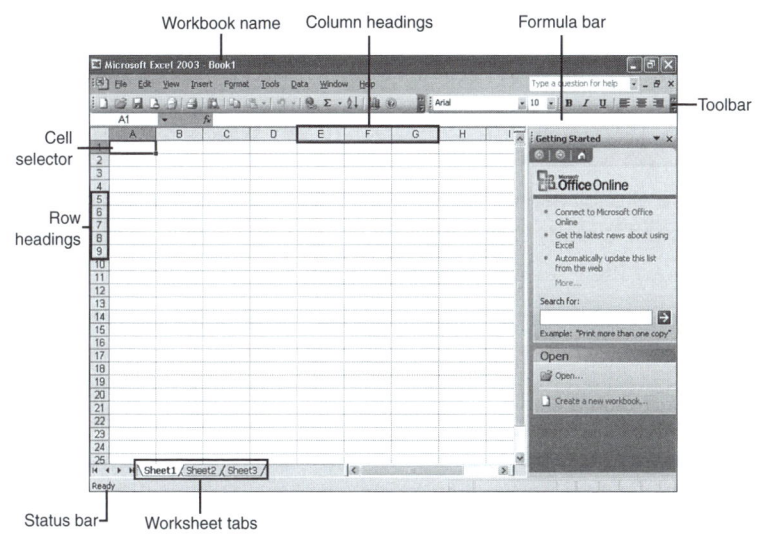

Figure 1.1 Excel provides a new workbook and the menus and toolbars necessary for doing some serious number crunching.

The Excel window shown here includes many of the various elements available in other Office applications, such as Word or PowerPoint. These elements include a menu bar (from which you select commands), a status bar (which displays the status of the current activity), and toolbars (which contain buttons and drop-down lists that provide quick access to various commands and features).

In addition, the window contains several elements that are unique to Excel, as shown in Table 1.1.

Creating a New Workbook **179**

Table 1.1 Elements of the Excel Window

Element	Description
Formula bar	When you enter information into a cell, it appears in the Formula bar. You can use the Formula bar to edit the data later. The cell's location also appears in the Formula bar.
Column headings	The letters across the top of the worksheet, which identify the columns in the worksheet.
Row headings	The numbers down the side of the worksheet, which identify the rows in the worksheet.
Cell selector	The dark outline that indicates the active cell. (It highlights the cell you are currently working in.)
Worksheet tabs	These tabs help you move from worksheet to worksheet within the workbook.

→ Starting a New Workbook

As you've already seen, when you start Excel, it opens a new blank workbook. It is ready to accept data entry, which is discussed in Lesson 2, "Entering Data into the Worksheet."

The empty workbook that appears when you start Excel is pretty much a blank canvas, but Excel also enables you to create new workbooks based on a template. A *template* is a predesigned workbook that you can modify to suit your needs. Excel contains templates for creating invoices, expense reports, and other common business accounting forms.

To create a new workbook, follow these steps:

1 Open the **File** menu and select **New**. The New Workbook task pane appears on the right side of the Excel window (if you did not close it as outlined earlier, it should already be open).

2 The New Workbook task pane enables you to create new blank workbooks or create workbooks based on an existing workbook or a template (see Figure 1.2).

Figure 1.2 The New Workbook task pane provides quick access to commands for creating new Excel workbooks.

3 To create a blank workbook, click the **Blank Workbook** icon. A new blank workbook opens in the Excel window.

> **Timesaver tip**
>
> **Instant Workbook** You can also quickly start a new blank workbook by clicking the **New** button on the Standard toolbar.

Blank templates are fine when you have a design in mind for the overall look of the workbook. However, for some help with workbook layout and formatting, you can base your new workbook on an Excel template. To use an Excel template, follow these steps:

1 Click the **On My Computer** link in the Templates pane of the New Workbook task pane. The Templates dialog box appears.

2 Click the **Spreadsheet Solutions** tab on the Templates dialog box. The various workbook template icons appear (see Figure 1.3).

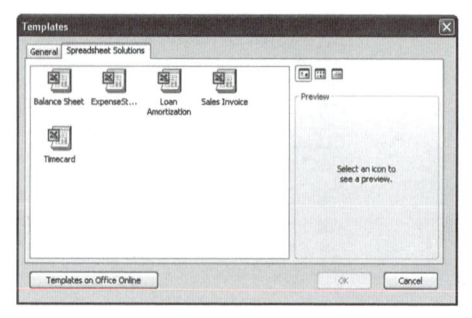

Figure 1.3 The Spreadsheet Solutions templates.

3 Select a template by clicking its icon, and then click **OK** or press **Enter**. A new workbook opens onscreen with a default name based on the template you chose. For example, if you chose the Timecard template, the new workbook is named Timecard1, as shown at the top of Figure 1.4.

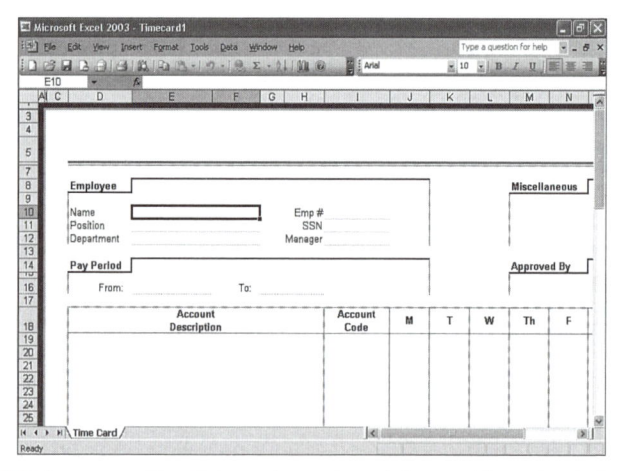

Figure 1.4 A new workbook based on a template provides a basic layout for a particular business form.

→ Saving and Naming a Workbook

Whether you build your workbook from a blank template or use one of the Excel templates, after you enter some data into the workbook, you should save the file (you learn about data entry in Lesson 2). Also, because changes that you make to the workbook are not automatically saved, you should occasionally save the edited version of your work.

The first time you save a workbook, you must name it and specify a location where it should be saved. Follow these steps to save your workbook:

1 Open the **File** menu and select **Save**, or click the **Save** button on the Standard toolbar. The Save As dialog box appears (see Figure 1.5).

2 Type the name you want to give the workbook in the **File Name** text box. You can use up to 218 characters, including any combination of letters, numbers, and spaces.

3 Normally, Excel saves your workbooks in the My Documents folder. To save the file to a different folder or drive (such as a network drive), select a new location using the **Save In** list.

Figure 1.5 Specify the name and location for your new workbook in the Save As dialog box.

Important

The Folder I Want to Save In Doesn't Exist! You can create a new folder from the Save As dialog box: click the **Create New Folder** button on the toolbar of the Save As dialog box, type a name for the new folder, and then press **Enter**.

4 Click **Save** to save your workbook and close the Save As dialog box.

To save changes that you make to a workbook that you have previously saved, just click the **Save** button on the Standard toolbar. You can also press the shortcut key combination of **Ctrl+S** to save changes to your workbook.

→ Saving a Workbook Under a New Name or Location

There might be an occasion when you want to save a copy of a particular workbook under a different name or in a different location. Excel makes it easy for you to make duplicates of a workbook. Follow these steps:

1 Select the **File** menu and select **Save As**. The Save As dialog box opens, just as if you were saving the workbook for the first time.

2 To save the workbook under a new name, type the new filename over the existing name in the **File Name** text box.

3 To save the new file on a different drive or in a different folder, select the drive letter or the folder from the **Save In** list.

4 To save the new file in a different format (such as WK4, which is a Lotus 1-2-3 format), click the **Save As Type** drop-down arrow and select the desired format.

5 Click the **Save** button or press **Enter**.

> **Timesaver tip**
>
> **Saving Excel Workbooks in Other File Formats** Occasionally, you might share Excel workbook data with coworkers or colleagues who don't use Excel. Being able to save Excel workbooks in other file formats, such as Lotus 1-2-3 (as discussed in step 4), enables you to provide another user a file that they can open in their spreadsheet program.

→ Opening an Existing Workbook

If you have a workbook you've previously saved that you would like to work on, you must open the file first, before you can make any changes. Follow these steps to open an existing workbook:

1 Open the **File** menu and select **Open**, or click the **Open** button on the Standard toolbar. The Open dialog box shown in Figure 1.6 appears.

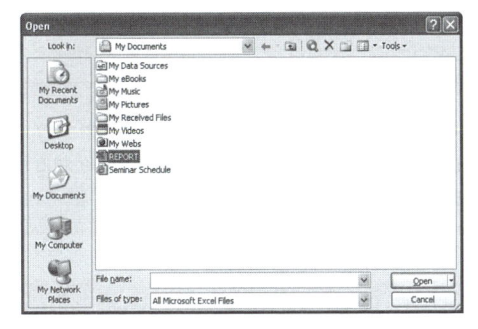

Figure 1.6 Use the Open dialog box to locate and open an existing Excel workbook.

2 If the file is not located in the current folder, open the **Look In** drop-down list box and select the correct drive and folder.

3 Select the file you want to open in the files and folders list.

4 To see a preview of the workbook before you open it, click the **Views** button and select **Preview**. Excel displays the contents of the workbook in a window to the right of the dialog box.

5 Click **Open** to open the currently selected workbook.

Timesaver tip

Recently Used Workbooks If the workbook you want to open is one of your four most recently used workbooks, you'll find it listed at the bottom of the File menu. It will also be listed at the top of the New Workbook task pane (if the task pane is active).

→ Closing Workbooks

When you have finished with a particular workbook and want to continue working in Excel, you can easily close the current workbook. Click the **Close** (**X**) button in the upper-right corner of the workbook. (There are two Close buttons; the one on top closes Excel, and the one below it closes the current workbook window.) You can also close the current workbook by selecting **File**, **Close**. If you have changed the workbook since the last time you saved it, you will be prompted to save any changes.

> **Timesaver tip**
>
> **It's Closing Time!** If you have more than one workbook open, you can close all of them at once by holding down the **Shift** key, selecting the **File** menu, and then selecting **Close All**.

→ Exiting Excel

When you have finished working with Excel, you need to exit the application. This closes all workbooks that are currently open. To exit Excel, select the **File** menu and select **Exit**. Or you can click the **Close** (**X**) button at the upper-right corner of the Excel window.

If you have changed any of the workbooks that you were working with, you are prompted to save changes to these workbook files before exiting Excel.

2 Entering Data into the Worksheet

In this lesson, you learn how to enter different types of data into an Excel worksheet.

→ Understanding Excel Data Types

When you work in Excel, you enter different types of information, such as text, numbers, dates, times, formulas, and functions (which is a special built-in formula provided by Excel). Excel data basically comes in two varieties: labels and values.

A label is a text entry; it is called a label because it typically provides descriptive information such as the name of a person, place, or thing. A label has no numerical significance in Excel; it's just there to describe accompanying values.

> **Jargon buster**
>
> **Label** Any text entry made on an Excel worksheet.

A value is data that has numerical significance. This includes numbers, dates, and times that you enter on your worksheet. Values can be acted on by formulas and functions. Formulas are discussed in Lesson 3, "Performing Simple Calculations."

> **Jargon buster**
>
> **Values** Entries, such as numbers and dates, that have numerical significance and can be acted upon by formulas or functions.

→ Entering Text

Text is any combination of letters, numbers, and spaces. By default, text is automatically left-aligned in a cell, whereas numerical data is right-aligned.

> **Timesaver tip**
>
> **Entering Numbers As Text** To enter a number that you want treated as text (such as a ZIP code), precede the entry with a single quotation mark ('), as in '46220. The single quotation mark is an alignment prefix that tells Excel to treat the following characters as text and left-align them in the cell. You do not have to do this to "text" numerical entries, but it ensures that they will not be mistakenly acted upon by formulas or functions.

To enter text into a cell, follow these steps:

1 Use your mouse or the keyboard arrows to select the cell in which you want to enter text.

2 Type the text. As you type, your text appears in the cell and in the Formula bar, as shown in Figure 2.1.

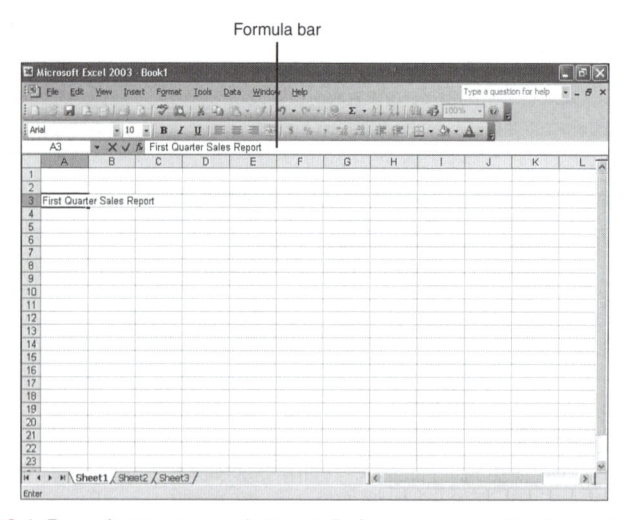

Figure 2.1 Data that you enter into a cell also appears in the Formula bar as you type it.

188 Brilliant Microsoft Office 2003 Pocket Book

3 Press **Enter**. Your text appears in the cell, left-aligned. The cell selector moves down one cell. You can also press **Tab** or an arrow key to enter the text and move to the next cell to the right (or in the direction of the arrow).

> **Important**
>
> **But My Entry Doesn't Fit!** When text does not fit into a cell (because of the column width set for that column), Excel displays the information in one of two ways: If the next cell is empty, the text overflows into that cell, allowing you to see your entire entry. If the cell to the right of your entry is not empty, you will be able to see only the portion of your entry that fits within the confines of the cell. This can easily be remedied by changing the column width.

Tips on Entering Column and Row Labels

Column and row labels identify your data. Column labels appear across the top of the worksheet beneath the worksheet title (if any). Row labels are entered on the left side of the worksheet.

Column labels describe what the numbers in a column represent. Typically, column labels specify time intervals such as years, months, days, quarters, and so on. Row labels describe what the numbers in each row represent. Typically, row labels specify data categories, such as product names, employee names, or income and expense items in a budget.

When entering your column labels, enter the first label and press the **Tab** key instead of pressing Enter. This moves you to the next cell on the right so that you can enter another column label. When entering row labels, use the down-arrow key or Enter instead of the Tab key. Figure 2.2 shows the various labels for a quarterly sales summary.

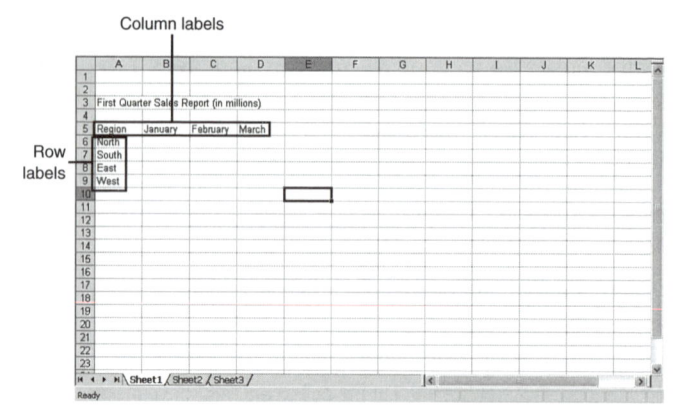

Figure 2.2 Column and row headings serve as labels for the data you enter on the worksheet.

If you need to enter similar data (such as a series of months or years) as column or row labels, you can enter them quickly as a series; this technique is discussed later in this lesson.

Adding Comments to Cells

You can add comments to particular cells, although the comments are not really considered cell content (such as labels and values). These comments allow you to associate information with a cell—information that does not appear (by default) with the worksheet when sent to the printer.

Comments are similar to placing a Post-it note on a cell, reminding you that an outstanding issue is related to that cell. For example, if you need to check the value that you've placed in a particular cell to make sure that it's accurate, you can place a comment in the cell (see Figure 2.3). Cells containing comments are marked with a red triangle in the upper-right corner of the cell. To view a comment, place the mouse pointer on the comment triangle.

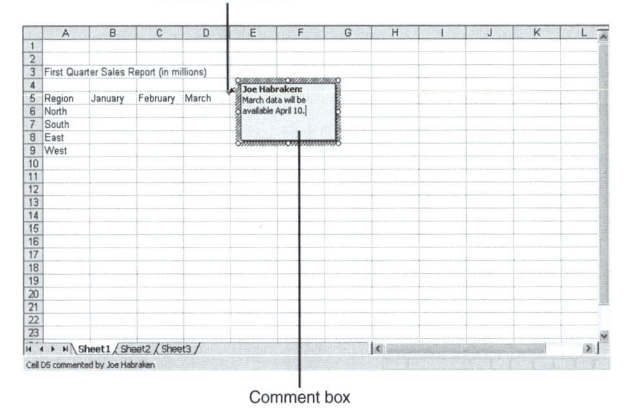

Figure 2.3 Comments can be added to cells as a kind of electronic Post-it note.

To insert a comment into a cell, follow these steps:

1 Click the cell in which you want to place the comment.
2 Select **Insert**, **Comment**. A comment box appears next to the cell.
3 Type your information into the comment box.
4 Click anywhere else in the worksheet to close the comment box.

You can also easily remove comments from cells. Select the cell, and then select **Edit** and point at **Clear**. On the cascading menu, select **Comments** to remove the comment.

Timesaver tip

Right-Click a Cell to Add Comment You can add a comment to a cell by right-clicking on the cell and then selecting **Insert Comment** from the shortcut menu that appears.

Entering Data into the Worksheet   **191**

→ Entering Numbers

Data that serves as the values in your workbooks can include the numeric characters 0–9. Because formulas are also considered values (you learn about simple calculations in Lesson 3), other valid value characters include symbols such as +, –, /, and *. You can also use characters such as a comma (,), a percent sign (%), or a dollar sign ($) in your values. You will find, however, that you can save yourself a few data-entry keystrokes and add these characters using different Excel formatting options.

For example, you could enter the dollar amount $700.00 including the dollar sign and the decimal point. However, it's probably faster to enter the 700 into the cell and then format all the cells that contain dollar amounts after you have entered all the data.

To enter a value, follow these steps:

1 Click in the cell where you want to enter the value.

2 Type the value. To enter a negative number, precede it with a minus sign or surround it with parentheses.

3 Press **Enter** or the **Tab** key; the value appears in the cell right-aligned. Figure 2.4 shows various values entered into a simple worksheet.

> **Timesaver tip**
>
> **What Are All Those Pound Signs?** If you enter a number and it appears in the cell as all pound signs (#######) or in scientific notation (such as 7.78E+06), the cell just isn't wide enough to display the entire number. To fix it, double-click the right border of the column's heading. The column expands to fit the largest entry in that column.

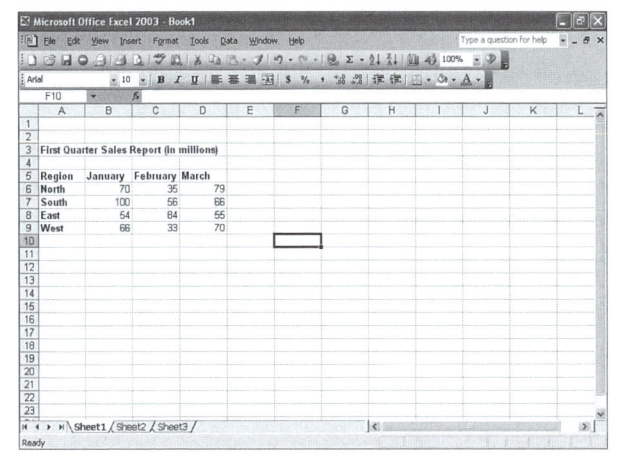

Figure 2.4 Values are right-aligned in a cell.

→ Entering Dates and Times

Dates that you enter into an Excel workbook have numerical significance. Excel converts the date into a number that reflects the number of days that have elapsed since January 1, 1900. Even though you won't see this number (Excel displays your entry as a normal date), the number is used whenever you use this date in a calculation. Times are also considered values. Excel sees them as the number of seconds that have passed since 12 a.m.

Follow these steps to enter a date or time:

1 Click in the cell where you want to enter a date or a time.

2 To enter a date, use the format MM/DD/YY or the format MM-DD-YY, as in 5/9/03 or 5-9-03.

To enter a time, be sure to specify a.m. or p.m., as in 7:21 p or 8:22 a.

Timesaver tip

A.M. or P.M.? Unless you type am or pm after your time entry, Excel assumes that you are using a 24-hour international clock. Therefore, 8:20 is assumed to be a.m., not p.m. (20:20 would be p.m.: 8 plus 12 hours). Therefore, if you mean p.m., type the entry as 8:20 pm (or 8:20 p). Note that you must type a space between the time and the am or pm notation.

Entering Data into the Worksheet

3 Press **Enter**. As long as Excel recognizes the entry as a date or a time, it appears right-aligned in the cell. If Excel doesn't recognize it, it's treated as text and left-aligned.

After you enter your date or time, you can format the cells to display the date or time exactly as you want it to appear, such as September 16, 2003, or 16:50 (international time). If you're entering a column of dates or times, you can format the entire column in one easy step. To format a column, click the column header to select the column. Then open the **Format** menu and select **Cells**. On the **Numbers** tab, select the date or time format you want to use.

→ Copying Data to Other Cells

Another way to enter labels or values onto a sheet is to use the Fill feature. You can copy (fill) an entry into surrounding cells. For example, suppose you have a list of salespeople on a worksheet, and they will each get a $100 bonus. You can enter the 100 once and then use the Fill feature to insert multiple copies of 100 into nearby cells. To use the Fill feature for copying, follow these steps:

1 Click the fill handle of the cell (the small block in the lower-right corner of the cell) that holds the data that you want to copy (see Figure 2.5).

2 Drag the fill handle down or to the right to copy the data to adjacent cells. A data tag appears to let you know exactly what data is being copied into the cells.

3 Release the mouse button. The data is "filled" into the selected cells.

When you release the mouse, a shortcut box for Fill options appears at the end of the cells that you filled. Copy Cells is the default option for the Fill feature, so you can ignore the shortcut box for the moment. It does come into play when you enter a series in the next section.

> **Information**
>
> **Watch That Fill!** The data you're copying replaces any existing data in the adjacent cells that you fill.

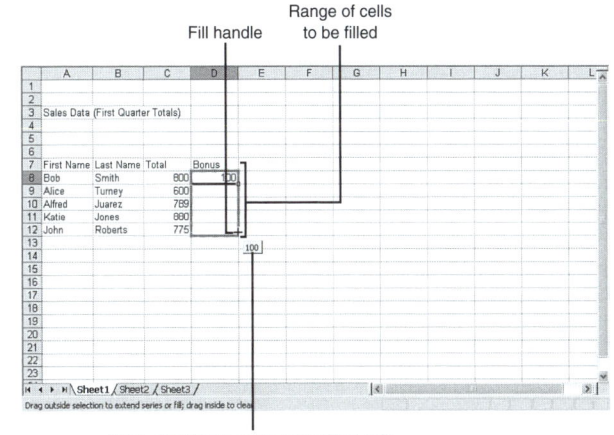

Figure 2.5 Drag the fill handle to copy the contents of a cell into neighboring cells.

Entering a Series of Numbers, Dates, and Other Data

Entering a value *series* (such as January, February, and March or 1, 2, 3, 4, and so on) is accomplished using the Fill feature discussed in the preceding section. When you use the Fill feature, Excel looks at the cell holding the data and tries to determine whether you want to just copy that information into the adjacent cells or use it as the starting point for a particular series of data. For example, with Monday entered in the first cell of the series, Excel automatically inserts Tuesday, Wednesday, and so on into the adjacent cells when you use the Fill feature.

Sometimes Excel isn't quite sure whether you want to copy the data when you use Fill or create a series. This is where the Fill options shortcut box comes in. It enables you to select how the Fill feature should treat the data that you have "filled" into the adjacent cells. Figure 2.6 shows the creation of a data series using Fill.

When you create a series using Fill, the series progresses by one increment. For example, a series starting with 1 would proceed to 2, 3, 4, and so on. If you want to create a series that uses some increment other than 1, you must create a custom series.

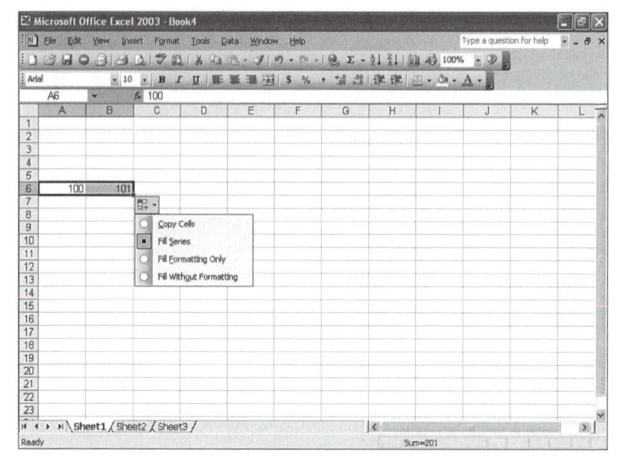

Figure 2.6 Fill can also be used to create a series of data in adjacent cells.

Entering a Custom Series

If you want to create a series such as 10, 20, 30, where the series uses a custom increment between the values, you need to create a custom series. Excel provides two ways to create a custom series. To create a custom series using Fill, follow these steps:

1 Enter the first value in the series into a cell.

2 Enter the second value in the series into the next cell. For example, you might enter **10** into the first cell and then **20** into the second cell. This lets Excel know that the increment for the series is 10.

3 Select both cells by clicking the first cell and dragging over the second cell.

4 Drag the fill handle of the second cell to the other cells that will be part of the series. Excel analyzes the two cells, sees the incremental pattern, and re-creates it in subsequent cells.

You can also create a custom series using the Series dialog box. This enables you to specify the increment or step value for the series and even specify a stop value for the series.

1 Enter the first value in the series into a cell.

2 Select the cells that you want included in the series.

3 Select the **Edit** menu, point at **Fill**, and then select **Series**. The Series dialog box opens (see Figure 2.7).

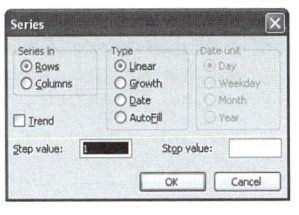

Figure 2.7 The Series dialog box enables you to create a custom series.

4 Enter the Step Value for the series. You can also enter a Stop Value for the series if you did not select the cells used for the series in step 2. For example, if you want to add a series to a column of cells and have clicked in the first cell that will receive a value, using a Stop Value (such as 100 for a series that will go from 1 to 100) will "stop" entering values in the cells when it reaches 100—the Stop Value.

5 Click **OK** to create the series.

> **Timesaver tip**
>
> **Different Series Types** Not only can you create a linear series using the Series dialog box (as discussed in the steps in this section), but you can also create growth and date series. In a growth series, the data you're copying replaces any existing data in the adjacent cells that you fill.

→ Taking Advantage of AutoComplete

Another useful feature that Excel provides to help take some of the drudgery out of entering information into a workbook is the AutoComplete feature. Excel keeps a list of all the labels that you enter on a worksheet by column. For example, suppose you have a worksheet tracking sales in Europe and you are entering country names, such as Germany, Italy, and so on, multiple times into a particular column in the worksheet. After you enter Germany the first time, it becomes part of the AutoComplete list for that column. The next time you enter the letter G into a cell in that column, Excel completes the entry as "Germany."

Entering Data into the Worksheet

You can also select an entry from the AutoComplete list. This allows you to see the entire list of available entries. Follow these steps:

1. Enter your text and value data as needed onto the worksheet.
2. If you want to select a text entry from the AutoComplete list, to fill an empty cell, right-click that cell. A shortcut menu appears.
3. Select **Pick from List** from the shortcut menu. A list of text entries (in alphabetical order) appears below the current cell.
4. Click a word in the list to insert it into the current, empty cell.

> **Timesaver tip**
>
> **Adding Data to Excel Using Voice Recognition** The Office Speech Recognition feature can also be used to enter data into an Excel worksheet and to perform voice commands. If you have a computer that is set up with a sound card and microphone, you can use this feature.

3 Performing Simple Calculations

In this lesson, you learn how to use formulas to calculate results in your worksheets.

→ Understanding Excel Formulas

One way to add calculations to an Excel workbook is to create your own formulas. Formulas are typically used to perform calculations such as addition, subtraction, multiplication, and division. More complex calculations are better left to Excel functions, which is a built-in set of formulas that provide financial, mathematical, and statistical calculations.

Formulas that you create typically include cell addresses that reference cells on which you want to perform a calculation. Formulas also consist of mathematical operators, such as + (addition) or * (multiplication). For example, if you wanted to multiply two cells, such as C3 and D3, and then divide the product by 3, you would design a formula that looks like this:

=(C3*D3)/3

Notice that the formula begins with the equal sign (=). This lets Excel know that the information that you are placing in the cell is meant to do a calculation. The parentheses are used to let Excel know that you want C3 multiplied by D3 before the result is divided by 3. Creating appropriate formulas requires an understanding of the order of mathematical operations, or what is often called the rules of precedence. The natural order of math operations is covered in the next section.

Formula Operators

As previously mentioned, you can create formulas that add, subtract, and multiply cells in the worksheet. Table 3.1 lists some of the operators that you can use and how you would use them in a simple formula.

Table 3.1   Excel's Mathematical Operators

Operator	Performs	Sample Formula	Result
^	Exponentiation	=A1^3	Enters the result of raising the value in cell A1 to the third power
+	Addition	=A1+A2	Enters the total of the values in cells A1 and A2
–	Subtraction	=A1–A2	Subtracts the value in cell A2 from the value in cell A1
*	Multiplication	=A2*A3	Multiplies the value in cell A2 by cell A3
/	Division	=A1/B1	Divides the value in cell A1 by the value in cell B1

Figure 3.1 shows some formulas that have been created for an Excel worksheet. So that you can see how I wrote the formulas, I've configured Excel so that it shows the formula that has been placed in a cell rather than the results of the formula (which is what you would normally see).

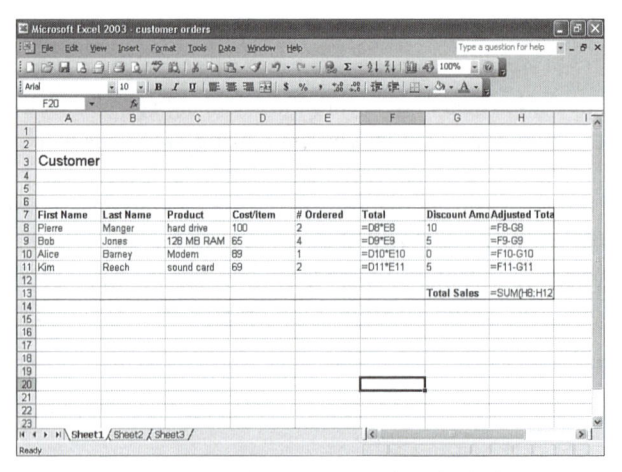

Figure 3.1   You can create formulas to do simple calculations in your worksheets.

200   Brilliant Microsoft Office 2003 Pocket Book

Order of Operations

The order of operations, or *operator precedence*, simply means that some operations take precedence over other operations in a formula. For example, in the formula =C2+D2*E2, the multiplication of D2 times E2 takes precedence, so D2 is multiplied by E2 and then the value in cell C2 is added to the result.

You can force the precedence of an operation by using parentheses. For example, if you want C2 and D2 added before they are multiplied by E2, the formula would have to be written =(C2+D2)*E2.

The natural order of math operators follows:

1. Exponent (^) and calculations within parentheses
2. Multiplication (*) and division (/)
3. Addition (+) and subtraction (–)

In the case of operations such as multiplication and division, which operate at the same level in the natural order, a formula containing the multiplication operator followed by the division operator will execute these operators in the order they appear in the formula from left to right. If you don't take this order into consideration, you could run into problems when entering your formulas. For example, if you want to determine the average of the values in cells A1, B1, and C1, and you enter **=A1+B1+C1/3**, you'll get the wrong answer. The value in C1 will be divided by 3, and that result will be added to A1+B1. To determine the total of A1 through C1 first, you must enclose that group of values in parentheses: **=(A1+B1+C1)/3**.

→ Entering Formulas

You can enter formulas in one of two ways: by typing the entire formula, including the cell addresses, or by typing the formula operators and selecting the cell references. Take a look at both ways.

To type a formula, perform the following steps:

1. Select the cell where you will place the formula.
2. Type an equal sign (=) into the cell to begin the formula.

3 Enter the appropriate cell references and operators for the formula. Figure 3.2 shows a simple multiplication formula. The formula also appears in the Formula bar as you type it. The cells that you specify in the formula are highlighted with a colored border.

4 Press **Enter** when you have finished the formula, and Excel calculates the result.

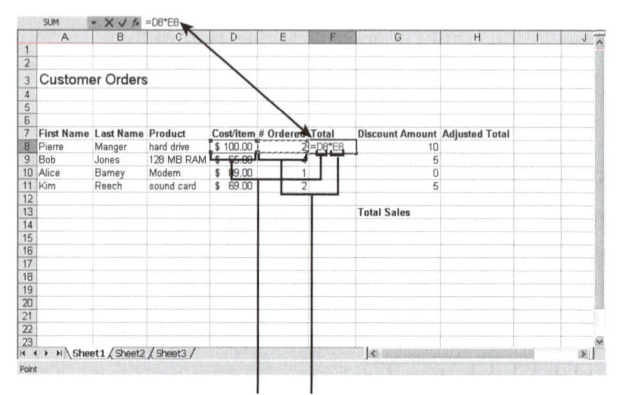

Cell border and cell text reference have matching color

Figure 3.2 The formula appears in the cell and in the Formula bar as you type it.

Timesaver tip

Unwanted Formula If you start to enter a formula and then decide you don't want to use it, you can skip entering the formula by pressing **Esc**.

To enter a formula by selecting cell addresses, follow these steps:

1 Click in the cell where you will place the formula.

2 Type the equal sign (=) to begin the formula.

3 Click the cell whose address you want to appear first in the formula. You can also click a cell in a different worksheet or workbook. The cell address appears in the cell and in the Formula bar.

4 Type a mathematical operator after the value to indicate the next operation you want to perform. The operator appears in the cell and in the Formula bar.

5 Continue clicking cells and typing operators until the formula is complete.

6 Press **Enter** to accept the formula and have Excel place its results into the cell.

> ### Important
>
> **Error!** If ERR appears in a cell, you probably made a mistake somewhere in the formula. Be sure you did not commit one of these common errors: dividing by zero, using a blank cell as a divisor, referring to a blank cell, deleting a cell used in a formula, or including a reference to the same cell in which the formula appears.

> ### Timesaver tip
>
> **Natural Language Formulas** Excel also enables you to create what are called Natural Language formulas. You can refer to a cell by its column heading name and the corresponding row label. For example, if you had a column labeled Total and a column labeled Discount for each customer, you can write a formula such as =Smith Total–Smith Discount. You are referring to cells by the labels that you have placed in the worksheet rather than the actual cell addresses.

→ Using the Status Bar AutoCalculate Feature

Using a feature that Excel calls , you can view the sum of a column of cells simply by selecting the cells and looking at the status bar. The values in the selected cells are added. You can also right-click the AutoCalculate area of the status bar and choose different formulas, such as average, minimum, maximum, and count.

This feature is useful if you want to quickly check the total for a group of cells or compute the average. It also allows you to "try out" an Excel function before actually entering it into a cell. You can also view the average, minimum, maximum, and count of a range of cells. To display something other than the sum, highlight the group of cells you want the operation performed on, right-click the status bar, and select the option you want from the shortcut menu that appears (see Figure 3.3).

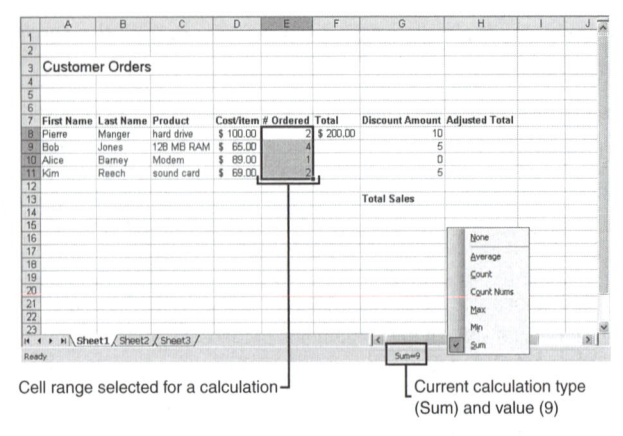

Figure 3.3 You can view the results of different built-in formulas in the status bar.

> **Timesaver tip**
>
> **Missing Status Bar?** If the status bar is not visible on your screen, you can display it by selecting the **View** menu and then selecting **Status Bar**.

→ Displaying Formulas

Normally, Excel does not display the formula in a cell. Instead, it displays the result of the calculation. You can view the formula by selecting the cell and looking in the Formula bar. However, if you're trying to review all the formulas in a large worksheet, it would be easier if you could see them all at once (and even print them). If you want to view formulas in a worksheet, follow these steps:

1. Open the **Tools** menu and choose **Options**.
2. Click the **View** tab.
3. In the Window options area of the View tab (near the bottom of the tab), click to select the **Formulas** check box.
4. Click **OK**.

→ Editing Formulas

Editing a formula is the same as editing any entry in Excel. The following steps show how you do it:

1 Select the cell that contains the formula you want to edit.

2 Click in the Formula bar to place the insertion point in the formula, or press **F2** to enter Edit mode (the insertion point is placed at the end of the entry in that cell).

> **Timesaver tip**
>
> **In-Cell Editing** To quickly edit the contents of a cell, double-click the cell. The insertion point appears inside the cell, and you can make any necessary changes.

3 Press the left-arrow key or the right-arrow key to move the insertion point within the formula. Then, use the **Backspace** key to delete characters to the left, or use the **Delete** key to delete characters to the right. Type any additional characters.

4 When you finish editing the data, click the **Enter** button on the Formula bar or press **Enter** to accept your changes.

4 Editing Worksheets

In this lesson, you learn how to change data and how to undo those changes if necessary. You also learn how to search for data and replace it with other data, how to spell check your work, and how to copy, move, and delete data.

→ Correcting Data

You've taken a look at entering text, values, formulas, and functions. There will definitely be occasions when you need to edit information in a cell. One way to change an entry in a cell is to replace it by selecting the cell and then entering new data. Just press **Enter** after entering the information. If you just want to modify the existing cell content, you can also edit data within a cell.

To edit information in a cell, follow these steps:

1. Select the cell in which you want to edit data.
2. To begin editing, click in the Formula bar to place the insertion point into the cell entry. To edit within the cell itself, press **F2** or double-click the cell. This puts you in Edit mode; the word Edit appears in the status bar.
3. Press the right- or left-arrow key to move the insertion point within the entry. Press the **Backspace** key to delete characters to the left of the insertion point; press the **Delete** key to delete characters to the right. Then, type any characters you want to add.
4. Press the **Enter** key when you have finished making your changes.

If you change your mind and you no longer want to edit your entry, click the **Cancel** button on the Formula bar or press **Esc**.

> **Timesaver tip**
>
> **Moving to the Beginning or End of a Cell Entry** In Edit mode, you can quickly move to the beginning or end of a cell's contents. Press **Home** to move to the beginning of the entry; press **End** to move to the end of the entry.

→ Undoing an Action

Although editing a worksheet is supposed to improve it, you might find that you've done something to a cell or range of cells that you had not intended. This is where the Undo feature comes in.

You can undo just about any action while working in Excel, including any changes you make to a cell's data. To undo a change, click the **Undo** button on the Standard toolbar (or select **Edit**, **Undo**).

You can also undo an undo. Just click the **Redo** button on the Standard toolbar.

> **Timesaver tip**
>
> **Undoing/Redoing More Than One Thing** The Undo button undoes only the most recent action. To undo several previous actions, click the **Undo** button multiple times or click the drop-down arrow on the Undo button and select the number of actions you want undone.

→ Using the Replace Feature

Suppose you've entered a particular label or value into the worksheet and find that you have consistently entered it incorrectly. A great way to change multiple occurrences of a label or value is using Excel's Replace feature; you can locate data in the worksheet and replace it with new data. To find and replace data, follow these steps:

1 Select the **Edit** menu, and then select **Replace**. The Find and Replace dialog box appears, as shown in Figure 4.1.

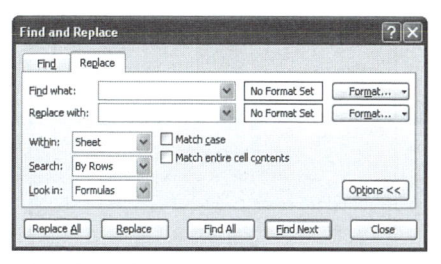

Figure 4.1 Find and replace data with the Find and Replace dialog box.

2 Type the text or value that you want to find into the **Find What** text box.

3 Click in the **Replace With** text box and type the text you want to use as replacement text.

4 To expand the options available to you in the dialog box, click the **Options** button (Figure 4.1 shows the dialog box in its expanded form).

5 If you want to match the exact case of your entry so that Excel factors in capitalization, click the **Match Case** check box. If you want to locate cells that contain exactly what you entered into the Find What text box (and no additional data), click the **Match Entire Cell Contents** check box.

6 To search for entries with particular formatting, click the **Format** button on the right of the Find What box. The Find Format dialog box appears (see Figure 4.2). You can search for entries that have been assigned number, alignment, font, border, patterns, or protection using the appropriate tab on the Find Format dialog box. After making your selection, click the **OK** button.

7 You can also replace your entries with a particular formatting. Click the **Format** button on the right of the Replace With box. The Replace Format dialog box appears. It is the same as the Find Format dialog box. Simply select any formats you want to assign to your replacement, and then click **OK**.

8 Click **Find Next** to find the first occurrence of your specified entry.

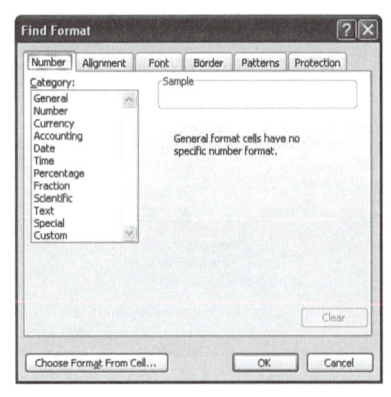

Figure 4.2 The Find Format dialog box enables you to search for entries that have been assigned a particular formatting.

- **9** When an occurrence is found, it is highlighted. Click **Replace** to replace only this occurrence and then click **Find Next** to find the next occurrence.
- **10** If you want to find all the occurrences, click **Find All**; you can also replace all the occurrences of the entry with **Replace All**.
- **11** When you have finished working with the Find and Replace dialog boxclick **Close**.

Timesaver tip

Search an Entire Workbook If you want to search an entire workbook for a particular entry, click the **Within** drop-down list in the Find and Replace dialog box and select **Workbook**.

If you don't need to replace an entry but would like to find it in the worksheet, you can use the Find feature. Select **Edit**, **Find**, and then type the data you want to locate into the Find What text box and click **Find Next**.

→ Checking Your Spelling

Because worksheets also include text entries, you might want to make sure that you check for any misspellings in a worksheet before printing the data. Excel offers a spell-checking feature that finds and corrects misspellings in a worksheet.

To run the Spelling Checker, follow these steps:

1 Click the **Spelling** button on the Standard toolbar (or select **Tools, Spelling**). The Spelling dialog box appears. Excel finds the first misspelled word and displays it at the top of the Spelling dialog box. A suggested correction appears in the Suggestions box (see Figure 4.3).

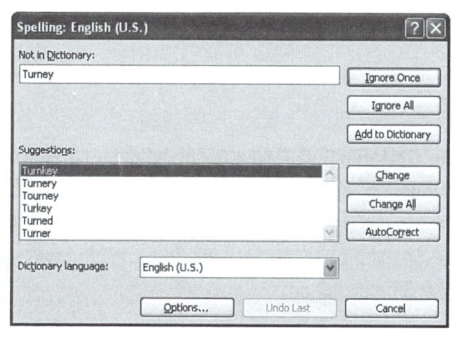

Figure 4.3 Correct spelling mistakes with the options in the Spelling dialog box.

2 To accept the suggestion in the Suggestions box, click **Change**, or click **Change All** to change all occurrences of the misspelled word.

3 If the suggestion in the Suggestions box is not correct, you can do any of the following:

- Select a different suggestion from the Suggestions box, and then click **Change** or **Change All**.

- Type your own correction into the Change To box, and then click **Change** or **Change All**.

- Click **Ignore Once** to leave the word unchanged.

- Click **Ignore All** to leave all occurrences of the word unchanged.

- Click **Add to Dictionary** to add the word to the dictionary so that Excel won't flag it as misspelled again.

- Click **AutoCorrect** to add a correctly spelled word to the AutoCorrect list so that Excel can correct it automatically as you type.

- If you make a mistake related to a particular entry, click the **Undo Last** button to undo the last change that you made.

4 You might see a message asking whether you want to continue checking spelling at the beginning of the sheet. If so, click **Yes** to continue. When the Spelling Checker can't find any more misspelled words, it displays a prompt telling you that the spelling check is complete. Click **OK** to confirm that the spelling check is finished.

> **Timesaver tip**
>
> **Setting Spelling Options** If you want to set options related to the Spelling feature, such as ignoring words in uppercase and words with numbers, click the **Options** button in the Spelling dialog box. This takes you to the Options dialog box for the Spelling Checker. Set options as needed and then click **OK** to return to the Spelling dialog box.

→ Copying and Moving Data

In Lesson 2, you learned how to use the Fill feature to copy a particular entry to multiple cells. In this section, you take a closer look at the Copy feature. When you copy or cut data in a cell, that data is held in a temporary storage area (a part of the computer's memory) called the Clipboard.

Excel 2003 (and all the Office 2003 applications) makes it easy for you to work with the Clipboard because it can be viewed in the Office Clipboard task pane (you look at the Clipboard later in this lesson). This enables you to keep track of items that you have copied or cut to the Clipboard. The Clipboard not only enables you to copy or move data with Excel, but it enables you to place Excel data directly into another application.

> **Jargon buster**
>
> **Clipboard** The Clipboard is an area of memory that is accessible to all Windows programs. The Clipboard is used to copy or move data from place to place within a program or between programs.

When you copy data, you create a duplicate of data in a cell or range of cells. Follow these steps to copy data:

1. Select the cell(s) that you want to copy. You can select any range or several ranges if you want.
2. Click the **Copy** button on the Standard toolbar. The contents of the selected cell(s) are copied to the Clipboard.
3. Select the first cell in the area where you would like to place the copy. (To copy the data to another worksheet or workbook, change to that worksheet or workbook first.)
4. Click the **Paste** button. Excel inserts the contents of the Clipboard at the location of the insertion point.

> **Important**
>
> **Watch Out!** When copying or moving data, be careful not to paste the data over existing data (unless, of course, you intend to).

You can copy the same data to several places by repeating the **Paste** command. Items remain on the Clipboard until you remove them.

Using Drag and Drop

The fastest way to copy something is to drag and drop it. Select the cells you want to copy, hold down the **Ctrl** key, and drag the border of the range you selected (see Figure 4.4). When you release the mouse button, the contents are copied to the new location. To insert the data between existing cells, press **Ctrl+Shift** as you drag.

To drag a copy to a different sheet, press **Ctrl+Alt** as you drag the selection to the sheet's tab. Excel switches you to that sheet, where you can drop your selection into the appropriate location.

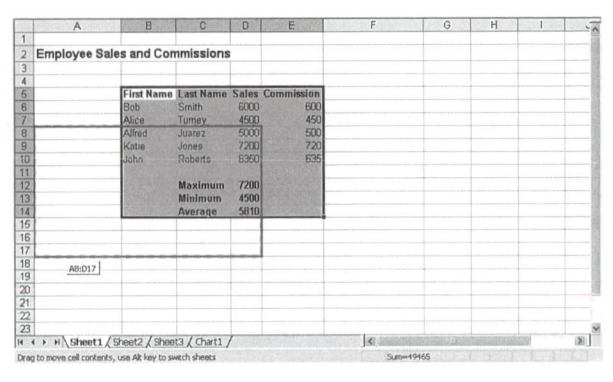

Figure 4.4 Dragging is the fastest way to copy data.

Moving Data

Moving data is similar to copying except that the data is removed from its original place and placed into the new location.

To move data, follow these steps:

1 Select the cells you want to move.

2 Click the **Cut** button.

3 Select the first cell in the area where you want to place the data. To move the data to another worksheet, change to that worksheet.

4 Click **Paste**.

Using Drag and Drop to Move Data

You can also move data using drag and drop. Select the data to be moved, and then drag the border of the selected cells to its new location. To insert the data between existing cells, press **Shift** while you drag. To move the data to a different worksheet, press the **Alt** key and drag the selection to the worksheet's tab. You're switched to that sheet, where you can drop your selection at the appropriate point.

→ Using the Office Clipboard

You can use the Office Clipboard to store multiple items that you cut or copy from an Excel worksheet (or workbook). You can then paste or move these items within Excel or to other Office applications. The Office Clipboard can hold up to 24 items.

> **Important**
>
> **What a Drag!** You can't use the drag-and-drop feature to copy or move data to the Office Clipboard.

The Office Clipboard is viewed in the Clipboard task pane. Follow these steps to open the Office Clipboard:

1 Select the **Edit** menu, and then select **Office Clipboard**. The Clipboard task pane appears. Any items that you have cut or copied appear on the Clipboard (see Figure 4.5).

Figure 4.5 The Clipboard provides a list of items that you have cut or copied.

2 To paste an item that appears on the Clipboard, click in a cell on the worksheet, and then click the item on the Clipboard. It is then pasted into the selected cell.

You can remove any of the items from the Clipboard. Place the mouse pointer on an item listed on the Clipboard and click the drop-down arrow that appears. Click **Delete** on the shortcut menu that appears.

You can also clear all the items from the Clipboard. Click the **Clear All** button at the top of the Clipboard task pane.

> **Timesaver tip**
>
> **Open the Clipboard from the System Tray** You can quickly open the Office Clipboard in any Office application by double-clicking the Clipboard icon in the Windows System Tray (at the far right of the Windows taskbar).

→ Deleting Data

To delete the data in a cell or range of cells, select them and press **Delete**. Excel also offers some additional options for deleting cells and their contents:

- With the **Edit**, **Clear** command, you can delete only the formatting of a cell (or an attached comment) without deleting its contents. The formatting of a cell includes the cell's color, border style, numeric format, font size, and so on. You'll learn more about this option in a moment.

- With the **Edit**, **Delete** command, you can remove cells and then shift surrounding cells over to take their place.

To use the Clear command to remove the formatting of a cell or a note, follow these steps:

1. Select the cells you want to clear.
2. Open the **Edit** menu and point at **Clear**. The Clear submenu appears.
3. Select the desired Clear option: **All** (which clears the cells of all contents, formatting, and notes), **Formats**, **Contents**, or **Comments**.

PowerPoint

1 Working in PowerPoint

In this lesson, you learn how to start and exit PowerPoint. You also learn about the PowerPoint presentation window.

→ Starting PowerPoint

PowerPoint is a powerful application that enables you to create presentations that can be viewed on a computer. Using PowerPoint, you can print handouts or create film slides for a presentation. PowerPoint also enables you to add animation and sound to your presentations, which makes it the perfect tool for business presentations or classroom lectures.

To start PowerPoint, follow these steps:

1. Click the **Start** button.
2. Move your mouse pointer to **Programs** (**All Programs** on Windows XP). A menu of programs appears. Point at the **Microsoft Office** icon.
3. Move your mouse pointer to the **Microsoft Office PowerPoint** icon and click it. The PowerPoint application window opens, as shown in Figure 1.1.

The first thing you see when you open PowerPoint is that the application window is divided into different areas. The default view for PowerPoint is the Normal view (you learn about the different PowerPoint views in Lesson 3, "Working with Slides in Different Views"). On the left of the screen is a pane that can be used to switch between an Outline and Slides view of the current presentation. In the center of the PowerPoint application window is the Slide pane; this is where you work individually on each slide in the presentation.

Below the Slide pane is the Notes pane, which enables you to add notes to the presentation for each slide. On the far right of the application window is the New Presentation task pane. The task pane provides different commands and features depending on what you are currently doing in PowerPoint.

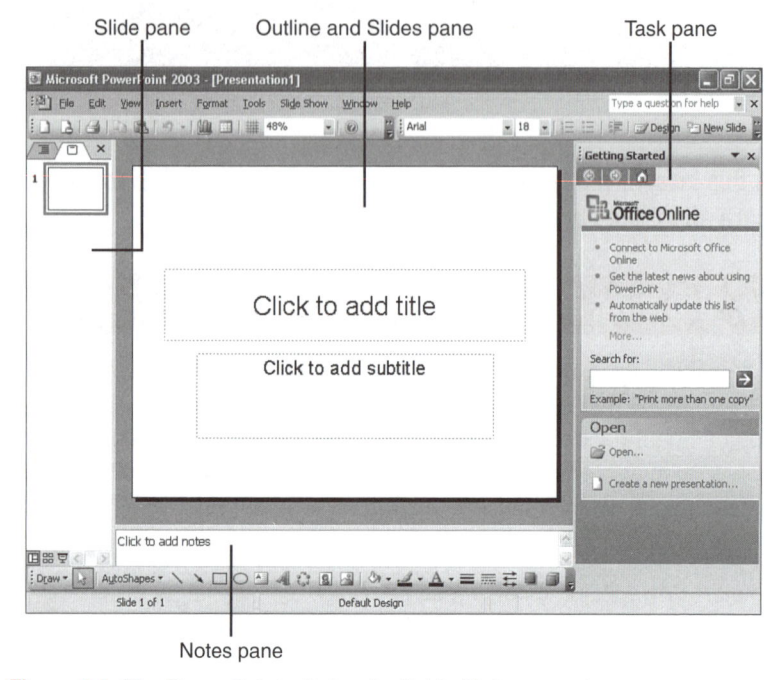

Figure 1.1 The PowerPoint window is divided into several panes.

→ Getting Comfortable with the PowerPoint Window

Although PowerPoint looks a little different from the other Office applications, such as Word and Excel, all the standard Office application components, such as the menu bar and various toolbars, are available to you as you design your presentations. The basic element of a presentation is a slide, to which you add text and other objects, such as images, using the Slide pane (which is discussed in the next lesson). PowerPoint provides several slide layouts; each layout provides the necessary text boxes or clip-art boxes for creating a particular type of slide.

Adding text to a slide is very straightforward. Each slide that you add to a presentation (Lesson 5, "Inserting, Deleting, and Copying Slides," discusses inserting slides into a presentation) contains placeholder text that tells you what to type into a particular text box on the slide. For example, Figure 1.2 shows a title slide. Note that the top text box on the slide says Click to Add Title.

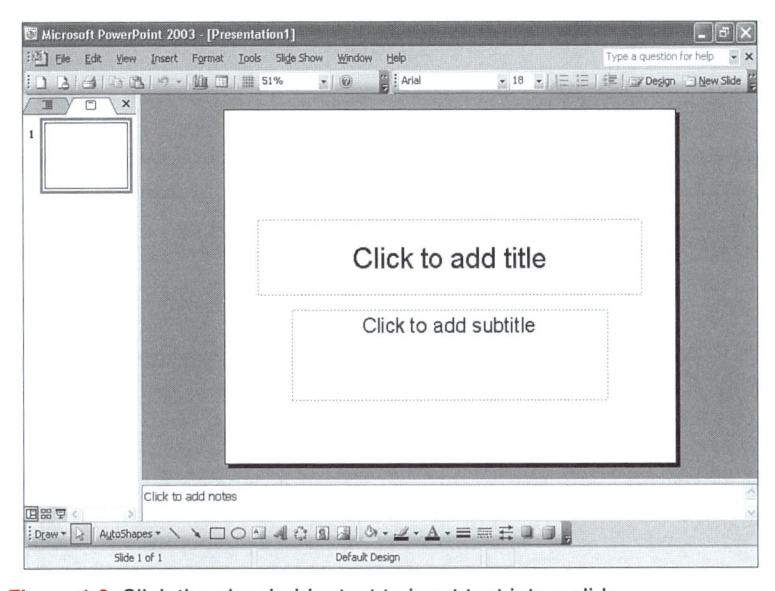

Figure 1.2 Click the placeholder text to input text into a slide.

To replace the placeholder text with your own text, just click the placeholder text. Then, you can type your entry into that text box.

Because a presentation consists of several slides, PowerPoint provides a thumbnail view of each slide in the presentation to the left of the Slides pane. Figure 1.3 shows an example of a complete presentation with a series of these thumbnail slides. This view can be used to keep track of your slides as you add them to the presentation and can even be used to rearrange slides in the presentation.

Because presentations require a certain logical arrangement of information, you can view the slides in the presentation as an outline. This enables you to make sure that you have the facts presented by each slide in the proper order for the presentation. The Outline pane also enables you to move topics within the presentation and even move information from slide to slide. Figure 1.4 shows the Outline pane for a presentation that contains several slides.

Working in PowerPoint   **221**

Figure 1.3 The Slides pane enables you to view thumbnails of the slides in the presentation.

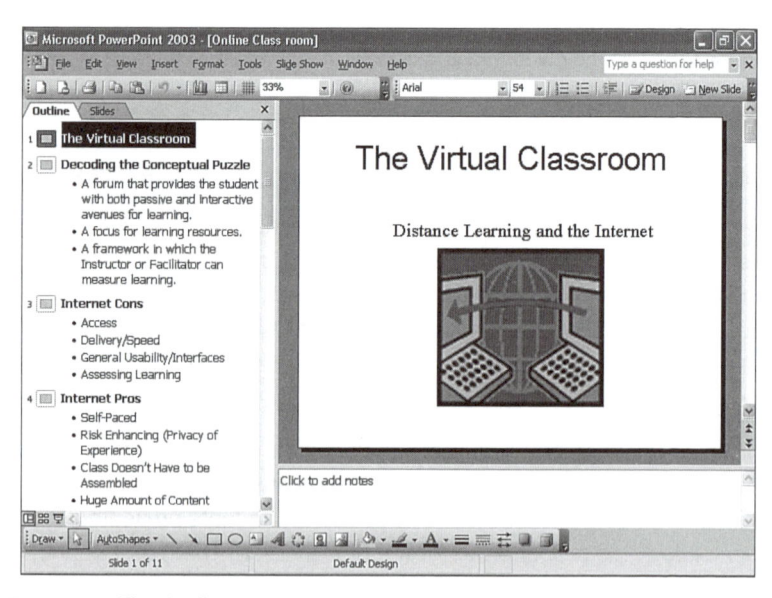

Figure 1.4 The Outline pane enables you to view the topic of each slide and each piece of text information included in a slide.

You learn about using the Slides and Outline pane in Lesson 3, "Working with Slides in Different Views."

Lesson 3 shows you how you can edit the presentation's text in either the Outline or the Slide pane. Changes in one pane are reflected in the other pane. When you want to place a nontext object on a slide (such as a graphic), you do so in the Slide pane.

→ Exiting PowerPoint

When you finish using PowerPoint, you can exit the application. This closes any open presentations (PowerPoint might prompt you to save changes to those presentations).

To exit PowerPoint, perform one of the following:

- Click the PowerPoint window's **Close (X)** button.
- Double-click the **Control Menu** icon in the left corner of the title bar, or click it once to open the Control menu and then select Close.
- Open the **File** menu and select **Exit**.
- Press **Alt+F4**.

2 Creating a New Presentation

In this lesson, you learn several ways to create a presentation. You also learn how to save, close, and open an existing presentation.

→ Starting a New Presentation

PowerPoint offers several ways to create a new presentation. Before you begin, decide which method is right for you:

- The AutoContent Wizard offers the highest degree of help. It walks you through each step of creating the new presentation. When you're finished, you have a standardized group of slides, all with a similar look and feel, for a particular situation. Each slide created includes dummy text that you can replace with your own text.
- A design template provides a professionally designed color, background, and font scheme that applies to the slides you create yourself. It does not provide sample slides.
- You can also start a new presentation based on an existing presentation. This "copies" all the slides in the existing presentation and allows you to save the new presentation under a new filename.
- You can start from scratch and create a totally blank presentation. That means that you build the presentation from the ground up and create each slide in the presentation. (Beginners might want to use the wizard or templates until they get a feel for the overall design approach used to create a cohesive slide presentation.)

> **Jargon buster**
>
> **Design Template** A design template is a preformatted presentation file (without any slides in it). When you select a template, PowerPoint applies the color scheme and general layout of the template to each slide you create for the presentation.

Creating a New Presentation with the AutoContent Wizard

With the AutoContent Wizard, you select the type of presentation you want to create (such as corporate, sales, or various projects), and PowerPoint creates an outline for the presentation.

The following steps describe how you use the AutoContent Wizard:

1 Select the **File** menu and select **New**. The New Presentation task pane appears on the right of the PowerPoint window, as shown in Figure 2.1 (if the Presentation task pane was already open in the window, you can skip to step 2).

Figure 2.1 Start the AutoContent Wizard from the task pane.

2 Click the **From AutoContent Wizard** link on the task pane.

3 The AutoContent Wizard starts. The opening wizard screen summarizes the process you should follow to create a new presentation. Click **Next** to continue.

4 The wizard provides you with category buttons for different categories of presentations: General, Corporate, Projects, and Sales/Marketing. Select a category by selecting the appropriate button (see Figure 2.2). A list of specific presentations will appear to the right of the category buttons. To see all the AutoContent presentations available, click the **All** button.

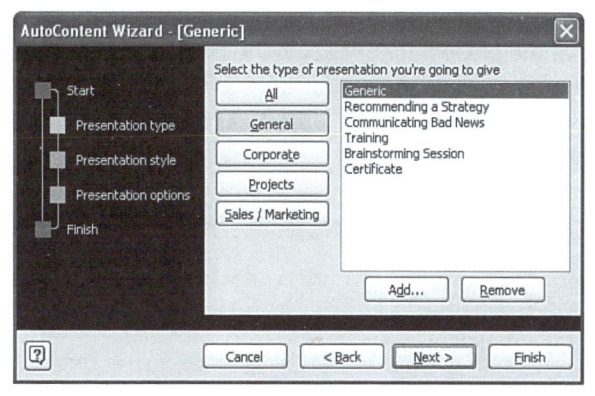

Figure 2.2 Select a category button to view a list of presentation types.

5 After selecting a particular category of presentations, select a presentation type in the list provided. You can choose to create a generic presentation, or presentations recommending a strategy, communicating bad news, or for a brainstorming session (among others). After selecting the type of presentation (I selected generic), click **Next** to continue.

6 On the next screen, you select how you will give the presentation. Select one of the following options:

- **Onscreen Presentation**—Choose this if you plan to use a computer and your PowerPoint file to present the show.

- **Web Presentation**—Choose this if you are planning to distribute the presentation as a self-running or user-interactive show.

- **Black-and-White Overheads**—Choose this if you plan to make black-and-white transparencies for your show.

- **Color Overheads**—Choose this if you plan to make color transparencies for your show.

- **35mm Slides**—Choose this if you plan to send your PowerPoint presentation to a service bureau to have 35mm slides made. (You probably don't have such expensive and specialized equipment in your own company.)

7 After selecting how you will give the presentation, click **Next** to continue.

8 On the next screen, type the presentation title into the text box provided (see Figure 2.3). If you want to add a footer (such as your name or other) that will appear at the bottom of each slide of the presentation, click in the Footer box and type the appropriate text. If you do not want a date and/or slide number on each slide, deselect the **Date Last Updated** and/or **Slide Number** check boxes.

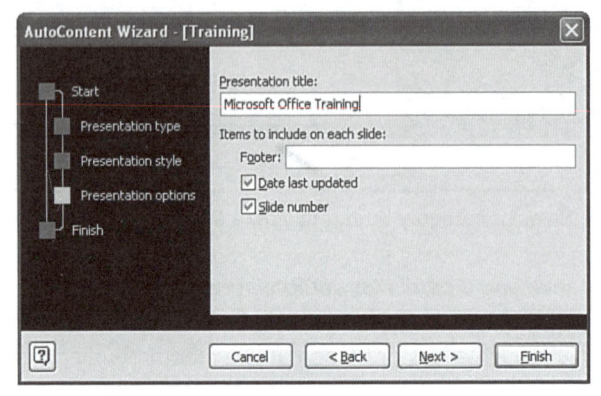

Figure 2.3 Provide a title for the presentation.

9 After supplying the presentation title and any optional information, click **Next** to continue.

10 PowerPoint takes you to the last wizard screen, where you should simply click **Finish**.

The title slide of your new presentation appears in the Slide pane. The entire presentation, including the dummy text placed on each slide, appears in the Outline pane on the left of the PowerPoint window (see Figure 2.4).

You can start working on your presentation right away by replacing the dummy text on the slides with your own text. Just select the existing text in a text box and type right over it. You learn about editing text in slide text boxes in Lesson 6, "Adding and Modifying Slide Text."

Creating a New Presentation with a Design Template

A template is the middle ground between maximum hand-holding (the AutoContent Wizard) and no help at all (Blank Presentation). Two kinds of templates are available: presentation templates and design templates.

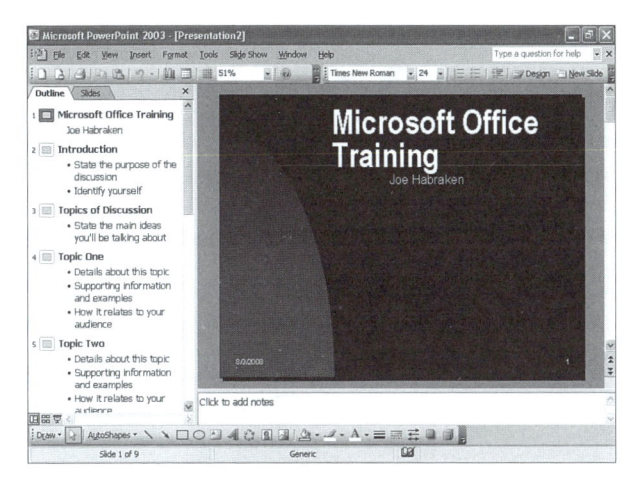

Figure 2.4 Your new presentation appears in the PowerPoint window.

When you use the AutoContent Wizard, you use a presentation template. It contains not only formatting, but also sample slides that contain placeholder text. The other kind of template is a design template. It contains the overall formatting for the slides of the presentation but does not actually create any slides. If you want to use a presentation template that includes placeholder text, use the AutoContent Wizard, as explained in the preceding section.

To start a new presentation using a design template, follow these steps:

1 Select the **File** menu and select **New**. The New Presentation task pane appears on the right of the PowerPoint window.

> **Timesaver tip**
>
> **Select Your Task Pane** If the task pane is already open for another PowerPoint feature, click the drop-down arrow on its title bar and select **New Presentation** from the list that appears.

2 On the New Presentation task pane, click the **From Design Template** link. PowerPoint switches to the Slide Design side pane, which displays a list of design templates, as shown in Figure 2.5. A blank title slide for the presentation appears in the Slide pane.

Creating a New Presentation   **229**

Figure 2.5 Design templates are listed in the task pane.

3 Click a template from the Available For Use section of the task pane. PowerPoint then formats the title slide in the Slide pane using the selected template.

You can select different templates to determine the best look for your presentation. When you have found the design template that you want to use, you can immediately start working on the slides for the presentation.

> **Timesaver tip**
>
> **The Next Step?** Add more slides by clicking the **New Slide** button on the toolbar. Inserting slides into a presentation is covered in Lesson 5, "Inserting, Deleting, and Copying Slides."

Creating a New Presentation from an Existing Presentation

Another alternative for creating a new presentation is to use an existing presentation. This creates a copy of the existing presentation (and all its slides) and allows you to quickly save the presentation under a new filename.

1 Select the **File** menu and select **New**. The New Presentation task pane appears on the right of the PowerPoint window.

2 Select **From Existing Presentation** in the New Presentation task pane. The New from Existing Presentation dialog box opens (see Figure 2.6).

3 Use the Look in drop-down list to locate the drive and the folder that holds the existing presentation. When you locate the existing presentation, select it and then click **Create New**.

4 A "copy" of the existing presentation will open in the PowerPoint window.

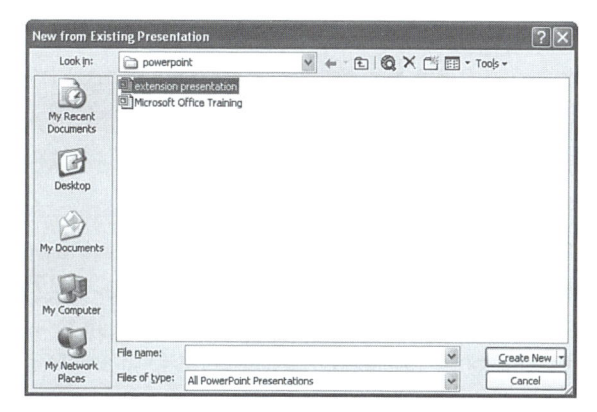

Figure 2.6 Open the existing presentation that the new presentation will be based on.

When you have the copy of the existing presentation open, you can edit it as needed. You can then save the presentation under a new filename as discussed later in this lesson.

Timesaver tip

What Is the Photo Album? An additional choice, Photo Album, appears on the New Presentation task pane. This new presentation option provides you with a quick way to create a presentation that contains pictures and other images. We discuss the Photo Album in Lesson 7, "Adding Graphics to a Slide."

Creating a Blank Presentation

Your fourth option for creating a new presentation is to create a blank presentation. This means that you have to create all the slides from scratch. A design for the slides can then be selected using the Slide Design task pane. You open this task pane by selecting **Format**, **Slide Design**. In the Slide Design task pane, be sure that the Design Templates icon is selected.

Creating a new, blank presentation takes only a click: Click the **New** button on the Standard toolbar or click the **Blank Presentation** link on the New Presentation task pane. The new presentation appears in the PowerPoint window. A blank title slide is ready for you to edit.

→ Saving a Presentation

After you create a new presentation, it makes sense to save it. To save a presentation for the first time, follow these steps:

1 Select **File**, **Save**, or just click the **Save** button on the Standard toolbar. The Save As dialog box appears (see Figure 2.7).

2 In the **File Name** text box, type the name you want to assign to the presentation. Your filenames can be as long as 255 characters and can include spaces.

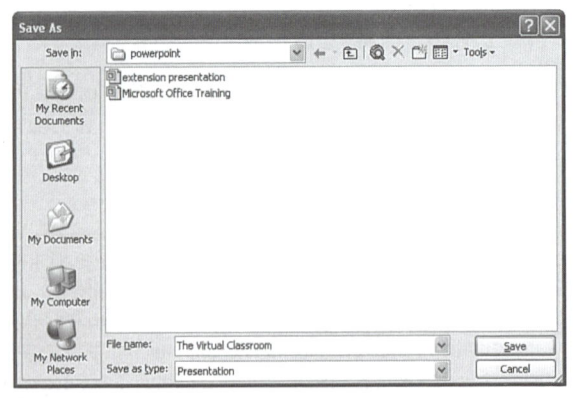

Figure 2.7 Type a name for your presentation into the Save As dialog box.

3 The Save In box shows in which folder the file will be saved. The default is My Documents. To select a different drive location for the file, click the **Save In** drop-down arrow and select one from the list that appears. To save to a specific folder in the drive location you've selected, double-click the folder in which you want to store the file.

4 Click **Save**.

Now that you have named the file and saved it to a disk, you can save any changes you make simply by pressing **Ctrl+S** or clicking the **Save** button on the Standard toolbar. Your data is saved under the filename you assigned to the presentation in the Save As dialog box.

To create a copy of a presentation under a different filename or location, select **File**, **Save As**. The Save As dialog box reappears; follow steps 2 to 4 as discussed in this section to give the file a new name or location.

→ Closing a Presentation

You can close a presentation at any time. Note that although this closes the presentation window, it does not exit PowerPoint as do the methods discussed in Lesson 1. To close a presentation, follow these steps:

1 If more than one presentation is open, click a presentation's button on the Windows taskbar to make it the active presentation, or you can select the **Window** menu and select the presentation from the list provided.

2 Select **File**, **Close**, or click the presentation's **Close** (**X**) button. (It's the lower of the two Close buttons; the upper one is for the PowerPoint window.) If you haven't saved the presentation or if you haven't saved since you last made changes, a dialog box appears, asking whether you want to save.

3 To save your changes, click **Yes**. If this is a new presentation that has never been saved, refer to the steps in the preceding section for saving a presentation. If you have saved the file previously, the presentation window closes.

→ Opening a Presentation

A presentation, like Rome, is not built in a day, so you will probably fine-tune a presentation over time. To open a saved presentation file that you want to work on, follow these steps:

Creating a New Presentation

1. Select **File**, **Open**, or click the **Open** button on the Standard toolbar. The Open dialog box appears (see Figure 2.8).

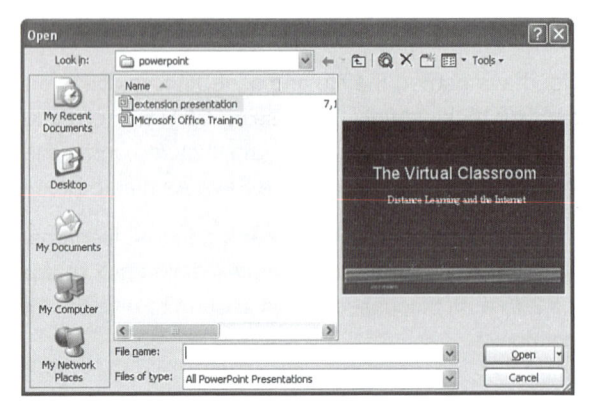

Figure 2.8 Select the presentation you want to open.

2. If the file isn't in the currently displayed folder, select the **Look In** drop-down arrow to choose from a list of other drives and/or folders.
3. Browse to the location containing the file and double-click it to open it in PowerPoint.

→ Finding a Presentation File

If you're having trouble locating your file, PowerPoint can help you look. Follow these steps to find a file:

1. Select **File**, **Open** (if the Open dialog box is not already open).
2. Click the **Tools** drop-down button in the Open dialog box and select **Search**. The File Search dialog box appears (see Figure 2.9).
3. In the **Search Text** box, type text that is contained in the presentation's filename. Use the Search In box to specify where you want the search to be conducted. In the Results Should Be box, specify the file types you want to be included in the search.
4. When you are ready to conduct the search, click the **Search** button.
5. Files that meet the search criteria are listed in the Results box (if you see your file in the Results box and the search is continuing, click the **Stop** button).

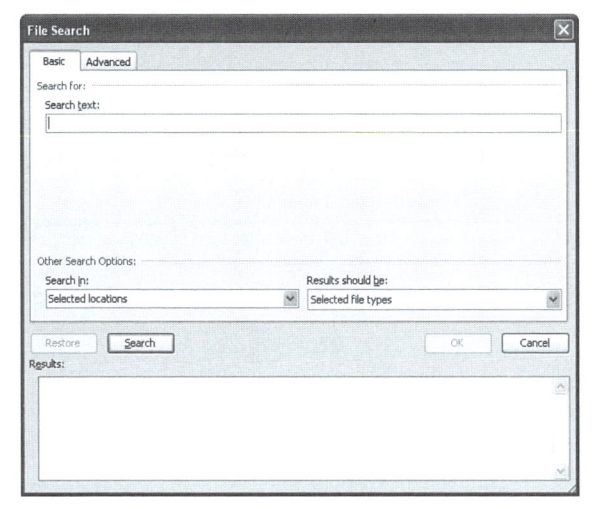

Figure 2.9 Use the File Search dialog box to find a presentation on your computer.

6 To open a file in the Results box, double-click the filename.

7 You are returned to the Open dialog box with the file listed in the File Name box. Click **OK** to open the file. A PowerPoint presentation then opens in the PowerPoint window.

3 Working with Slides in Different Views

In this lesson, you learn how to display a presentation in different views and how to edit slides in the Outline and Slide views.

→ Understanding PowerPoint's Different Views

PowerPoint can display your presentation in different views. Each of these views is designed for you to perform certain tasks as you create and edit a presentation. For example, Normal view has the Outline/Slides, Slide, and Notes panes; it provides an ideal environment for creating your presentation slides and for quickly viewing the organization of the slides or the information in the presentation (using the Outline or the Slides tabs). Another view, the Slide Sorter view, enables you to quickly rearrange the slides in the presentation (and is similar to the Slides view that shares the pane with the Outline tab when you are in the Normal view).

To change views, open the **View** menu and choose the desired view: **Normal**, **Slide Sorter**, **Slide Show**, or **Notes Page**.

- **Normal**—The default, three-pane view (which is discussed in Lesson 1, "Working in PowerPoint").
- **Slide Sorter**—This view shows all the slides as thumbnails so that you can easily rearrange them by dragging slides to new positions in the presentation (Figure 3.1 shows the Slide Sorter).
- **Slide Show**—A specialized view that enables you to preview and present your show onscreen. It enables you to test the presentation as you add slides, and it is used later when your presentation is complete.
- **Notes Page**—This view provides a large pane for creating notes for your speech. You can also type these notes in Normal view, but Notes Page view gives you more room and allows you to concentrate on your note text.

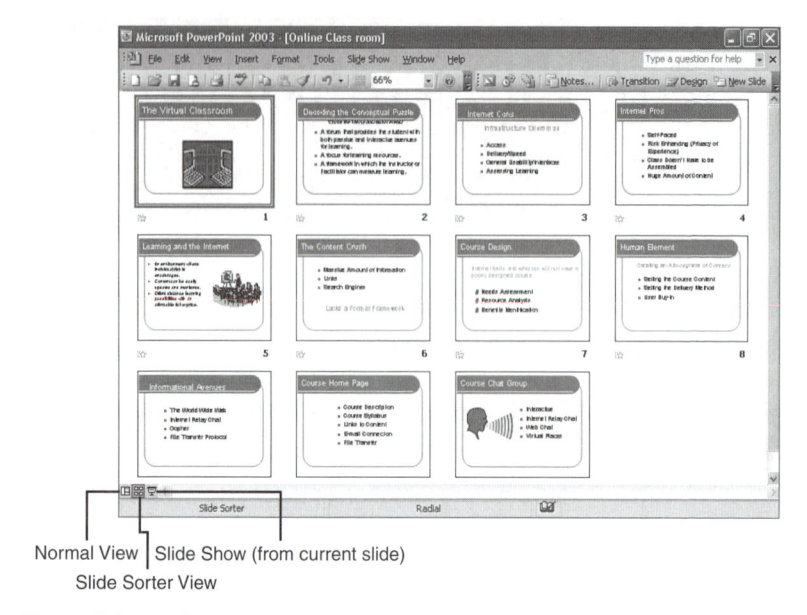

Figure 3.1 The Slide Sorter view is used to rearrange the slides in a presentation.

An even faster way to switch to certain views is to use the view buttons that are provided along the lower-left corner of the PowerPoint window. These buttons, from left to right, are Normal View, Slide Sorter View, and Slide Show (from current slide) button. A button not provided for the Notes view.

→ Moving from Slide to Slide

PowerPoint provides several ways to move from slide to slide in the presentation. The particular view you are in somewhat controls the procedure for moving to a specific slide.

In the Normal view, you can move from slide to slide using these techniques:

- Click the **Outline** tab on the far left of the window. To go to a particular slide in the outline, click the slide icon next to the slide number (see Figure 3.2). The slide opens in the Slide pane.
- Press the **Page Up** or **Page Down** keys to move to the previous or next slide, respectively.

- Click the **Previous Slide** or **Next Slide** button just below the vertical scrollbar (refer to Figure 3.2), or drag the scroll box inside the vertical scrollbar until the desired slide number is displayed.
- Click the **Slides** tab on the far left of the PowerPoint window. This enables you to move from slide to slide in the Normal view by selecting a particular slide's thumbnail. When you click the thumbnail, the slide appears in the Slide pane.

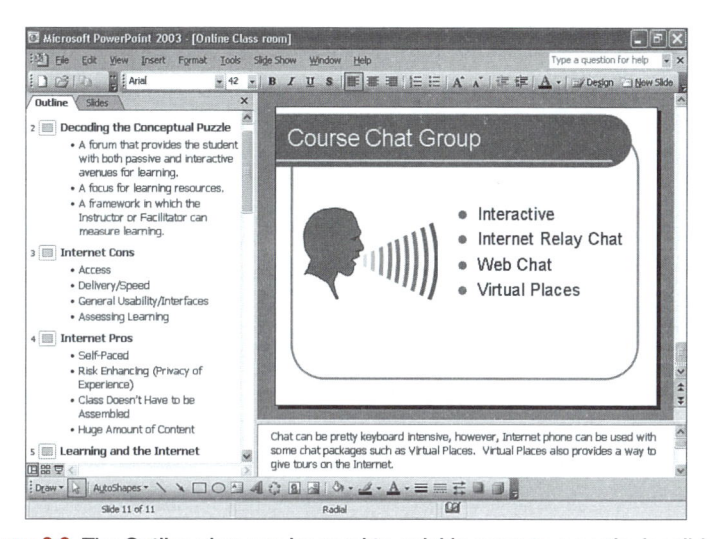

Figure 3.2 The Outline view can be used to quickly move to a particular slide.

You can also move from slide to slide in other views, such as the Slide Sorter view or the Slide Show view. In the Slide Sorter view (refer to Figure 3.1), just click a slide's thumbnail to move to that slide. You then can use any of the tools that PowerPoint provides to format the selected slide (or delete it). If you want to actually open a slide when you are working in the Slide Sorter view, so that you can edit the text it contains, double-click the slide. You are returned to the Normal view.

When you are actually showing a presentation in the Slide Show view, you can use the **Page Up** or **Page Down** keys to move from slide to slide (unless you have set up timers to change slides). You can also click a slide with the mouse to move to the next slide.

→ Introduction to Inserting Slide Text

If you created a presentation in Lesson 2 using the AutoContent Wizard, you already have a presentation that contains several slides, but they won't contain the text you want to use. Slides created by the wizard contain placeholder text that you must replace. If you created a blank presentation or based a new presentation on a design template, you have only a title slide in that presentation, which, of course, needs to be personalized for your particular presentation. This means that additional slides will need to be added to the presentation. Lesson 5, "Inserting, Deleting, and Copying Slides," covers the creation of new slides for a presentation.

The sections that follow in this lesson look at the basics of inserting text into the text boxes provided on slides. You will look at adding new text boxes and formatting text in text boxes in Lesson 6, "Adding and Modifying Slide Text." Upcoming lessons also discuss how to add pictures and other objects to your PowerPoint slides.

> **Jargon buster**
>
> **Object** An object is any item on a slide, including text, graphics, and charts.

→ Editing Text in the Slide Pane

The text on your slides resides within boxes (all objects appear on a slide in their own boxes for easy manipulation). As shown in Figure 3.3, to edit text on a slide, click the text box to select it and then click where you want the insertion point moved, or select the text you want to replace.

When you work with the Slide pane, you might want to close the Outline/Slides pane. Just click the pane's **Close** button (X) to provide the Slide pane with the entire PowerPoint window (refer to Figure 3.3). In Lesson 6, "Adding and Modifying Slide Text," you'll learn more about adding text to a slide, including creating your own text boxes on a slide.

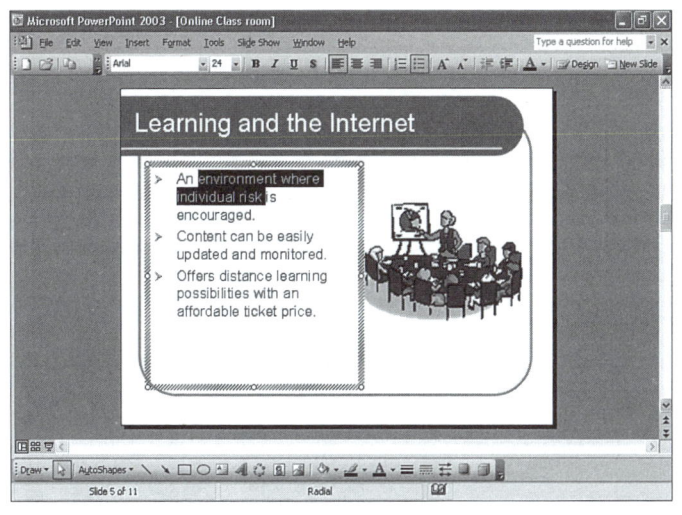

Figure 3.3 You can edit your text directly on the slide in the Slide pane.

> **Timesaver tip**
>
> **Opening the Outline Pane** If you close the Outline pane to concentrate on the Slide pane, click **View**, **Normal (Restore Panes)** to restore it to the application window.

Editing Text in the Outline Pane

The Outline pane provides another way to edit text in a slide. To switch to the Outline view on the Outline/Slides pane, click the **Outline** tab. You simply click to move the insertion point where you want it (or select the range of text you want to replace) in the outline, and then type your text (see Figure 3.4). If you've placed the insertion point in the slide text (without selecting a range), press the **Delete** key to delete characters to the right of the insertion point or press the **Backspace** key to delete characters to the left. If you've selected a range of text, either of these keys deletes the text. If you want to move the highlighted text, simply drag it to where you want it moved.

> **Timesaver tip**
>
> **Larger Outline** You might want to enlarge the Outline pane by dragging its divider to the right in the Normal view.

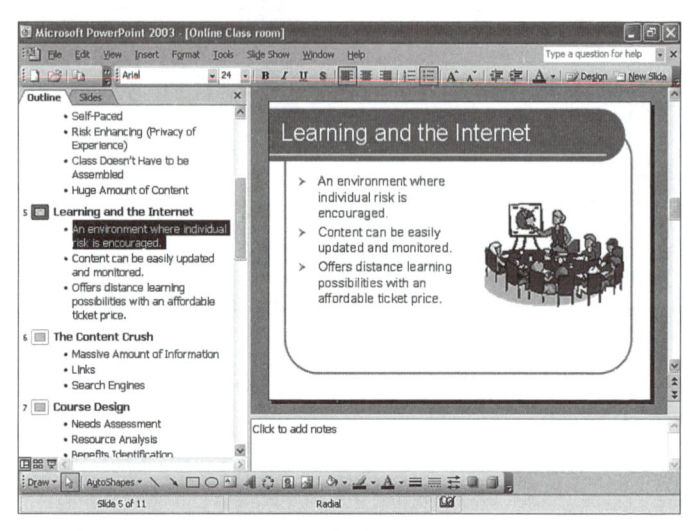

Figure 3.4 You can edit your text in Outline view.

> **Timesaver tip**
>
> **Auto Word Select** When you select text, PowerPoint selects whole words. If you want to select individual characters, open the **Tools** menu, select **Options**, click the **Edit** tab, and click the **When Selecting, Automatically Select Entire Word** check box to turn it off. Click **OK**.

Moving Text in the Outline Pane

As you work in the Normal view, you can also view your presentation slides as an outline using the Outline pane. This provides you with a quick way to move text items around on a slide or move them from slide to slide. Just select the text and drag it to a new position.

As already mentioned, you can also drag text from one slide to another. All you have to do is select a line of text in the Outline pane and drag it to another slide. You can also move a slide in the Outline pane. Drag the slide's icon in the Outline pane to a new position (under the heading for another slide).

If you aren't that confident with your dragging skills, PowerPoint provides you with help in the form of the Outlining toolbar. It provides buttons that make it easy to move text up or down on a slide (with respect to other text on the slide) or to move a slide up or down in the presentation.

To turn on the Outlining toolbar, right-click one of the PowerPoint toolbars and select **Outlining**. Figure 3.5 shows the Outlining toolbar on the left side of the Outline pane (the Outline pane has also been expanded to take up more of the PowerPoint window).

- To move a paragraph or text line up in a slide, select it and click the **Move Up** button.
- To move a paragraph or text down in a slide, select it and click the **Move Down** button.

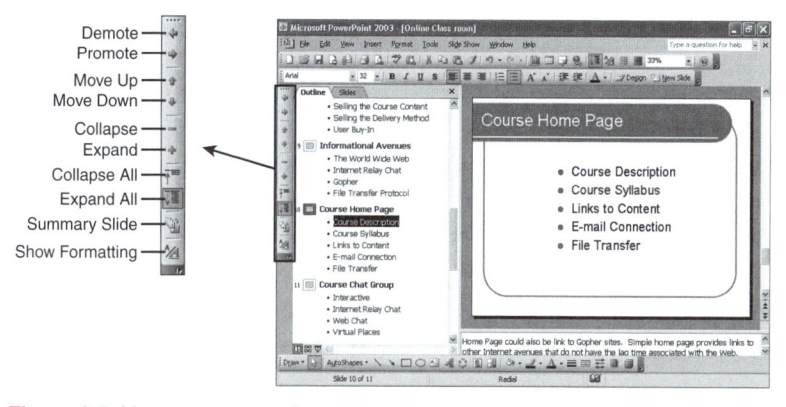

Figure 3.5 You can use the Outlining toolbar to move text and slides in the presentation.

You can also use the **Move Up** and **Move Down** buttons to move entire slides up or down in the presentation. Click the slide's icon and then use the appropriate button (it might take several clicks to move a slide up or down with respect to another slide).

If you want to see how the text is actually formatted on the slides that you are viewing in the Outline pane, click the **Show Formatting** button on the Outlining toolbar. Viewing the text as it is formatted can help you determine where the text should appear on a slide as you move the text (or whether you will have to reformat the text later).

Working with Slides in Different Views

Rearranging Text in the Outline Pane

As you can see from Figure 3.5, your presentation is organized in a multilevel outline format. The slides are at the top level of the outline, and each slide's contents are subordinate under that slide. Some slides have multiple levels of subordination (for example, a bulleted list within a bulleted list).

You can easily change an object's level in Outline view with the Tab key or the Outlining toolbar:

- To demote a paragraph in the outline, click the text, and then press the **Tab** key or click the **Demote** button on the Outlining toolbar.
- To promote a paragraph in the outline, click the text, and then press **Shift+Tab** or click the **Promote** button on the Outlining toolbar.

In most cases, subordinate items on a slide appear as items in a bulleted list.

> **Timesaver tip**
>
> **Create Summary Slides in the Outline Pane** If you would like to create a summary slide for your presentation that contains the headings from several slides, select those slides in the Outline pane (click the first slide, and then hold down the **Shift** key and click the last slide you want to select). Then, click the **Summary Slide** button on the Outlining toolbar. A new slide appears at the beginning of the selected slides containing the headings from the selected slides. You then can position the Summary slide anywhere in the presentation as you would any other slide.

4. Changing a Presentation's Look

In this lesson, you learn various ways to give your presentation a professional and consistent look.

→ Giving Your Slides a Professional Look

PowerPoint comes with dozens of professionally created designs and color schemes that you can apply to your presentations. These designs include background patterns, color choices, font choices, and more. When you apply a design template to your presentation, it applies its formatting to a special slide called the Slide Master.

The Slide Master is not really a slide, but it looks like one. It is a master design grid that you make changes to; these changes affect every slide in the presentation. When you apply a template, you are actually applying the template to the Slide Master, which in turn applies it to each slide in the presentation.

> **Jargon buster**
>
> **Master Slide** A slide that contains the master layout and color scheme for the slides in a presentation.

You don't have to work with the Slide Master itself when you apply template or color scheme changes to your presentations. Just be aware that you can open the Slide Master (select **View**, point at **Master**, and then select **Slide Master**) and change the style and fonts used by the text boxes in a presentation (see Figure 4.1). You can also select a custom background color for the slides in the presentation. Any changes that you make to the Slide Master affect all the slides in the presentation.

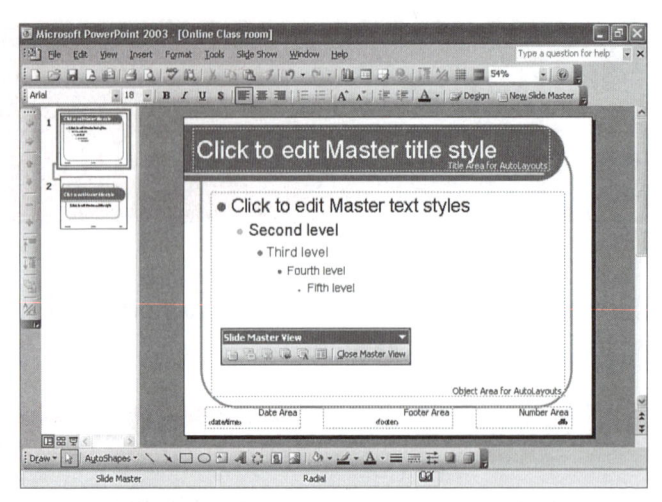

Figure 4.1 The Slide Master holds the default design and color options for the entire presentation.

You will probably find that PowerPoint provides enough template and color scheme options that you won't need to format the Slide Master itself very often. Edit its properties only if you have a very strict formatting need for the presentation that isn't covered in the templates and color schemes provided. For example, one good reason to edit the Slide Master would be a situation in which you want a graphic to appear on every slide (such as a company logo); you can place the image on the Slide Master instead of pasting it onto each slide individually.

Timesaver tip

Close the Slide Master If you open the Slide Master, you can close it by clicking **Close Master View** on the Master View toolbar.

→ Applying a Different Design Template

You can apply a different template to your presentation at any time, no matter how you originally created the presentation. To change the design template, follow these steps:

1 Select **Format**, **Slide Design** to open the Slide Design task pane. Then, if necessary, click the **Design Templates** icon at the top of the task pane. This provides a listing of PowerPoint's many design templates (see Figure 4.2).

2 Click the template that you want to use in the list. The template is immediately applied to the slide in the Slide pane.

3 When you have decided on a particular template (you can click on any number of templates to see how they affect your slides), save the presentation (click the **Save** button on the toolbar).

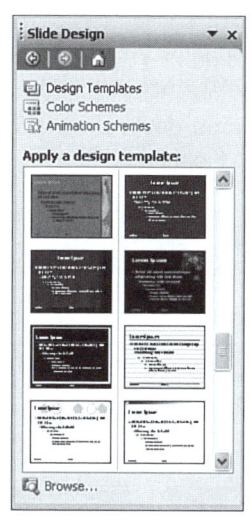

Figure 4.2 Choose a different template from the Design Templates task pane.

Important

The Design Template Changes Custom Formatting If you spent time bolding text items on a slide or changing font colors, these changes are affected (lost) when you select a new design template. For example, if you have customized bold items in black in your original design template and switch to another template that uses white text, you lose your customizations. You should choose your design template early in the process of creating your presentation. Then, you can do any customized formatting at the end of the process so that it is not affected by a design template change.

When you work with design templates, you can apply them to all the slides in the presentation (as discussed in the steps provided in this section), or you can apply the template to selected slides in the presentation. Follow these steps to apply a template to a selected group of slides in a presentation:

1. Switch to the Slide Sorter view (select **View**, **Slide Sorter**).
2. Open the Slide Design task pane as outlined in the previous steps.
3. Now you must select the slide (or slides) to which you want to apply the template. Click the first slide you want to select, and then hold down the **Ctrl** key as you click other slides you want to select. To select a series of slides, click the first one and then Shift+click on the last slide to select them all.
4. Point at the design template you want to use in the Slide Design task pane; a drop-down arrow appears.
5. Click the template's drop-down arrow and select **Apply to Selected Slides** (see Figure 4.3).

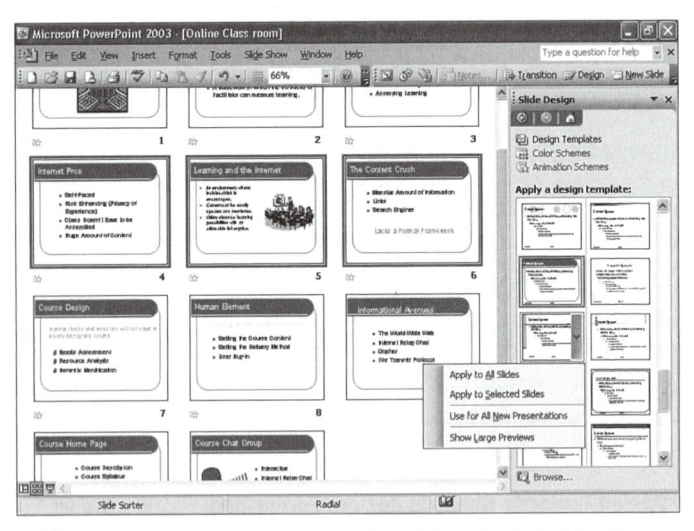

Figure 4.3 Design templates can be assigned to selected slides in a presentation.

The template's design is then applied to the selected slides.

> **Timesaver tip**
>
> **View a Larger Design Sample** To expand the view of the design templates, click the drop-down arrow on the template and select **Show Large Previews**.

→ Using Color Schemes

Design templates enable you to change the overall design and color scheme applied to the slides in the presentation (or selected slides in the presentation, as discussed in the previous section). If you like the overall design of the slides in the presentation but would like to explore some other color options, you can select a different color scheme for the particular template that you are using.

The number of color schemes available for a particular design template depends on the template itself. Some templates provide only three or four color schemes, whereas other templates provide more. As with design templates, you can assign a new color scheme to all the slides in the presentation or to selected slides.

To change the color scheme for the presentation or selected slides, follow these steps:

1 In the Normal or Slide Sorter view (use the Slide Sorter view if you want to change the color scheme for selected slides), open the task pane by selecting **View**, **Task Pane** (if the task pane is already open, skip to the next step).

2 Select the task pane's drop-down arrow and then select **Slide Design-Color Schemes**. This switches to the Color Schemes section of the Slide Design task pane. The color schemes available for the design template that you are using appear in the Apply a Color Scheme section (see Figure 4.4).

3 (Optional) If you are in the Slide Sorter view and want to assign a new color scheme only to selected slides, select those slides (click the first slide and then hold down **Ctrl** and click additional slides).

4 To assign the new color scheme to all the slides in the presentation, click a scheme in the Slide Design task pane. If you are assigning the color scheme only to selected slides, point at the color scheme and click its drop-down arrow. Select **Apply to Selected Slides**.

The new color scheme is applied to the slides in the presentation (or selected slides in the presentation). If you decide you don't like the color scheme, select another scheme from the task pane.

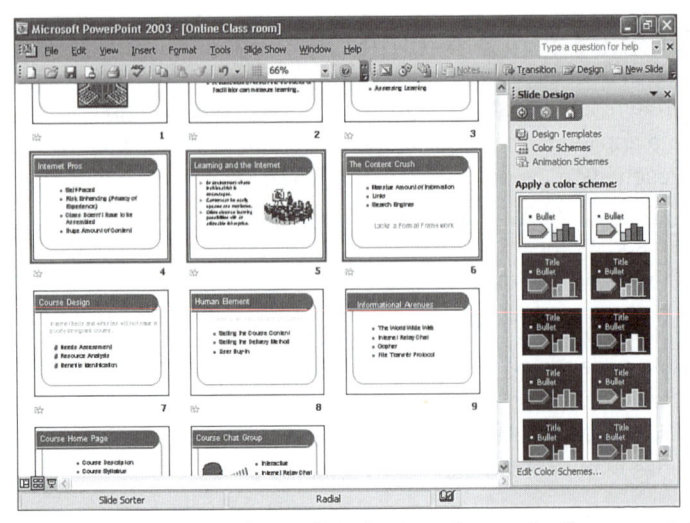

Figure 4.4 You can choose from a list of color schemes for the presentation or selected slides.

→ Changing the Background Fill

You can also fine-tune the color scheme that you add to a slide or slides by changing the background fill. This works best in cases where the design template and color scheme that you selected don't provide a background color for the slide or slides. You must be careful, however, because you don't want to pick a background color that obscures the text and graphics that you place on the slide or slides.

To change the background fill on a slide or slides, follow these steps:

1. Switch to the Slide Sorter view (select **View**, **Slide Sorter**).
2. (Optional) If you are going to change the background fill for selected slides, select those slides in the Slide Sorter window.
3. Select the **Format** menu and then select **Background**. The Background dialog box appears (see Figure 4.5).
4. Click the drop-down arrow at the bottom of the dialog box and choose a fill color from the color palette that appears.
5. To assign the fill color to all the slides in the presentation, click **Apply to All**. To assign the fill color to selected slides (if you selected slides in step 2), click **Apply**.

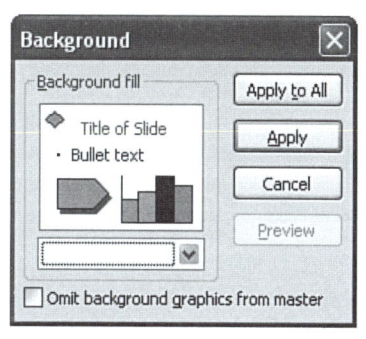

Figure 4.5 Use the Background dialog box to add a fill color to a slide or slides.

5 Inserting, Deleting, and Copying Slides

In this lesson, you learn how to insert new slides, delete slides, and copy slides in a presentation.

→ Inserting Slides into a Presentation

You can insert slides into your presentation. You can insert blank slides or you can insert slides from other presentations.

Let's look at inserting blank slides. Then we can look at inserting existing slides from another presentation.

Inserting a New, Blank Slide

You can insert a slide into a presentation at any time and at any position in the presentation. To insert a new slide, follow these steps:

1 On the Outline or Slides pane, select the slide that appears just before the place where you want to insert the new slide (you can also insert a new slide in the Slide Sorter view, if you want).

2 **New Slide** Choose the **Insert** menu and then **New Slide**, or click the **New Slide** button on the PowerPoint toolbar. A new blank slide appears in the PowerPoint window, along with the Slide Layout task pane (see Figure 5.1).

3 In the Slide Layout task pane, select the slide layout that you want to use for the new slide. Several text slide layouts and layouts for slides that contain graphics are provided.

4 Follow the directions indicated on the slide in the Slide pane to add text or other objects. For text boxes, you click an area to select it and then type in your text. For other object placeholders, you double-click the placeholder.

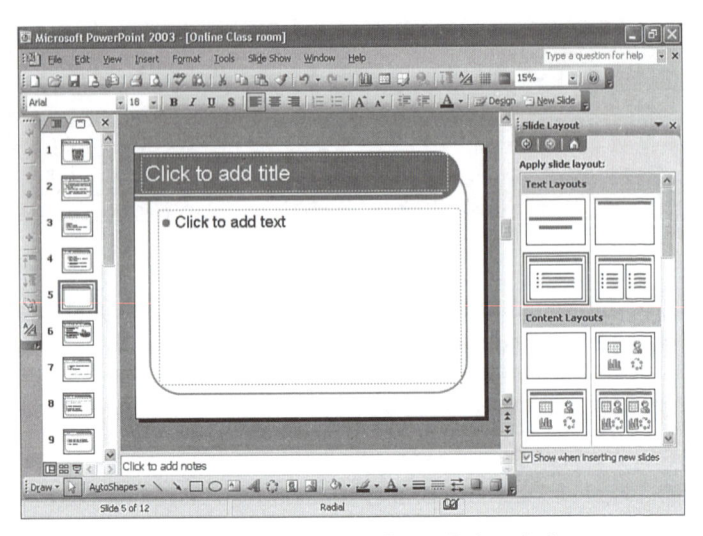

Figure 5.1 Your new slide appears in the PowerPoint window.

Timesaver tip

Cloning a Slide To create an exact replica of an existing slide (in any view), select the slide you want to duplicate. Click **Insert** and then select **Duplicate Slide**. The new slide is inserted after the original slide. You can then choose a different layout for the slide if you want.

Inserting Slides from Another Presentation

If you want to insert some or all of the slides from another presentation into the current presentation, perform these steps:

1 Open the presentation into which you want to insert the slides.

2 Select the slide located before the position where you want to insert the slides.

3 Select the **Insert** menu and select **Slides from Files**. The Slide Finder dialog box appears (see Figure 5.2).

4 Click the **Browse** button to display the Browse dialog box. In the Browse dialog box, locate the presentation that contains the slides that you want to insert into the current presentation (use the **Look In** drop-down arrow to switch drives, if necessary).

5 When you locate the presentation, double-click it.

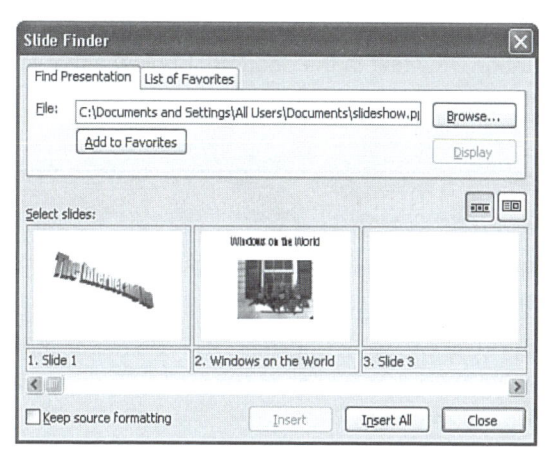

Figure 5.2 Use the Slide Finder dialog box to insert slides from another presentation.

6 The slides in the presentation appear in the Slide Finder's Select Slides box. To select the slides that you want to insert into the current presentation, click the first slide and then hold down **Ctrl** and click any subsequent slides.

7 When you have selected all the slides you want to insert, click **Insert** (if you want to insert all the slides, click **Insert All**).

8 PowerPoint inserts the slides into the presentation at the point you originally selected. Click **OK** to close the Slide Finder dialog box.

→ Creating Slides from a Document Outline

If you have created a document in Word that includes outline-style headings and numbered or bulleted lists, PowerPoint can pull the headings and the text from the document and create slides. To create slides from a document outline, follow these steps:

1 Choose the **Insert** menu, and then choose **Slides from Outline**. The Insert Outline dialog box appears (it is similar to the Open dialog box used to open a presentation or other file).

2 Use the **Insert Outline** dialog box to locate the document file you want to use.

3 Double-click the name of the document file.

PowerPoint then uses all the first-level headings to create slides for your presentation. Any text in the document below a first-level outline heading is added to the slide in an additional text box.

→ Deleting Slides

You can delete a slide from any view. To delete a slide, perform the following steps:

1. Select the slide you want to delete. You can delete multiple slides by selecting more than one slide (on the Outline or Slides pane or in the Slide Sorter view).
2. Choose the **Edit** menu, and then choose **Delete Slide**. The slide is removed from the presentation.

> **Timesaver tip**
>
> **Use the Delete Key** You can quickly delete slides by selecting the slide or slides and then pressing the **Delete** key on the keyboard.

> **Important**
>
> **Oops!** If you deleted a slide by mistake, you can get it back. Select **Edit**, **Undo**, or press **Ctrl+Z**. This works only if you do it immediately. You cannot undo the change if you exit PowerPoint and restart the application.

→ Cutting, Copying, and Pasting Slides

Although dragging slides to new positions in the Slide Sorter is probably the easiest way to move slides, you can use the **Cut**, **Copy**, and **Paste** commands to move or copy slides in the presentation. Follow these steps:

1. Change to Slide Sorter view, or display Normal view and work with the Outline or Slides panes.
2. Select the slide(s) you want to copy or cut.

3 Open the **Edit** menu and select **Cut** or **Copy** to either move or copy the slide(s), respectively, or you can use the **Cut** or **Copy** toolbar buttons.

> **Timesaver tip**
>
> **Quick Cut or Copy** From the keyboard, press **Ctrl+C** to copy or **Ctrl+X** to cut.

4 In Slide Sorter view, select the slide after which you want to place the cut or copied slide(s), or on the Outline pane, move the insertion point to the end of the text in the slide after which you want to insert the cut or copied slide(s).

5 Select the **Edit** menu and choose **Paste**, or click the **Paste** toolbar button. PowerPoint inserts the cut or copied slides.

> **Timesaver tip**
>
> **Keyboard Shortcut** You can also press **Ctrl+V** to paste an item that you cut or copied.

6 Adding and Modifying Slide Text

In this lesson, you learn how to add text boxes to a slide and change the text alignment and line spacing.

→ Creating a Text Box

As you learned in Lesson 3, "Working with Slides in Different Views," the text on slides resides in various text boxes. To edit the text in a text box, click in the box to place the insertion point, and then enter or edit the text within the box. If you want to add additional text to a slide that will not be contained in one of the text boxes already on the slide, you must create a new text box.

> **Jargon buster**
>
> **Text Box** A text box acts as a receptacle for the text. Text boxes often contain bulleted lists, notes, and labels (used to point to important parts of illustrations).

To create a text box, perform the following steps:

1. If necessary, switch to the Normal view (select **View**, **Normal**). Use the Slides or Outline tab on the left of the workspace to select the slide that you want to work on. The slide appears in the Slide pane.
2. Click the **Text Box** button on the Drawing toolbar (if the Drawing toolbar isn't visible, right-click any toolbar and select **Drawing**).
3. Click the slide where you want the text box to appear. A small text box appears (see Figure 6.1). (It will expand as you type in it.)
4. Type the text that you want to appear in the text box. Press **Enter** to start a new paragraph. Don't worry if the text box becomes too wide; you can resize it after you are done typing.

5 When you are finished, click anywhere outside the text box to see how the text appears on the finished slide.

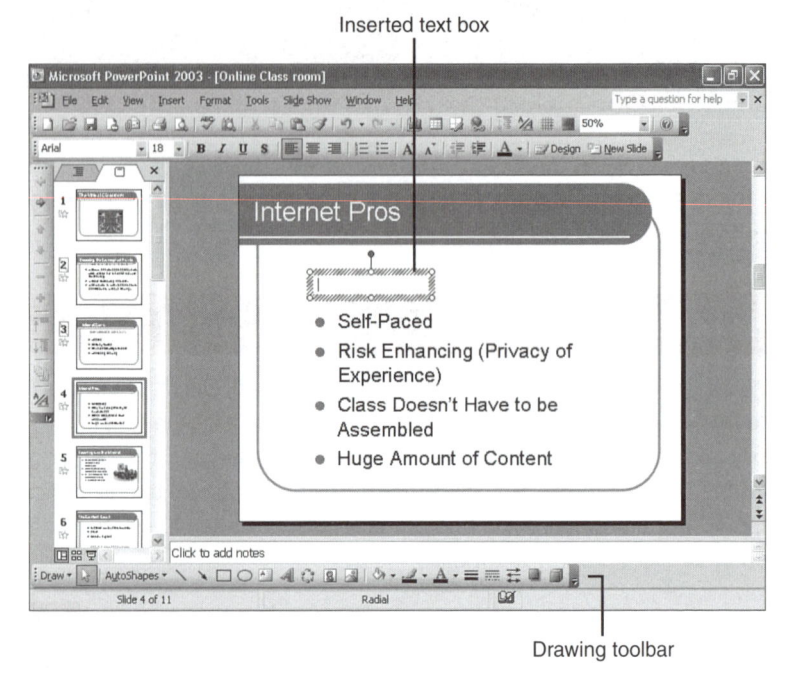

Figure 6.1 Text boxes can be inserted from the Drawing toolbar.

If the text does not align correctly in the text box, see the section "Changing the Text Alignment and Line Spacing" later in this lesson to learn how to change it.

You can also add a text box via the Insert menu. Select **Insert**, then **Textbox**. Then use the mouse to "draw" the text box on the slide. Using this command set to create a textbox actually allows you to create the width of the text box before you enter the text.

Sizing and Moving Text Boxes

You can size any of the text boxes on a slide. You can also move them on the slide. To size a text box follow these steps:

1 Select the text box.

2 Place the mouse on any of the sizing handles that appear on the box (they will be small round circles).

3 When you place the mouse on the sizing handle a sizing tool appears. Click and drag the sizing handle to change the size of the box. To retain the height-width ratio of the text box, use a sizing handle on any of the text box corners and drag on the diagonal. To move a text box, place the mouse pointer on any of the box borders. The mouse pointer becomes a move tool. Drag the box to any location on the slide.

> **Timesaver tip**
>
> **Rotate a Text Box** You can rotate a text box using the green rotation handle that appears at the top center of a selected text box. Place the mouse pointer on the handle, and the rotation icon appears. Use the mouse to drag the rotation handle to the desired position to rotate the box.

Deleting a Text Box

You can delete text boxes from your slides. Select the text box (so that handles appear around it and no insertion point appears inside it), and then press the **Delete** key.

If you want to delete multiple text boxes, select the first text box and then select other text boxes with the mouse while holding down the **Ctrl** key. This will select each additional text box. Press the **Delete** key to delete the text boxes.

→ Changing Font Attributes

You can enhance your text by using the Font dialog box or by using various tools on the Formatting toolbar. Use the Font dialog box if you want to add several enhancements to your text at one time. Use the Formatting toolbar to add one font enhancement at a time.

> **Jargon buster**
>
> **Fonts, Styles, and Effects** In PowerPoint, a font is a family of text that has the same design or typeface (for example, Arial or Courier). A style is a standard enhancement, such as bold or italic. An effect is a special enhancement, such as shadow or underline.

Adding and Modifying Slide Text

Using the Font Dialog Box

The font dialog box offers you control over all the attributes you can apply to text. Attributes such as strikethrough, superscript, subscript, and shadow are available as check boxes in this dialog box.

You can change the font of existing text or of text you are about to type by performing the following steps:

1 To change the font of existing text, select text by clicking and dragging the I-beam pointer over the text in a particular text box. If you want to change font attributes for all the text in a text box, select the text box (do not place the insertion point within the text box).

2 Choose the **Format** menu and then choose **Font**. The Font dialog box appears, as shown in Figure 6.2.

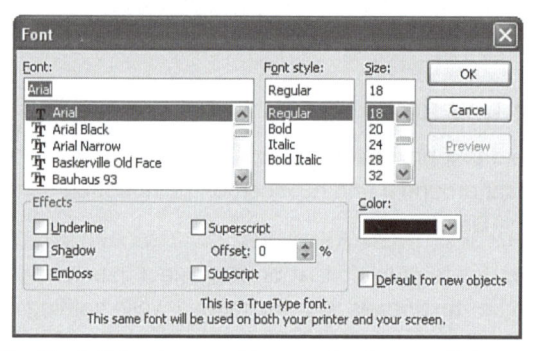

Figure 6.2 The Font dialog box enables you to change all the text attributes for selected text.

> **Timesaver tip**
>
> **Right-Click Shortcut** You can right-click the text and select **Font** from the shortcut menu to open the Font dialog box.

3 From the **Font** list, select the font you want to use.

4 From the Font Style list, select any style you want to apply to the text, such as **Bold** or **Italic**. (To remove styles from text, select **Regular**.)

5 From the Size list, select any size in the list, or type a size directly into the box. (With TrueType fonts—the fonts marked with the TT logo—you can type any point size, even sizes that do not appear on the list.)

6 In the Effects box, select any special effects you want to add to the text, such as **Underline**, **Shadow**, or **Emboss**. You can also choose **Superscript** or **Subscript**, although these are less common.

7 To change the color of your text, click the arrow button to the right of the Color list and click the desired color. (For more colors, click the **More Colors** option at the bottom of the Color drop-down list; to select a color, use the dialog box that appears.)

8 Click **OK** to apply the new look to your selected text.

> **Timesaver tip**
>
> **Title and Object Area Text**   If you change a font on an individual slide, the font change applies only to that slide. To change the font for all the slides in the presentation, you need to change the font on the Slide Master. Select **View**, point at **Master**, and then select **Slide Master**. Select a text area and perform the preceding steps to change the look of the text on all slides. Be careful, however, because these changes override any font styles that are supplied by the design template assigned to the presentation.

Formatting Text with the Formatting Toolbar

The Formatting toolbar provides several buttons that enable you to change font attributes for the text on your slides. It makes it easy for you to quickly bold selected text or to change the color of text in a text box.

To use the different Formatting toolbar font tools, follow these steps:

1 To change the look of existing text, select the text, or select a particular text box to change the look of all the text within that box.

2 To change fonts, open the **Font** drop-down list and click the desired font.

3 To change font size, open the **Font Size** drop-down list, click the desired size or type a size directly into the box, and then press **Enter**.

> **Timesaver tip**
>
> **Incrementing the Type Size**   To increase or decrease the text size to the next size up or down, click the Increase Font Size or Decrease Font Size buttons on the Formatting toolbar.

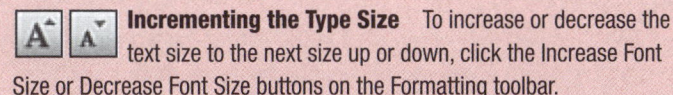

Adding and Modifying Slide Text   **263**

4 To add a style or effect to the text (bold, italic, underline, and/or shadow), click the appropriate button(s):

B Bold

I Italic

U Underline

S Shadow

As you have already seen, you can change the font color through the Font dialog box. You can also change it with the Font Color button on the Formatting toolbar. Just do the following:

1. Select the text for which you want to change the color.

2 Click the down-pointing arrow next to the **Font Color** button on the Formatting toolbar. A color palette appears (see Figure 6.3).

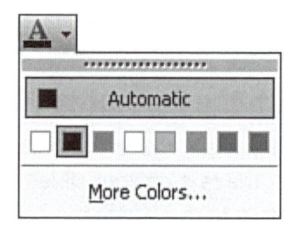

Figure 6.3 When you click the arrow next to the Font Colors button, a color palette appears.

3 Do one of the following:

- Click a color on the palette to change the color of the selected text or the text box (the colors available are based on the design template and color scheme you have selected for the presentation).

- Click the **More Font Colors** option to display a Colors dialog box. Click a color on the Standard tab or use the Custom tab to create your own color. Then click **OK**. The color is applied to the text.

→ Copying Text Formats

If your presentation contains text with a format you want to use, you can copy that text's format and apply it to other text on the slide (or other slides). To copy text formats, perform the following steps:

1. Highlight the text with the format you want to use.
2. Click the **Format Painter** button on the toolbar. PowerPoint copies the format.
3. Drag the mouse pointer (which now looks like the Format Painter icon) across the text to which you want to apply the format.

If you want to apply a format to different text lines or even different text boxes on a slide or slides, double-click the Format Painter button. Use the mouse to apply styles to as many text items as you want. Then, click the Format Painter button again to turn off the feature.

→ Changing the Text Alignment and Line Spacing

When you first type text, PowerPoint automatically places it against the left edge of the text box. To change the paragraph alignment, perform the following steps:

1. Click anywhere inside the paragraph you want to realign (a paragraph is any text line or wrapped text lines followed by a line break—created when you press the **Enter** key).
2. Select the **Format** menu and then select **Alignment**. The Alignment submenu appears (see Figure 6.4).
3. Select **Align Left**, **Center**, **Align Right**, or **Justify** to align the paragraph as required.

> **Timesaver tip**
>
> **Some Alignment Shortcuts** To quickly set left alignment, press **Ctrl+L** or click the **Align Left** button on the Formatting toolbar. For centered alignment, press **Ctrl+C** or click the **Center** button. For right alignment, press **Ctrl+R** or click the **Align Right** button.

Adding and Modifying Slide Text

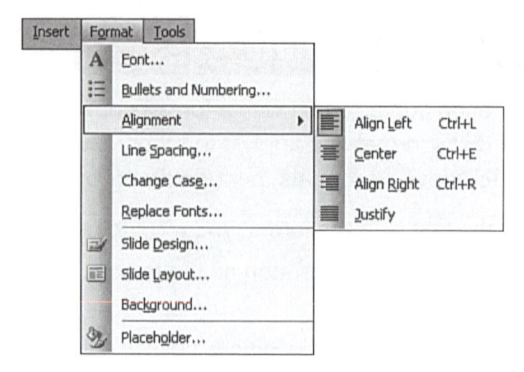

Figure 6.4 You can align each text line or paragraph in a text box.

If you want to align all the text in a text box in the same way (rather than aligning the text line by line), select the entire text box (click the box border) and then use the Alignment menu selection or the alignment buttons on the Formatting toolbar.

You can also change the spacing between text lines (remember, PowerPoint considers these to be paragraphs) in a text box. The default setting for line spacing is single space. To change the line spacing in a paragraph, perform these steps:

1 Click inside the paragraph you want to change, or select all the paragraphs you want to change by selecting the entire text box.

2 Select **Format**, **Line Spacing**. The Line Spacing dialog box appears, as shown in Figure 6.5.

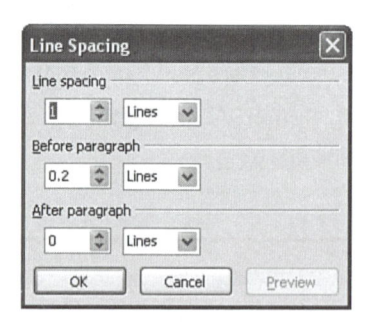

Figure 6.5 Select Format, Line Spacing to open the Line Spacing dialog box.

3 Click the arrow buttons to the right of any of the following text boxes to change the spacing for the following:

266 Brilliant Microsoft Office 2003 Pocket Book

- **Line Spacing**—This setting controls the space between the lines in a paragraph.
- **Before Paragraph**—This setting controls the space between this paragraph and the paragraph that comes before it.
- **After Paragraph**—This setting controls the space between this paragraph and the paragraph that comes after it.

4 After you make your selections, click **OK**.

> **Timesaver tip**
>
> **Lines or Points?** The drop-down list box that appears to the right of each setting enables you to set the line spacing in lines or points. A line is the current line height (based on the current text size). A point is a unit commonly used to measure text. One point is 1/72 of an inch.

→ Adding a WordArt Object

PowerPoint comes with an add-on program called WordArt (which is also available in other Office applications, such as Word and Excel) that can help you create graphical text effects. You can create text wrapped in a circle and text that has 3D effects and other special alignment options. To insert a WordArt object onto a slide, perform the following steps:

1 In the Slide view, display the slide on which you want to place the WordArt object.

2 Click the **Insert** menu, point at **Picture**, and then select **WordArt** (or select the WordArt button on the Drawing toolbar). The WordArt Gallery dialog box appears, showing many samples of WordArt types.

3 Click the sample that best represents the WordArt type you want and click **OK**. The Edit WordArt Text dialog box appears (see Figure 6.6).

4 Choose a font and size from the respective drop-down lists.

5 Type the text you want to use into the Text box.

6 Click **OK**. PowerPoint creates the WordArt text on your slide, as shown in Figure 6.7.

Figure 6.6 Enter the text, size, and font to be used into the Edit WordArt Text dialog box.

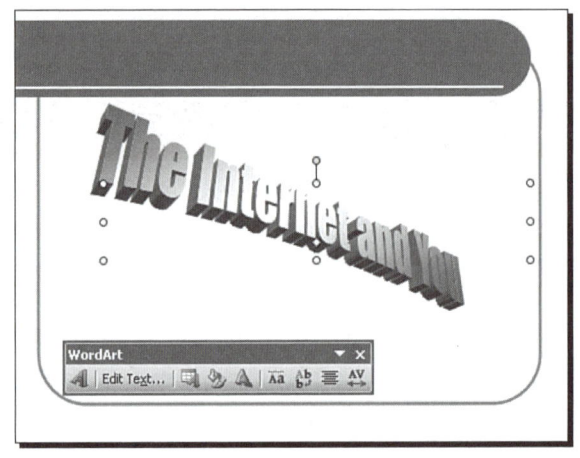

Figure 6.7 The WordArt toolbar is available when your WordArt object is selected.

After you have created WordArt, you have access to the WordArt toolbar, shown in Figure 6.7. You can use it to modify your WordArt. Table 6.1 summarizes the toolbar's buttons.

Table 6.1 Buttons on the WordArt Toolbar

To Do This	Click This
Insert a new WordArt object	
Edit the text, size, and font of the selected WordArt object	Edit Text...
Change the style of the current WordArt object in the WordArt Gallery	
Open a Format WordArt dialog box	
Change the shape of the WordArt	
Make all the letters the same height	
Toggle between vertical and horizontal text orientation	
Change the text alignment	
Change the spacing between letters	

You can rotate a WordArt object by dragging the rotation handle on the WordArt box. To edit the WordArt object, double-click it to display the WordArt toolbar and text entry box. Enter your changes and then click outside the WordArt object. You can move the object by dragging its border or resize it by dragging a handle.

7 Adding Graphics to a Slide

In this lesson, you learn how to add PowerPoint clip art to your presentations and how to add images from other sources.

→ Using the Clip Art Task Pane

The Clip Art task pane provides you access to all the clip art provided with Microsoft Office. It also includes a search engine that you can use to search for clip art, photographs, movies, and sounds that are stored on your computer. You can also search for clip art and other items using Microsoft's online clip library. (You must be connected to the Internet when using PowerPoint to access the Microsoft online library.)

Figure 7.1 shows the Clip Art task pane. You can use this task pane to search for and insert images onto your slides, or you can take advantage of slides that use a layout that contains a placeholder for images and clip art.

You learn about using the Clip Art task pane and slide layouts that provide image placeholders in this lesson.

> **Jargon buster**
>
> **Clip Art** A collection of previously created images or pictures that you can place on a slide. Microsoft Office provides clip art and other media types, such as movies and sounds.

You can open the Clip Art task pane in any of these ways:

- Click the **Insert Clip Art** button on the Drawing toolbar.
- Select the **Insert** menu, point at **Picture**, and then choose **Clip Art**.

- Open the task pane, click the task pane drop-down arrow, and then select **Insert Clip Art** to switch to the Clip Art task pane.

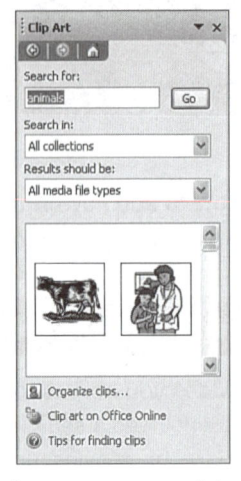

Figure 7.1 The Clip Art task pane manages pictures, motion clips, and sounds—all in one convenient place.

When you use the Clip Art task pane, you search for images by keywords. In the following sections, you take a look at inserting clip art from the task pane and learn how you can insert clip art using some of the slide layouts (that provide a clip art placeholder on the slide).

Timesaver tip

Clip Organizer Scan The first time you open the Clip Art task pane, PowerPoint prompts you to allow the Clip Organizer (which is discussed later in the lesson) to search your hard drive. Clip Organizer then creates category folders and image indexes from the clip art and images that it finds there. Click **Yes** to allow this process to take place.

→ Inserting an Image from the Task Pane

As previously mentioned, the Clip Art task pane allows you to search for clip art files using keywords. If you wanted to search for clip art of cats, you would search for the word "cats." To insert a piece of the clip art using the task pane, follow these steps:

1. Select the slide on which you want to place the image so that it appears in the Slide pane.
2. Select **Insert**, point at **Picture**, and then select **Clip Art**. The Clip Art task pane appears.
3. Type keywords into the Search Text box in the task pane that will be used to find your clip art images.
4. Click the **Search** button. Images that match your search criteria appear in the task pane as thumbnails.
5. In the Results list, locate the image that you want to place on the slide. Then click the image, and the clip art is placed on the slide (see Figure 7.2).

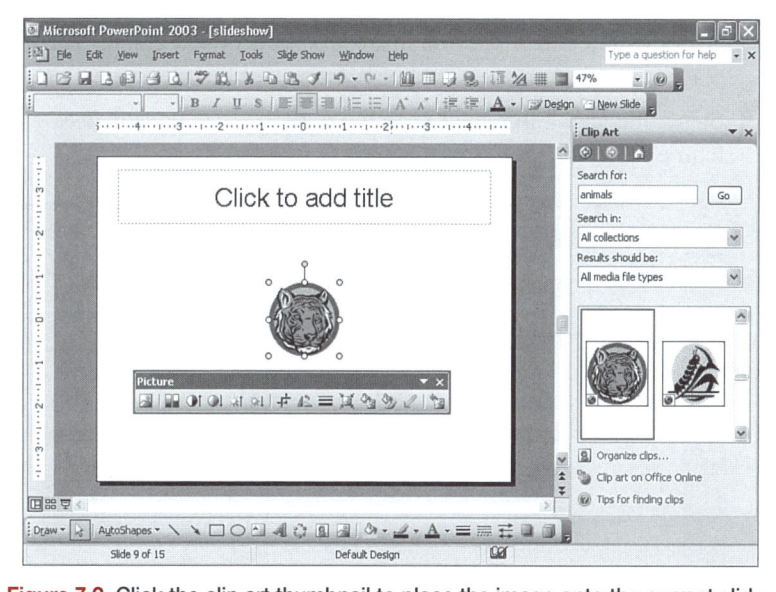

Figure 7.2 Click the clip art thumbnail to place the image onto the current slide.

You can use the sizing handles on the image to size the clip art box. Or you can drag the clip art box to a new location on the slide.

→ Inserting an Image from an Image Box

Another way that you can add clip art images to a slide in your presentation is to create the slide using a slide format that supplies a clip art placeholder box on the slide. These slide layout types are called content layouts because they make it easy to insert objects such as clip art, charts, and other items onto a slide. You can then use the object placeholder on the slide to access the clip art library and insert a particular image onto the slide.

Follow these steps:

1. Create a new slide or select the slide you want to assign a layout to that contains a clip art placeholder box.

2. Open the task pane (**View**, **Task Pane**) and then click the task pane drop-down menu and select **Slide Layout** (the Slide Layout task pane automatically opens if you've just created a new slide).

3. Scroll down through the layouts provided until you locate either the Content layout or the Text and Content layout. Both of these layout categories provide slide layouts that contain object placeholders or object placeholders and text boxes, respectively.

4. Select the layout that best suits the purpose of your slide (see Figure 7.3).

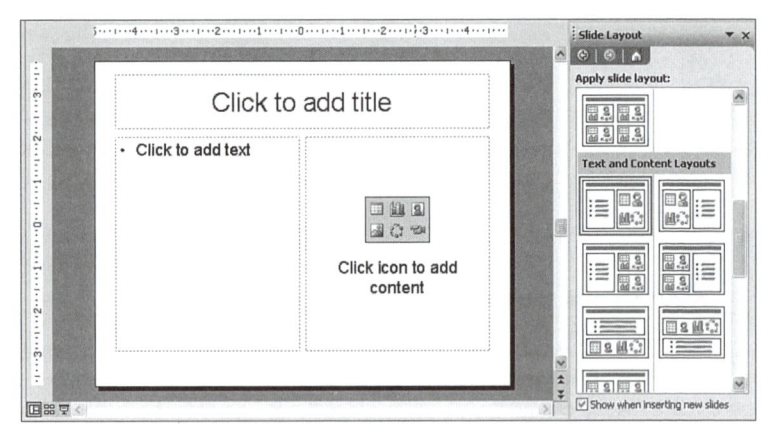

Figure 7.3 Select a slide layout that contains an object placeholder.

5. The slide layout you choose provides you with a placeholder box that contains icons for tables, charts, clip art, and other objects. Click the **Insert Clip Art** icon in the placeholder box. The Select Picture dialog box appears (see Figure 7.4).

6. Scroll down through the list of clip art and other images to find a particular image (the list will be lengthy because it includes all the Office Clip Art and any other images that were located on

your computer when the Clip Organizer cataloged the images on your computer).

7 If you want, you can search for particular images by keyword. Type the search criteria into the Search Text box and then click **Search**. Images that match the search criteria appear in the Select Picture dialog box.

8 Click the picture thumbnail that you want to place on the slide. Then click **OK**.

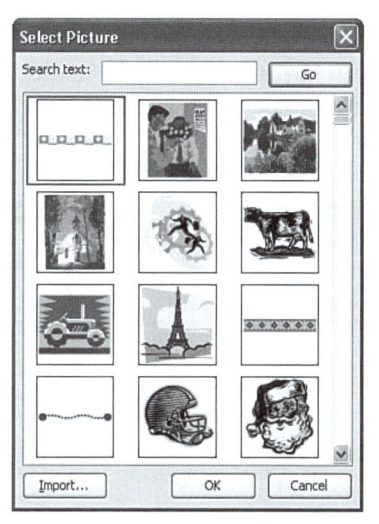

Figure 7.4 The Select Picture dialog box enables you to scroll through or search through the entire clip art and image library on your computer.

PowerPoint places the image on the slide in the object placeholder box. You can size the box or move it on the slide.

→ Inserting a Clip from a File

If you have an image stored on your computer that you would like to place on a slide, you can insert the picture directly from the file. This means that you don't have to use the Clip Art task pane to search for and then insert the image.

To place a graphical image on a slide directly from a file, follow these steps:

1. Select the slide on which the image will be placed.
2. Select the **Insert** menu, point at **Picture**, and then select **From File**. The Insert Picture dialog box appears (see Figure 7.5).
3. Select the picture you want to use. You can view all the picture files in a particular location as thumbnails. Select the **Views** button, and then select **Thumbnails** on the menu that appears.
4. Click **Insert** to place the image on the slide.

If the picture is too big or too small, you can drag the selection handles (the small squares) around the edge of the image to resize it. Hold down the **Shift** key to proportionally resize the image (this maintains the height/width ratio of the image so that you cannot stretch or distort it).

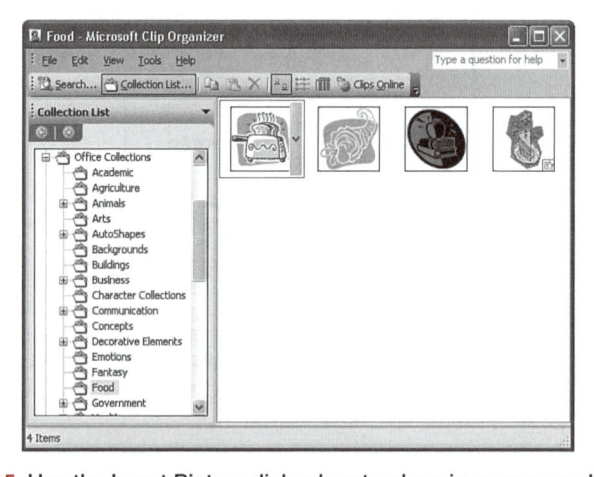

Figure 7.5 Use the Insert Picture dialog box to place images on a slide.

Timesaver tip

Link It Up You can link a graphic to the presentation so that whenever the original changes, the version in the presentation changes, too. Just open the drop-down list on the Insert button in the Insert Picture dialog box (refer to Figure 7.5) and choose **Link to File**.

→ Managing Images in the Clip Organizer

Occasionally, you might want to add or delete clip art images from folders on your computer. Managing images is accomplished using the Clip Organizer. When you install Microsoft Office 2003 (using the default installation), a fairly large library of clip art is placed on your hard drive in different category folders. You can manage these clip art images and other images on your computer, such as scanned images or pictures from a digital camera. To open the Clip Organizer, follow these steps:

1 With the Clip Art task pane open in the PowerPoint window, click the **Clip Organizer** link near the bottom of the task pane to open the Clip Organizer.

2 (Optional) The first time you open the Organizer, you will be given the opportunity to catalog all the media files (clip art, photos, videos) on your computer. Click the **Now** button to catalog all media.

3 To view the clip art categories Microsoft Office has provided, click the plus sign (+) to the left of the Office Collections folder in the Collection list (this folder is located on the left side of the Clip Organizer window). Category folders such as Academic, Agriculture, and so on will appear in the Collection list.

4 Click one of the category folders to view the clip art that it holds (for example, click **Food**). The clip art in that category folder appears in the Clip Organizer window (see Figure 7.6).

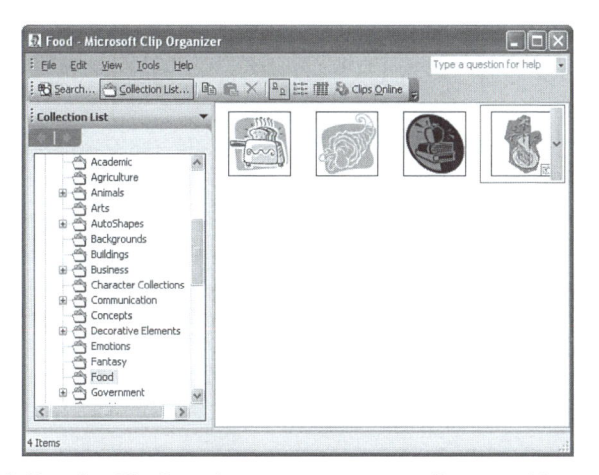

Figure 7.6 Use the Clip Organizer to manage your clip art and image files.

Adding Graphics to a Slide   **277**

Not only does the Clip Organizer allow you to browse the various clip art and other images on your computer, it allows you to copy, delete, or move images. For example, if you find an image you no longer want to store on your computer, select the image in the Clip Organizer window and press **Delete**. A dialog box appears, letting you know that this image will be removed from all collections on the computer. Click **OK** to delete the image.

You can also use the Clip Organizer to copy or move clip art images from a location on your hard drive to one of the clip art collections. Locate the images you want to move or copy to a particular collection and then select them.

To move the images to a collection, select the **Edit** menu, and then **Move to Collection**. The Move to Collection dialog box appears (see Figure 7.7). Select a location in the dialog box and click **OK** to move the selected image or images.

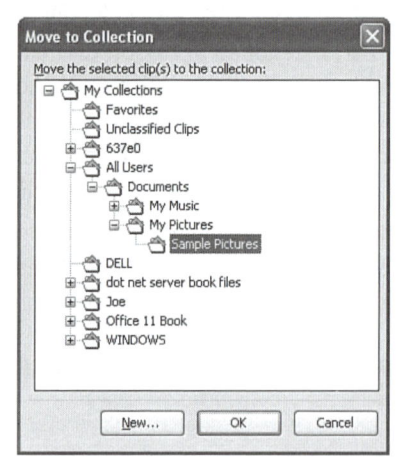

Figure 7.7 You can move images from one location to another using the Clip Organizer.

You can also copy images to a new location using the Copy to Collection command. Select the images in a particular folder on your computer using the Clip Organizer window. Select the **Edit** menu and then **Copy to Collection**. Select a location in the Copy to Collection dialog box where you would like to place copies of the images, and then click **OK**.